Effective Classroom Pract

Effective Classroom Practice

Alison Kington, Pam Sammons, Elaine Regan,
Eleanor Brown, and James Ko, with Scott Buckler

Mc
Graw
Hill
Education   Open University Press

Open University Press
McGraw-Hill Education
McGraw-Hill House
Shoppenhangers Road
Maidenhead
Berkshire
England
SL6 2QL

email: enquiries@openup.co.uk
world wide web: www.openup.co.uk

and Two Penn Plaza, New York, NY 10121-2289, USA

First published 2014

A catalogue record of this book is available from the British Library

ISBN-13: 978-0-335-24712-7
ISBN-10: 0-335-24712-1
eISBN: 978-0-335-24713-4

Library of Congress Cataloging-in-Publication Data
CIP data applied for

Typeset by Aptara, Inc.

Fictitious names of companies, products, people, characters and/or data that may be used
herein (in case studies or in examples) are not intended to represent any real individual,
company, product or event.

Praise for this book

"I am impressed! Based on meticulous research this book offers powerful insights into a range of classroom practices to help both beginning and experienced teachers advance their teaching skills and is a 'must-have' for all education professionals."

Prof. Dr. Wim van de Grift, director of the Department of Teacher Education of the University of Groningen

"This book is unusually lucid for a publication based on research written by academics. I would go further; it is engaging, accessible and enjoyable to read. This is not a book for teachers; nor is it a book for researchers. It is a book for everyone and that is a rare thing. The authors draw authoritatively on a wide range of research studies to locate their own findings into a much broader landscape. Usually in books such as this, the 'methods' chapter is either omitted or is uninteresting resulting in it often being skipped over. This is not the case here. Chapter 3 is illuminative and engaging, taking the reader into the procedures and strategies which supported the research. I think this book will be enjoyed by teachers, researchers and teacher educators. Furthermore, it should be on a required reading list for policy makers and politicians!"

Peter Gates, Associate Professor, University of Nottingham, UK

"This book is a shining example of what educational research should aspire to in terms of combining illuminating insights with indisputably 'hard' evidence - drawn not only from a large-scale longitudinal study (funded initially by central government and subsequently by the Economic and Social Research Council), but also from other relevant and high-quality research studies. The chapters in this clearly-structured book address different topics on perennially important themes, including effective classroom practice, the teaching career path and teachers' professional development. Where necessary, the book does some judicious conceptual work to explicate some of the complexities involved in pedagogical practice - and to dispel some of the simplistic myths around 'effectiveness' - but without over-burdening the reader with theory. The book should be required reading for education policy-makers and strategists at local and national levels, in the public, private and charitable sectors."

Lesley Saunders, Visiting Professor, Institute of Education

For Joseph

Contents

---

[1]Sammons, P., Ko, J. and Bakkum, L. (2014) Effective teaching and effective teachers: an overview of research and evidence. In A. Kington, P. Sammons, E.Brown, E. Regan. and J. Ko, *Effective Classroom Practice,* Maidenhead: Open University Press.

[2]Sammons, P., Kington, A., Robertson, D. and Lindorff-Vijayendran, A. (2014) The Impact of Effective Practice: learning from student voices. In A. Kington, P. Sammons, E.Brown, E. Regan. and J. Ko, *Effective Classroom Practice,* Maidenhead: Open University Press.

About the authors

Dr. Alison Kington. After training as a primary teacher, Alison completed a PhD at the University of Bristol and has been subsequently employed as a research assistant at the Roehampton Institute of Education and the Institute of Education (London), Senior Research Officer at the National Foundation for Educational Research, and Senior Research Fellow at the University of Nottingham. She took up her current post as Principal Lecturer at the University of Worcester in September 2012. Alison's research focuses on 'classroom life'; that is, the experiences, relationships and perceptions of children and staff in schools, with an emphasis on the utilization and application of research to improve professional practice. To that end, she has developed experience in mixed methods research design with specific expertise in classroom observation, critical event narrative and repertory grid techniques. Alison has led a range of international and national research projects funded by research councils and government agencies, including a four-year research project investigating variations in the work and lives of teachers, a study of effective classroom practice and an exploration of early years education for 2-year-olds. She is co-author of *Teachers Matter* (2007), and co-editor of *The Role of Theory and Research in Educational Practice* (2008) and *Paradigms and Research of Educational Practice* (2012).

Professor Pamela Sammons. Pam is a Professor of Education at the Department of Education, University of Oxford and a Senior Research Fellow at Jesus College, Oxford. Previously she was a Professor at the University of Nottingham, and at the Institute of Education, University of London, where she directed the International School Effectiveness and Improvement Centre (1999–2004). Her research focuses on school effectiveness and improvement, teaching effectiveness, the early years, and promoting equity and inclusion in education. She is a Principal Investigator for the longitudinal Effective Pre-school, Primary & Secondary Education study, investigating children's development from age 3 to 16+ years (EPPSE 3-16+). She is also a Principal Investigator on the Evaluation of Children's Centres in England. Pam is an adviser working with OUP on its School Improvement model. She is a governor of a primary school in Oxfordshire and a secondary school in Oxford.

Dr. Elaine Regan. Elaine is a Postdoctoral Research Associate in the School of Social Science and Public Policy, King's College London. Her research interests encompass student participation in science, inquiry-based science education, effective classroom practice, continuing professional development for teachers and informal science educators, and learning outside the classroom. She is lead researcher on the European Union INQUIRE project for botanic garden educators across 11 countries and is currently working in partnership with the Science Museum, London. She is a frequent contributor to international education and science education conferences and expert in designing and implementing mixed methods research designs. She was formerly a Research Fellow in the School of Education, University of Nottingham.

Dr. Eleanor J. Brown. Eleanor is a research fellow at the University of York. She recently completed her PhD in Development Education at the University of Nottingham, where she worked for several years as a researcher on projects on peace education, school leadership and effective classroom practice. Her primary research interests are in transformative learning and participative pedagogies. Eleanor spent a year conducting research based at the University of Granada, Spain, and has a masters degree in international relations. Prior to this she taught English as a foreign language for four years in Barcelona, Spain, and San Jose, Costa Rica.

Dr. James Ko. James is an Assistant Professor of Department of Education Policy and Leadership, Hong Kong Institute of Education. He was an ESL teacher for 14 years at a secondary school and the Head of the Discipline Team and the Counselling and Guidance Team for 10 years. He co-founded the junior form Integrated Humanities unit. He had extensive training in linguistics, psychology and education, with degrees from Canada, Hong Kong and the UK. He worked in numerous large-scale research projects funded by the DfES and ESRC in England and RGC in Hong Kong. Now he is a grant reviewer for, and grant holder of, the Research Grants Council, Hong Kong. He has also published in, and reviewed for, numerous international journals, including *School Effectiveness and School Improvement, School Leadership and Management, Journal of Educational Administration* etc. He does mixed method research and his research interest is now focusing on issues related to educational effectiveness, its assessment and improvement.

Dr. Scott Buckler. Scott originally worked as a primary teacher in London and Birmingham before his employment as a Senior Lecturer at the University of Worcester. He was appointed for his work in special educational needs although he has diversified over the years to pursue how psychology can be applied to education. Scott is actively involved in the field of transpersonal psychology and has a particular research interest in redefining the context of transpersonal education. Scott has published several textbooks notably *Psychology for Teachers* and *Your Dissertation in Education*.

List of tables and figures

Foreword

Ian Menter
Professor of Teacher Education, University of Oxford
President of the British Educational Research Association,
2013–15

This book: '. . . argues . . . that greater attention need[s] to be given to the positive contribution that research findings can make in helping to support teachers' professional development as autonomous and reflective practitioners' (p. 10).

Perhaps more than for most people, those of us working in education at present find that we live in interesting times. Never has there been more political interest in education and within that general prioritization ('Education, Education, Education' as one former UK prime minster put it), we see the growing significance of teaching and teachers – *The Importance of Teaching*, as the English White Paper of 2010 called it (DfE 2010). Encouraged by the increasing range of evidence that it is not just schools 'that matter', but most importantly teachers 'that matter', politicians across the world have taken an increasing interest is the teaching profession.

Of course, at one level, such interest is entirely welcome. For those of us who teach or have taught in schools, or who now work in teacher education, we entered the profession very much because we wanted to make a difference to the lives of children, and so we do tend to have a very deep assumption that teaching is important, indeed crucial.

On the other hand, such has been politicians' concern about the quality of teaching (some of us remember Keith Joseph's White Paper of 1983, *Teaching Quality*, DES 1983), that they seem to have been led to making increasingly direct interventions into what had historically been a domain mainly for professional determination and judgement. The number of incursions into teacher education and the practice of teaching has steadily increased. We have seen the complete transformation of the governance of teacher education in England through the creation of various government bodies, from the Council for the Accreditation of Teacher Education in 1984 through to the National College for Teaching and Leadership (NCTL) in 2013, with many intermediate bodies such as the (largely unlamented) Teacher Training Agency in between. The fact that the NCTL, as now constituted, is not even a quango (quasi-autonomous non-government organization), but has been incorporated within the government's Department for Education, shows just how much control the current government seeks to exert over the profession and concomitantly how little trust now resides within the profession. On the other hand the likely emergence of a College of Teaching, led by members of the profession, indicates a growing recognition among teachers that there should be a significant degree of self-regulation and development for teachers.

Against this backdrop, this book by Alison Kington and her colleagues could not be more timely. The study it reports and the findings that emerge are entirely consistent with the recognition of the importance of teaching. However, the findings are not at all consistent with the reductionist and technicist views of teaching and teacher development that are so regrettably promoted in some quarters by some politicians. In this book we see the full complexity of the task of effective teaching emerging. We read through the voices of teachers and of school students about the multiple challenges that teachers face every day and the huge range of decisions that they have to make minute by minute, hour by hour. There are certainly significant craft elements in teaching – and therefore it is crucial that much of teacher learning does take place in school settings – but the work of teaching has such a wide range of intellectual elements that the view that it is predominantly a craft, rather than a fully-fledged profession, is deeply flawed and counterproductive. The effective teacher, as described in this book, is someone who not only knows their subject matter well, who is capable of forming positive relationships with a wide range of pupils, who is able to plan carefully and systematically, but who can also adapt and amend those plans even during the process of implementation, who can assess students' learning, collaborate with colleagues, who can, in short, perform multiple tasks successfully while working around 52 hours per week during term time. How does that match up with the European directive on working time? Effectiveness in teaching is not a term to be treated simplistically and the authors of this text are careful to use it critically and to ensure that a broadly based holistic definition underpins the study.

The work by Kington *et al.* falls within a continuing tradition of studies looking at the work of teachers, drawing on a range of research methods. Indeed, many important previous studies are cited in the book, including, in the English context, the groundbreaking ORACLE study carried out in the 1970s (Galton *et al.* 1980); the first school effectiveness study from the 1980s by Mortimore and his colleagues (and one of that team, Pamela Sammons, is part of the present team) (Mortimore *et al.* 1988); as well as, more recently, the Variations in Teachers' Work, Lives and their Effects on Pupils (VITAE) project led by Day and Sammons, which was one of the first multi-method studies to attempt to connect questions of effectiveness with the working experiences, indeed the wider lives and career phases, of teachers (Day *et al.* 2007). The present book therefore can be seen as an excellent example of research which does build on previous work. One of the criticisms levelled at UK education research in the critiques of the 1980s and 1990s was that it was not 'cumulative'. Well, this work can certainly not be accused of that. But nor is the book narrowly English in its focus. Not only does the research make use of instruments that were developed internationally but the analysis throughout connects to work carried out around the globe.

The research methods deployed are set out very clearly in the text and this will serve as an exemplary exposition for students of education seeking to gain a deep understanding of the value of mixed methods approaches in our field. But in addition to the mixed methods we are also offered multiple perspectives. Recognizing the increased attention being paid to the experiences of learners as well as of teachers, we clearly hear the pupil voice coming through in this study as well as the voice of teachers.

However it is with teachers' voices that I wish to conclude. One of the most heartening aspects of reading this important book is the reminder that in spite of the lack of trust, in spite of the shockingly high proportion of teachers in the study who are either stressed or highly stressed (29 per cent), there are teachers who manage to get deep fulfilment from their work and are resistant to their work becoming commodified, across the phases of schooling. These extracts are taken from Chapter 6:

> I'm still as committed to the job as I ever was, just because I think I deserve it to the children to be as committed, irrespective of motivation or levels, each one of those children deserve to get the best out of me.
>
> (Benjamin, Year 6 teacher, FSM 3)

or

> It is motivating for you to see the children making progress and you look back in their books and see where they were in the beginning of the year and where they were at the end, that's really rewarding to see the progress that they're making and to have them responding and I guess things like parents evenings, when you share the work of the children and the parents are really pleased with the progress and things, that's very rewarding.
>
> (Amy, Year 2 teacher, FSM 2)

or

> We lead research and development groups every Monday and one of my roles on the leadership team is to make sure that everything we do, we come back to thinking about teaching and learning because there is a danger in management that you start to run the whole thing like a business and start treating children just as commodities and making profits and we forget about the teaching and learning.
>
> (Michael, Year 9 maths teacher, FSM 1)

As we proceed to consider the development of the teaching profession over the years ahead and continue to prioritize the work of the profession as being central to a future characterized by social and economic well-being, let us ensure that the working environment for all teachers is one where such experiences and perspectives become the norm. Effective teachers appear to be those who can work well in collegial settings and who have some real control over their own work and their own career development. In short, they have a degree of 'agency' in their work. If this book is read by politicians (and I hope it will be), then the biggest implication for them is to step back and to encourage confidence and self-determination within the teaching profession. Reading this book, they should have little doubt about the commitment and resilience which exists within the workforce nor any doubt about the capability within the profession to take on such responsibility.

However, as implied by the quotation from the book that I included at the beginning of this foreword, this is also the kind of study that should inform teacher education programmes across the country and beyond – student teachers, early career and later career teachers, as well as school leaders and teacher educators will all find an enormous amount which is relevant to their work within it.

References

Day C., Sammons, P., Stobart, G., Kington, A. and Gu, Q. (2007) *Teachers Matter.* Maidenhead: Open University Press.

Galton, M., Simon, B. and Croll, P. (1980) *Inside the Primary Classroom.* London: Routledge & Kegan Paul.

Mortimore, P., Sammons, P., Stoll, L., Lewis, D. and Ecob, R. (1988) *School Matters: The Junior Years.* Wells: Open Books.

DES (1983) *Teaching Quality: White Paper* (Cm 8836). London: HMSO.

DfE (2010) *The Importance of Teaching: The Schools White Paper* (Cm 7980). London: HMSO.

Acknowledgements

We would like to express our gratitude to all the teachers, headteachers and students who participated in the Effective Classroom Practice (ECP) project which forms the basis of this book. We also wish to thank the Economic and Social Research Council (ESRC) for funding this innovative research study.

There are also many colleagues who have made valuable contributions to our work and thinking on effective classroom practice throughout the project's journey: in particular Dr Judith Gunraj, Dr Dan Robertson, Linda Bakkum, Ariel Lindorff-Vijayendran, Joanne Towle and Hayley McCalla. Special thanks go to Dr Scott Buckler and Caryn Thorogood for their help, support and patience. On a personal note, I also wish to acknowledge my co-directors on the project, Professor Pam Sammons and Professor Christopher Day for their support and encouragement.

Finally, this book is dedicated to my son, Joseph Kington (aged 6), who would have preferred me to write a book about pirates and knights!

PART 1

1 Exploring effective classroom practice

The chapters in this book draw primarily upon the results of a national research project, 'Effective Classroom Practice' (ECP). The project aims to provide a holistic picture of the work of teachers in primary and secondary schools in England who were judged to be effective and more effective for a sustained period of at least three consecutive years in terms of their pupils' measured progress and attainment. The project not only observes them in action but also places what they did in the contexts of their career phases, workplaces, and personal and professional lives. The book links the project's results with the wider literature on effective teaching and explores the implications of the research for policy-makers and practitioners who seek to enhance the quality of education. This first chapter, **Exploring effective classroom practice**, introduces the different but complementary perspectives which are elaborated in each chapter of the book and which, together, form the complex web of influence upon teachers and their practice. These perspectives explore their sense of self and professional identity; and the values, qualities, strategies and behaviours which they hold, develop and display in sustaining their effectiveness in the classroom. While there are numerous small-scale qualitative studies of teachers' work and lives and a steady stream of larger-scale quantitative studies of teacher and school effectiveness, there are few which combine qualitative and quantitative classroom observation, self-report, and pupils' views in the context of external measures of teacher effectiveness. This is what the ECP does, and the different chapters highlight these key elements and what we can learn from them (Kington *et al.* 2011).

Within each chapter, also, is a consideration of associated research by others internationally. This book is not, therefore, simply a report of a particular project, but a series of accounts and informed discussions which connect and go beyond its various parts in order to understand and explain what it is that enables some teachers, in primary and secondary schools in a range of socio-economic contexts and in different phases of their teaching lives, to be effective and others to be even more effective, what that looks like in practice and what influences seem to help and challenge their capacities to sustain their effectiveness.

The project itself and its findings cannot be isolated, either, from its immediate, large-scale predecessor, 'Variations in Teachers' Work, Lives and their Effects on Pupils' (VITAE), a four-year, large-scale, mixed methods project in which members of this team and others engaged in research with 300 teachers in 100 primary and secondary schools in seven local authorities (school districts/municipalities) across England (Day *et al.* 2007; Sammons *et al.* 2007). The findings from that project informed and created a springboard for much of the new research reported in this book.

We took our definition of effectiveness originally from VITAE. The teachers who were selected from that and one other project in which we were engaged, and whose lives and classroom practices are illustrated and unpacked in different ways in this book, are those who were defined as demonstrating 'relative' value-added effectiveness – that is when the progress and attainment of their students over at least a three-year consecutive period had been at or above the level expected on the basis of previous progress and attainment when compared with the results of pupils of teachers with similar experience and working in similar contexts. In addition, in the VITAE research we also found that these teachers' effectiveness was also 'relational': that is, albeit within their overall relative and relational effectiveness, they experienced and managed fluctuations through, for example, anticipated and unanticipated challenges and changes in their own personal circumstances and professional life phase 'scenarios' which influenced their sense of efficacy and professional identity. We explore these aspects in more depth in this book. While these findings in general replicate those of the VITAE study (Day *et al.* 2007; Sammons *et al.* 2007), they add an important new observational element. They are able, therefore, to provide further understandings about the work of a particular group of teachers who had been identified as not only demonstrating both 'relative' and 'relational 'effectiveness in the original studies but also having continued to do so.

Although effectiveness was defined initially by the progress and test results of their students, the ECP project was able to provide more detailed pictures of the influences of the organizational landscapes in which these effective and more effective teachers worked, the scenarios which tested their resolve, the strategies they used in their classroom practices and the ways in which they and their teaching were perceived by their students. The majority of studies of schools, teachers and classrooms have provided important understandings of 'effectiveness' in general. However, most have focused almost exclusively on what happens in the classroom (e.g. observational studies), the results of what happens in the classroom on pupil outcomes (e.g. quantitative studies), the lives of teachers (e.g. qualitative studies), the characteristics of teachers (e.g. psychologically driven studies), or classroom and school conditions for teachers and teaching (e.g. sociologically driven studies). Large-scale econometric studies (e.g. seeking correlations between student results and teaching qualifications) have looked at inputs and outputs without venturing into the 'black box' of the classroom action. The result has been, with few exceptions, that they have not been able to provide a holistic picture of the ways in which influences and conditions outside the classroom and inside the school are managed successfully by effective teachers.

The added value of this research, therefore, is that it focused upon what happens in the classrooms of teachers identified as effective and more effective in terms of the progress and attainment of their pupils through observations of the classroom action itself and through listening to their own accounts.

The second chapter, **Effective teaching and effective teachers: an overview of research and evidence** begins by examining further the meaning of effectiveness begun in the VITAE project, by asking the question, 'Who are considered to be "effective" teachers and what does effective teaching mean?'. The chapter provides an overview of the evidence from different sources of research and practice internationally and notes that the term 'effectiveness' varies according to the definitions of educational objectives of those who use it. For example, it notes that, from a policy-maker perspective, teacher effectiveness is generally referred to in terms of pupil test and examination results and the teacher behaviours and classroom processes that promote these. However, we suggest that while this definition is essential, it is only a partial indicator of teacher effectiveness. The chapter draws evidence in support of this from, for example, Ofsted (the Office for Standards in Education, the independent inspection watchdog for school standards in England) which details a number of qualities and characteristics of what good teaching looks like and what it shows:

- good subject knowledge: an essential prerequisite of good teaching;
- well-structured lessons sharing a number of key characteristics;
- the skilful use of well-chosen questions to engage and challenge learners and to consolidate understanding;
- effective assessment for learning.

The chapter extends this general framework through which the quality of teaching is often observed and judged. Summarizing the research, it suggests that effective teachers:

- are clear about their teaching and learning goals;
- are knowledgeable about curriculum content and the strategies for teaching it;
- communicate to their students what is expected of them;
- make expert use of existing teaching and learning materials in order to devote more time to practices that enrich and clarify the content;
- are knowledgeable about their students, adapting teaching to their needs and anticipating misconceptions to their existing knowledge;
- teach students meta-cognitive strategies and give them opportunities to master them;
- address higher- as well as lower-level cognitive objectives;
- monitor students' understanding by offering regular appropriate feedback;
- integrate their instruction with that in other subject areas;
- accept responsibility for student outcomes.

By detailing the key features of classroom practice that help to illuminate the concepts of effective teaching and effective teachers, the chapter provides a research-informed baseline against which to observe the approaches to teaching of the 'effective' teachers who participated in the ECP project. However, it acknowledges, also, that observation and pupil results are both insufficient means of providing a deep understanding of teaching and learning.

Drawing upon the VITAE findings, the chapter asserts, also, that 'we should not view teacher effectiveness as an isolated characteristic of a teacher, but a consequence of many interacting factors' and that, 'a teacher may be more or by contrast less effective in different circumstances and at different times, and thus there is a need to examine the factors that affect teachers' observed teaching behaviours, their overall teaching effectiveness, and their variation and stability over time'.

Chapter 3, **Studying effective classroom practice**, describes the integrated mixed methods design which enabled the research to investigate effective teachers and effective teaching across different school contexts and professional life phases, and to place the observations of their practices, strategies and methods in these. The chapter will be of particular interest to researchers and those who undertake research as part of their university degree programmes. It provides a conceptual map of the factors identified as being most likely to influence pupil outcomes – school climate; pupil characteristics; adult–pupil interactions and relationships; teaching organization and management; classroom climate; and teacher characteristics – and sets the scene for the examination in subsequent chapters of the relationships across 45 teachers in 22 primary and 36 teachers in 11 secondary schools, between observed classroom practice and policy, school context, teacher professional life phase and professional identity, together with the views of 1,250 pupils from those schools. The sample in this study reinforces a key finding of the VITAE project that there is a statistically significant association between teacher motivation, commitment and effectiveness, when applied to effective and more effective teachers. The teacher and pupil surveys, teacher and leadership interviews, classroom observation protocols and repertory grid technique, and the use of NVivo as an analytical tool in the integration and synthesis of the qualitative and quantitative strands of the data are also described in some detail, together with the use of 'Narrative Teacher Profiles', through which a range of data were combined to construct a concentrated story of each teacher.

Chapter 4, **Exploring effective teaching: learning from classroom observation**, provides a summary of teacher effectiveness research and inspection evidence on the characteristics of effective classroom practice, presents and discusses the quantitative analysis of the classroom observations of the teachers, identifying from this a number of models of the classroom behaviour of effective teachers and, finally, discusses the implications for training and continuing professional development. The chapter lays to rest simplistic but long-held differences in the ways teaching has been characterized as, for example, either a 'craft', an 'art' or a 'science'. It represents examples from the last 30 years of key studies which have investigated classroom practice and pupil outcomes together with teaching factors associated with success, which have been identified by school inspectors in England.

It draws attention to the need to adopt well-developed tools for systematic classroom observation to complement the qualitative insights from field notes. By using international observation instruments the research could use existing powerful lenses to study the practice of teachers in the ECP project.

The chapter presents the two innovative classroom observation instruments used. These were 'The International System for Teacher Observation and Feedback', an internationally applicable instrument developed by researchers and experts in over 20 countries (Teddlie *et al.* 2006) and 'The Quality of Teaching Schedule' based on an instrument used by school inspectors in the Netherlands (Van de Grift *et al.* 2004; Van de Grift 2007).

The detailed quantitative analysis of the results of the use of the observation schedules revealed support for a generic view of overall effectiveness such that we can say with a high degree of confidence that effective teachers in this study, whether male or female, less or more experienced, working in primary or secondary schools, regardless of their level of socio-economic advantage or disadvantage, score very highly in the following ways:

- clear and coherent lessons in supportive learning climates;
- engage students with assignments and activities;
- exercise positive classroom management;
- ensure purposeful learning;
- provide quality questioning and feedback to students.

We also found, however, that there was variation in relation to:

- the use of differentiation of work and instructional strategies for different groups of students;
- responsiveness to student needs;
- engagement of students in active learning;
- adaptation of teaching;
- teaching learning strategies.

Secondary school teachers obtained a lower score in these respects than primary school teachers, as did teachers in schools in more disadvantaged contexts. These findings hint at possible differences between the 'effective' group of teachers in this study and their 'more effective' counterparts. By adopting a mixed methods approach, we were able to examine possible differences and similarities qualitatively also.

Chapter 5, **Being an effective practitioner: learning from teachers' accounts and perceptions**, builds on what we observed from teachers' practice, by exploring what it means to be an effective practitioner according to the accounts and perceptions of teachers themselves. The data are drawn from interviews with teachers both before and after their lesson observations, and in many ways supports the findings of the observations in terms of the need for supportive lesson climates and proactive lesson management. We look at the effective teachers as one group, rather than differentiating between 'effective' and 'highly effective' teachers. This allows us to identify the key trends in teachers' accounts of their effectiveness. In this group we find that teachers place great importance on planning well-organized lessons with clear objectives, where students are engaged with the activities. They value positive classroom management and providing feedback to students, both as a means of achieving learning objectives and as a way to support positive relationships.

By focusing on teachers' perceptions we are able to explore in depth how teachers understand effectiveness, how it is built on their motivation and professional development and how they reflect on their practice in the classroom. The chapter is divided into two main sections: the first looks at characteristics of effective practitioners, finding them to be highly motivated people who enjoy their work. They have high levels of job satisfaction and are keen to develop their professional skills. Effective practitioners love seeing their students' progress and are interested in learning more about their subject and developing their professional skills. Teachers referred to a strong sense of motivation, commitment, self-efficacy and well-being with regard to their effectiveness.

The second section considers what effective practitioners do. This explores the ways that they build relationships with students, how this relates to giving praise and feedback and the ways in which teachers communicate high expectations to their students. Developing positive relationships was interpreted in different ways and influenced by a number of factors. Some essential dimensions of building relationships were getting to know the students well, establishing good rapport and interaction, using humour, listening to what the students had to say and communicating effectively with them. Relationships needed to be based on fairness, consistency and support, and tied into the ways that teachers communicated high expectations to students. These had to be clear, consistent and understood by students with rules and boundaries set out clearly at the outset.

In the final part of this second section, there is a discussion of the accounts teachers give of their lessons and how they work towards teaching creative, flexible and student-led classes, which acknowledge different learning styles and ability levels. The lesson and the learning environment were important dimensions of effective practice and were created through careful and well-directed planning, but it was also important that there was room for creativity and flexibility in planning and in the classroom.

The chapter concludes by summarizing ten key features of an effective practitioner:

- highly motivated and committed to their students;
- value professional development and look for opportunities to improve their subject knowledge and teaching practice;
- build strong relationships with their students and ensure they know them well, so that they can understand their needs;
- are firm but fair, positive, open and supportive;
- communicate clearly with students, particularly in terms of expectations and feedback;
- have high expectations of their students;
- give positive praise and feedback to students, carefully adapted to the individual's needs;
- are flexible with lesson plans and are able to adapt and enrich lessons in ways appropriate for their students;
- plan creative, enjoyable and stimulating lessons to engage students in learning, by considering a range of different learning styles;
- encourage students to take control of their own learning and ask questions to guide their own intellectual enquiry.

These features allowed us to develop a model of an effective practitioner from the perspective of the teachers themselves. This has three intersected dimensions: teacher-student relationships, praise and feedback and high expectations. These feed into teachers' values of being fair and consistent, demanding and supportive, positive and open, and are influenced by factors affecting self-efficacy, including job satisfaction, commitment to professional development and ability to plan flexible and creative lessons.

In Chapter 6, **The impact of effective practice: learning from student voices,** we present the results of a survey and focus group interviews of 1,250 pupils taught by the teachers in the study. In any study which seeks to understand the effectiveness of teachers and their teaching in the classroom, it is essential to listen to the voices of the pupils who are the focus of teachers' efforts. Over many years now, research has shown that pupils' voices are regarded as authentic and trustworthy indicators of the efficacy, efficiency and effectiveness of teachers and their teaching, and have an important part to play in decision-making at all levels. They are increasingly sought out, though for a variety of purposes. We begin the chapter with a summary of these purposes, from the United Nations Convention on the rights of all children to be heard and their views being given 'due weight' (UN General Assembly 1989) through to, in the UK, their use as a component in the school inspection system, engagement in school governance, evaluation of teaching and learning, as a basis from which to create more democratic interaction, and as researchers with the power to influence school change (MacBeath and Mortimore 2001). We point to the 'four core values' theoretical framework offered by Robinson and Taylor (2007): a conception of communication as dialogue; the necessity of participation and democratic inclusivity; acknowledgement of power relations and inequality; and the potential for change and transformation. Pupils' responses were largely very positive in all Year 2, 6 and 9 year groups taught by the ECP teachers in our sample, the exception being their negative views of the behaviour of some of their peers, and we detail their responses in the chapter. The most important broad categories for each year group were identified as:

Year 2

- pupil enjoyment and security;
- positive teacher support and reassurance;
- teacher approachability;
- clarity of teacher instruction and teacher expectations;
- attachment to school;
- positive working experience;
- working arrangements.

Year 6

- positive teacher support and reassurance;
- attachment to school;
- pupil motivation and feedback;
- pupil understanding of work;
- teacher feedback and resources.

Year 9

- pupil enjoyment and security;
- teacher approachability and organization;
- pupil behaviour and resources;
- positive teacher support and reassurance;
- understanding of work and teacher feedback;
- positive teacher feedback;
- clarity of instruction.

However, we note that pupils' responses also indicated differences in relation to the level of social disadvantage of the school context (measured by the free school meals – FSM – status of their school)[1]. For example, while pupils in schools serving high disadvantaged communities indicated high levels of enjoyment and security, they scored working arrangements, clarity of instruction and teacher expectations lower than other pupils.

These survey findings match well with the classroom observational data reported in this chapter, with pupils describing their teachers as knowing them well, caring and considerate, energetic, organized, reassuring and 'making everyone feel good about their learning'. The key factors which influenced the large majority of the pupils were: teachers' characteristics; learning involvement with teacher and with other pupils; classroom environment; activity and pace of the lesson; negative pupil behaviour; relevance of work to self; difficulty of task; communication; engagement; and frequency and quality of feedback.

Earlier chapters focused on the different classroom, school, personal and professional contexts which influence the work and lives of teachers in order to illustrate how they contribute to the quality of their teaching and its effectiveness. In Chapter 7, **Career phase and teacher effectiveness**, we examine how experience of teaching may play its part in influencing teachers' capacity for effectiveness. We again draw upon our earlier VITAE work (Day *et al.* 2007) in which we provided a conceptual framework of six professional life phases, based on years of experience in teaching rather than age. Teachers were placed and placed themselves in one or another according to a number of characteristics associated with experience, concerns and sense of commitment. In the ECP project, we explored the variations between the teachers by placing them in the three broader categories:

- **Early-career phase**: professional life phases 0–3 and 4–7 combined
- **Mid-career phase:** professional life phases 8–15 and 16–23 combined
- **Later-career phase:** professional life phases 24–3- and 31+ combined

Our analyses revealed patterns of both similarities and differences within and across these phases which influenced their levels of effectiveness. It was apparent, for example, that there were substantial differences between the three phases in terms of teachers' concerns. For early-career teachers, establishing positive, close working relationships with pupils and successfully managing behaviour in the classroom were central to their sense of self-efficacy, job satisfaction and commitment. For this group, also, the quality of leadership support was a vital ingredient in their sense of early success. For mid- and later-career teachers, positive pupil-teacher relationships were associated with low levels of behavioural problems as these teachers had developed their ability to regulate pupils' social, emotional and cognitive skills. It was the quality of the teacher-pupil interactions and expectations which counted most. Teachers who were in the later phases of their career spoke of their teaching as 'an integrated whole' in which, again, positive teacher-pupil interactions and relationships were primary satisfiers. Contrary to the 'disengagement' among later career teachers found by Huberman in his study of secondary school teachers (Huberman 1989, 1993), these effective teachers reported their continuing commitment. While for all these teachers, increases in bureaucracy, paperwork and workload were negative features of their lives, they had not allowed them to become dominant. The chapter goes on to provide illustrations from the teachers, in and across the three career phases, of the important influences on their ability to teach effectively. This includes:

- teacher-student relationships;
- praise and feedback to students;
- teacher (high) expectations;
- teacher creativity and flexibility;
- personal factors: motivation, commitment and job satisfaction; well-being; sense of self-efficacy.

The chapter ends with a brief but important discussion about the importance of 'emotional effectiveness' and the identification, within each career phase, of teachers who through the analyses of classroom observations, pupil progress and attainment data, and pupil feedback, were either 'effective' (N = 52) or 'highly effective' (N = 29). We present profiles of this range of teachers and begin to tease out similarities and differences between the two groups.

An important indicator of effectiveness or otherwise is how teachers feel about themselves as professionals. This will relate also to how they feel others see them, for example, as respected members of the community, valued for their knowledge, skills and work ethic and duty of care for the children and young people they teach; or as those who contribute to the failure of children and young people's education rather than to its success. There is much literature on the challenges to teachers' sense of professionalism, especially in times of continuing and often intensive government reform, the rise of technologies for learning which inevitably affect teachers' traditional roles as knowledge-holders, and changes in the social norms and expectations of family life which affect children and young people's behaviour in school.

In Chapter 8, **Professional identity and effective classroom practice**, we focus first upon what has been written about the nature of teacher identity as a source of meaning and experience, drawing upon empirical data from the ECP project. Previous chapters have drawn attention to effective and more effective teachers' practices, qualities and virtues through the lenses of pupil experience, self-report and classroom observation, and there is a sense in which these may be seen to combine to form teachers' sense of self or identity through the different phases of their careers, the different classroom and school contexts, and changes in the broader policy and social demands which are made upon them. The VITAE research identified the various factors which can contribute to teachers' sense of identity and, importantly, the fluctuations in their sense of positive and negative identity caused by both anticipated and unanticipated personal, workplace, socio-cultural and policy changes.

The evidence from a range of sources about effective and more effective teachers in the ECP study provides additional empirical support for this hypothesis. All had stable positive identities with direct effects of commitment upon relationships with pupils and pupils' learning and attainment; and a key feature of these teachers was their ability to manage the complex interactions between structure, agency and action.

The chapter identifies, as did the VITAE project, three dimensions which together constituted the major influences upon teachers' sense of professional identity. These are: personal, workplace and socio-cultural and policy. However, we find differences from the VITAE research, because of the focus on effective and more effective practitioners in this research. Teachers also told us of four 'scenarios' which they experienced which challenged their capacities to build and sustain a stable, positive sense of identity. In the first scenario, each dimension was able to be held in balance despite minor fluctuations. In Scenario 2, one dimension required more attention than the other two; in Scenario 3 two dimensions dominated and in Scenario 4 teachers experienced turbulence in all three dimensions. While all four scenarios needed energy, Scenarios 2, 3 and 4 required more time and energy, thus detracting from the reserves of energy and 'everyday resilience' (Day and Gu 2014) needed to teach to their best and sustain their positive sense of professional identity. None of those teachers identified as highly effective experienced Scenarios 3 and 4. The chapter identifies teacher-student relationships and self-efficacy as having the strongest influence on professional identity, regardless of scenarios experienced, and provides three case studies of teachers as illustrations of the challenges faced and overcome in managing Scenarios 1, 2 and 3. We also note in this chapter associations between self-efficacy and career phase.

The book provides a discussion and conclusion in the last chapter that draws together the key findings and examines their implications for policy and practice. In particular it cautions against current moves that seek to create high-stakes systems to measure teacher effectiveness for use in ways to reward or sanction teachers, by recognizing the complexities inherent in studying teacher effectiveness and classroom practice. It argues instead that greater attention needs to be given to the positive contribution that research findings can make in helping to support teachers' professional development as autonomous and reflective practitioners.

Note

1. FSM groups were based on the percentage of pupil eligibility for FSM: FSM 1 = 0–8%, FSM 2 = 9–20%, FSM 3 = 21–35%, FSM 4 = 36% and above.

References

Day, C. and Gu, Q. (2014) *Resilient Teachers, Resilient Schools: Building and Sustaining Quality in Testing Times (Teacher Quality and School Development)*. London: Routledge.

Day, C., Stobart, G., Sammons, P. and Kington, A. (2007) Variations in the work and lives of teachers: relative and relational effectiveness, *Teachers and Teaching: Theory and Practice*, 12(1): 169–92.

Huberman, M. (1989) The professional life cycle of teachers, *Teachers College Record*, 91(1): 31–57.

Huberman, M. (1993) *The Lives of Teachers*. London: Cassell.

Kington, A., Sammons, P., Day, C. and Regan, E. (2011) Stories and statistics: describing a mixed methods study of effective classroom practice, *Journal of Mixed Methods Research*, 5(2): 103–25.

MacBeath, J. and Mortimore, P. (eds) (2001) *Improving School Effectiveness*. Maidenhead: Open University Press.

Robinson, C. and Taylor, C. (2007) Theorizing student voice: values and perspectives, *Improving Schools*, 10(1): 5–17.

Sammons, P., Day, C., Kington, A., Gu, Q., Stobart, G. and Smees, R. (2007) Exploring variations in teachers' work, lives and their effects on pupils: key findings and implications from a longitudinal mixed methods study, *British Educational Research Journal*, 33(5): 681–701.

Teddlie, C., Creemers, B., Kyriakides, L., Muijs, D. and Yu, F. (2006) The International System for Teacher Observation and Feedback: evolution of an international study of teacher effectiveness constructs, *Educational Research and Evaluation*, 12(6): 561–82.

UN General Assembly. (1989) *Resolution adopted by the General Assembly: Convention on the Rights of the Child*. Geneva: United Nations, retrieved 15 December 2013 from www.ohchr.org/EN/ProfessionalInterest/Pages/CRC.aspxhttp://www.ohchr.org/EN/ProfessionalInterest/Pages/CRC.aspx.

Van de Grift, W. (2007) Quality of teaching in four European countries: a review of the literature and application of an assessment instrument, *Educational Research*, 49(2): 127–52.

Van de Grift, W., Matthews, P., Tabak, l. and de Rijcke, F. (2004) *Comparative Research into the Inspection of Teaching in England and the Netherlands*, HMI 2251. London: Ofsted.

2 Effective teaching and effective teachers: an overview of research and evidence

Introduction

We sought to ground our research in the relevant literature. It was important to study literature on teaching and on teachers and their effectiveness. We needed to explore how the concept of 'effectiveness' has been developed and applied by researchers and others in education systems who make judgements about standards and quality of provision. Who are considered to be 'effective' teachers and what does 'effective teaching' mean? How does this link with the broader concepts of what 'good' teaching may involve? In this chapter we provide an overview of evidence. We examine definitions of effectiveness and outline why we need to examine different perspectives and sources of evidence from different stakeholders. We pay attention to inspection evidence that has exerted a powerful influence in the UK, reflecting the high-stakes accountability system in operation since the introduction of published inspection reports by Ofsted in 1993. We also investigate the international teacher effectiveness research tradition. We conducted an in-depth review to inform the development of our research but this has been updated and extended to place our present research results from the Effective Classroom Practice (ECP) project in context (see Darling Hammond *et al.* 2010; Ko *et al.* 2013 for more detailed discussions). This chapter provides an overview of the main areas covered.

Defining effectiveness

The term 'educational effectiveness' was developed to provide a more confined definition than notions of 'good' or 'quality' education. Effectiveness can be examined throughout nearly all levels of an education system, from nationally to individual schools, departments and teachers (Ko *et al.* 2013: 5). Importantly, the concept of effectiveness should be considered in relation to a number of issues, such as outcomes, referring to the goals of education for students, time period, concerning change and improvement over time, and effectiveness in relation to promoting outcomes for different groups of students (by gender or/ethnic group, for example) (Sammons 1996). Creemers also emphasizes the need for criteria for effectiveness. These criteria refer to 'objectives of education in general and of teaching in particular' (1999: 51). At national level the criteria can be influenced by what is deemed important by policy-makers, and more locally they can be influenced by individual schools or departments (Stufflebeam and Shinkfield 1995; Sammons 1996). The chosen criteria, Creemers explains, 'are the result of a political and societal debate, but educational professionals, teachers and schools can also take part in it' (1999: 51). He also points out that 'although objectives of education show changes over time, language, reading and mathematics remain the core studies'.

Students' academic achievement is often a top priority, which is reflected in a definition of teacher effectiveness given by Campbell *et al.* They note that 'a teacher is effective if he/she can accomplish the planned goals and assigned tasks in accordance with school goals' (2004: 61). The objectives of education and the definitions of effectiveness are closely linked. Therefore, effective teaching should be defined in relation to understanding the objectives of education (Ko *et al.* 2013: 6). Moreover, in the research literature, instructional effectiveness, teacher effectiveness, and teaching effectiveness have regularly been used interchangeably (Scheerens 2004, 2008), reflecting that a substantial part of the teacher's work is instructional. The interchangeable manner in which the terms have been used can in part be explained by the fact that sometimes the 'focus is on the teacher's influence on student outcomes, and at other times on the classroom behaviours and practices that teachers use to promote better outcomes for students' (Ko *et al.* 2013: 6). Teacher effectiveness however, is generally referred to in terms of a focus on student outcomes and the teacher behaviours and classroom processes that promote better student outcomes (Ko *et al.* 2013: 2). As the role of teacher often extends beyond the classroom, some authors prefer a broader definition of effectiveness, which includes references to factors beyond the classroom processes (Medley 1982; Cheng 1995; Cheng and Tsui 1996; Campbell *et al.* 2004).

Finally, analyses of students' progress or learning gains measured in achievement tests can be used to produce value-added indicators of teacher effectiveness. However, these can provide only a partial source of evidence if the achievement tests do not reflect the wider goals and outcomes of education. This will be further discussed in a later part of the chapter.

Perspectives of teacher effectiveness

Examining teacher effectiveness can be done in a number of ways, such as classroom observation, interviews, inspection evidence, examination and testing of data about student achievement, policy documentation and questionnaire surveys. Not only that, but there are also different informants offering perspectives from key stakeholders in the system, including inspectors, school principals, heads of departments, teachers and students.

Student attainment data and value-added measures

Educational effectiveness research has frequently studied teacher effects on student attainment. Such research typically seeks to investigate teacher effects on the educational attainment of particular classes of students. Since the advent of multi-level modelling techniques that take into account different sorts of clustering in educational data (e.g. students nested in classes, classes nested in schools), it has been possible to provide better estimates of teacher and school effects. However, it is stressed that estimates are just that, and as with any assessments they are not perfect measures and are affected by statistical uncertainty. Such research draws attention to the need to control for differences in the prior attainments and background characteristics of student intakes to schools and individual classes in order to measure student progress and make fairer 'like with like' comparisons across schools and classes (Hanushek and Rivkin 2006; Darling Hammond et al. 2010).

Estimates suggest that schools account for around 5–15 per cent of the variation in student attainment outcomes after taking account of students' prior attainment and background, while teacher effects are generally much larger at 20–40 per cent when progress is examined over an academic year. Research indicates that teacher effects on student learning (measured by attainment progress over time) can be sizeable and may match or overcome the effects of social disadvantage (Darling Hammond et al. 2010: 87). Attainment data can be used to provide 'value-added' estimates of teacher effectiveness. This is one of the reasons why student attainment data is a popular approach to identifying effective teachers, which in turn can help to identify effective teaching behaviours and practices (Muijs and Reynolds 2000; Day et al. 2006). There have been a number of reviews of teacher effectiveness research (Porter and Brophy 1988; McBer 2000; Muijs and Reynolds 2000, 2005; Hattie 2009; Slavin 2010) which reveal consistent patterns of teaching practices that promote better outcomes for students, providing a valuable source of evidence on some key features of effective teaching.

In calculating estimates of individual teacher effects it is important to recognize that each has associated confidence intervals attached, thus it is not appropriate to make fine rank-ordered distinctions between individual teachers. Only statistically significantly different outliers (very high or very low effective teachers in terms of student value-added progress) can be distinguished reliably. Moreover, value-added measures of teacher effects may vary between years and across different classes as shown in the Variations in Teachers' Work, Lives and their Effects on Pupils (VITAE) research (Day et al. 2007; Sammons et al. 2007). Value-added data may further vary by type of attainment measure used, how well it links with the curriculum and by school contexts. For these reasons we argue for caution in the use of value-added measures or other measures of individual teacher effects in isolation. We strongly argue that value-added estimates are not suited to making 'high-stakes' judgements about individual teachers (e.g. in terms of career or pay). Rather, such data are best used for research purposes and in combination with other evidence to study more effective practice and support professional development.

The majority of research on value-added teacher effectiveness is quantitative, though there is a growing recognition that a qualitative element can provide additional insight to the statistical data (Day et al. 2007; Siraj-Blatchford et al. 2011) by studying the practice of teachers identified as more or less effective in more depth. As part of a broader study Hill et al. (2011) compared 24 middle school mathematics teachers' value-added scores with survey and observation-based indicators of teacher quality, instruction and student characteristics. They found that teachers' value-added scores were positively correlated with expert ratings of their instruction. However, although many teachers were classified similarly by their value-added and observational scores, a minority were not and the correlations were by no means perfect.

Inspection evidence

In addition to student attainment data, inspection evidence can provide a major source of evidence on effective teaching. Reasons for carrying out school inspections vary per country, and can be for quality assurance and/or helping and supporting teachers' and schools' developing practices. In England for example, Ofsted's aim was improvement through inspection (2009). As inspectors are often trained and experienced, and their judgements are checked for reliability, inspection evidence can inform practitioners about what practices are considered to be most 'effective', 'high quality' or 'good' and the features of 'unsatisfactory' 'good' and 'excellent' teaching are defined according to the professional judgements of inspectors. A 1994 Ofsted report on primary teaching in England showed a number of general teacher/teaching features associated with high standards of achievement. In a later study, analysing inspection judgements, Barber and Mourshed (2007) highlight some of the features of good teaching in England.

Ofsted's (1994, 1999) key findings in inspections of primary schools in the 1990s in England produced a guide to what effective teaching looks like in primary schools:

- good subject knowledge;
- good questioning skills;
- an emphasis upon instruction;
- a balance of grouping strategies;
- clear objectives;
- good time management;
- appropriate range of teacher assessment techniques;
- well-established classroom routines;
- effective planning;
- good classroom organization;
- effective use of other adults in the classroom.

Good teaching involves:

- good subject knowledge (an essential prerequisite for good teaching);
- well-structured lessons sharing a number of key characteristics;
- the skilful use of well-chosen questions to engage and challenge learners and to consolidate understanding is an important feature of good teaching.
- effective assessment for learning (a vital ingredient in good teaching).

Ofsted also published a report on good secondary school teaching in subject departments which suggests a number of questions for teachers that could be used as the starting points for teacher self-evaluation and departmental or whole-school review. These included questions such as: 'as a subject teacher, do I: have a detailed, up-to-date knowledge of the subject(s) I teach, plan lessons and units of work to ensure continuity in learning, and use questioning skilfully to probe and extend pupils' thinking' (for the whole list, see Ofsted 2002: 73–4).

A criticism of high-stakes school inspection, as in England, is that it can reduce teachers' freedom to be creative and so may damage their professional autonomy. Inspection is also claimed to have added to teachers' and schools' workload, increased stress on teachers and decreased job satisfaction. Nonetheless, there is evidence that in combination with other reforms, such as a national curriculum and investment in professional development, inspections have helped raise standards, particularly in weaker schools (Gray 2000; Matthews and Sammons 2004; Sammons 2008).

Teachers' perceptions

Teacher perceptions of effective teaching are often collected in surveys, instruction logs and interviews (Ball and Rowan 2004; Day et al. 2008). However, these are not entirely unproblematic; for example, Camburn and Barnes (2004) found that teacher and researcher reports did not always correspond, raising the question of validity as well as differences in values, understanding, interpretation and evaluation. In addition to investigating teachers' perceptions of what constitutes effective teaching, another interesting point is how teachers view their own effectiveness over time.

A study using a more global self-report measure of teachers' perceived effectiveness, and a measure of their relative effectiveness based on value-added analyses of pupil progress, sought to investigate teacher effectiveness in more depth, known as 'Variations in Teachers' Lives and Work and their Effects on Pupils (VITAE) (Day et al. 2007, 2008)'. VITAE showed that teacher effectiveness is not merely a result of age and experience but is influenced by variations in the individual teachers' work, lives and identities, which shape their senses of professional identity in their various professional life phases. This, in turn, influences their relative commitment and resilience, as well as teachers' capacities to manage these variations to sustain their teaching effectiveness. These findings are important in two ways. First, they suggest that studies that simply control for age and teaching experience would miss important roles of personal, situated and contextual factors that help to shape teachers' professional identities and their capacities to manage variations and sustain their effectiveness over the course of their teaching careers. Second, the results suggest that we should not view teacher effectiveness as an isolated characteristic of the teacher, but a consequence of many interacting factors. This research suggests that a teacher may be more or, by contrast, less effective in different circumstances and at different times, and thus there is a need to examine the factors that affect teachers' observed teaching behaviours, their overall teaching effectiveness, and their variation and stability over time.

Student perceptions

Despite some concerns about students' ability to appreciate the full context of teaching and worries about views of teachers' personalities or students' own grades affecting their ratings, students' views can be an insightful approach to examine teacher effectiveness (Ko *et al.* 2013). The validity and reliability of using students' course evaluations to understand teacher effectiveness has been established in various studies (Marsh 1984, 1987; Baker 1986; Follman 1992, 1995; Patrick and Smart 1998; Worrell and Kuterbach 2001; Kyriakides 2005; Shirbagi 2007) based on a range of measures, such as for example the Students' Evaluation of Education Quality intrument (SEEQ) by Marsh (1982), the Teacher Evaluation Questionnaire by the University of Queensland Tertiary Education Institute (Moses 1986) and the Course Experience Questionnaire by Ramsden (1991). The SEEQ measures a number of different items, such as instructor's enthusiasm, organization, group interaction and individual rapport. These items are very similar to other measures which will be discussed later. However, surveys of student ratings of teachers rarely concern classroom instruction only. They can also include what goes on beyond the classroom such as feedback on exams, or relevance of readings (Marsh 1982). As well as improving our understanding of effective teaching, Murray (1997) comments that when used with expert consultation, student ratings can be used to enhance teaching quality. Moreover, studies including a focus on teaching in higher education have shown that student evaluations of university teachers can identify clear dimensions related to effective teaching (Marsh 1984, 2007; Marsh and Hocevar 1991; Marsh and Bailey 1993; Marsh and Cheng 2008). Recent research as part of the Effective Provision of Pre-school Education project in England has shown that students' reports on their schools and on teachers can provide robust indicators of their learning environments (Sammons *et al.* 2011a, 2011b).

In addition to questionnaire-type student ratings of teacher effectiveness, other approaches of listening to the student 'voice' are becoming increasingly popular and these include small-group interviews with students, students engaging in their own action research in schools, students giving teachers feedback on their lessons and student involvement in teacher selection interviews.

The characterization challenge

The ultimate aim of characterizing effective teaching practices involves identifying the generic features and dimensions of effective teaching to provide a guide for the improvement of professional practice. There is a growing interest in many systems to measure the relative impacts of teacher effects on students' learning outcomes, and to establish whether particular contextual conditions (especially the level of disadvantage and prior ability of the students in some schools) influences teacher effectiveness. The first task begins with summarizing results of research that has sought to provide profiles of effective teachers and effective teaching. There have been many reviews synthesizing previous research on effective teaching behaviours (Light and Smith 1971; Rosenshine 1971; Bloom 1976; Glass 1977; Gage 1978; Good *et al.* 1983; Brophy and Good 1986; Walberg 1986; Wittrock 1986) and these reveal some agreement on the general features of effective teachers. The list below presents a general profile of effective teachers.

Effective teachers:

- are clear about instructional goals;
- are knowledgeable about curriculum content and the strategies for teaching it;
- communicate to their students what is expected of them – and why;
- make expert use of existing instructional materials in order to devote more time to practices that enrich and clarify the content;
- are knowledgeable about their students, adapting instruction to their needs and anticipating misconceptions in their existing knowledge;
- teach students meta-cognitive strategies and give them opportunities to master them;
- address higher- as well as lower-level cognitive objectives;
- monitor students' understanding by offering regular appropriate feedback;
- integrate their instruction with that in other subject areas;
- accept responsibility for student outcomes.

Unsurprisingly, ineffective teaching has been shown to exhibit contrasting characteristics.

Inconsistent approaches to the curriculum and teaching:

- inconsistent expectations for different learners that are lower for disadvantaged students from low socio-economic status families;
- an emphasis on supervising and communicating about routines;
- low levels of teacher-student interaction;
- low levels of student involvement in their work;
- student perceptions of their teachers as not caring, unhelpful, underappreciative of the importance of learning and their work;
- more frequent use of negative criticism and feedback.

It is important to note the effect that culture has on what constitutes effective teachers or effective teaching. Studies in Hong-Kong, for example, reveal many similarities to the western studies mentioned above, such as classroom climate and classroom management. However, there were also striking differences: the effective teacher is seen as a figure of authority, morality and benevolence, conforming to the Confucian concept of 'ren' and the social hierarchy of teachers in Chinese society (Jin and Cortazzi 1998). Additionally, research carried out in Hong Kong by Pratt and colleagues shows learning processes such as structured tasks, drills and memorization of materials to have greater focus than deep learning. Moreover, reflecting Chinese school culture, promoting students' attainment in external examinations and tests is given very high priority (Pratt et al. 1999).

Some researchers have tried to go even further than simply profiling effective teachers, by systematically categorizing different teaching behaviours and analysing links between these categories and student achievement. Consequently, there is not only a vast body of literature on general teaching behaviour, but also about effective teaching skills (Wragg 1984; Clark and Peterson 1986; Muijs and Reynolds

2005; Kyriacou 2007; Philpott 2009), different teaching styles (Bennett 1976; Galton *et al.* 1980; Opdenakke and Van Damme 2006) and different models of teaching which specify particular types of learning environment and approaches to teaching (Joyce *et al.* 2005, 2008). These studies have revealed that teacher effectiveness in the classroom is strongly affected by variations in their teaching behaviour. Moreover, these results are mostly in agreement with the generic features of effective teaching.

As noted earlier, cultural or philosophical beliefs may affect what constitutes an effective teacher and this is no different for teaching behaviours. The debate of teacher-directed (explicit) instruction versus a student-centred (constructivist) approach is a good example of this. In many western countries, the student-centred approach has been given high priority in teacher training courses and school systems, whereas Asian contexts have been known to adopt more teacher-centred approaches. An alternative approach to constructivist methods is direct instruction, which provides clear and constructive feedback on how to improve. However, studies show that when teaching younger children or disadvantaged students, teacher-directed approaches are more successful in promoting student learning (Galton *et al.* 1980; Mortimore *et al.* 1988; Muijs and Reynolds 2000; Rowe 2006). This does not mean there are no merits to adopting student-centred approaches, although Rowe stresses the importance of students having the basic knowledge and skills (best provided initially by direct instruction) before engagement in 'rich' constructivist learning activities (2006: 14).

Research on direct instruction indicates that learning can be greatly accelerated if instructional presentations are clear, minimize misinterpretations and facilitate generalizations. Furthermore, the approach is based on a number of important assumptions (Rowe 2006: 5):

- all children can learn, regardless of their intrinsic and context characteristics;
- the teaching of basic skills and their application in higher-order skills is essential to intelligent behaviour and should be the main focus of any instructional programme, and certainly prior to student-directed learning activities;
- instruction with students experiencing learning difficulties must be highly structured and permit large amounts of practice.

At primary schools in England, the Literacy and Numeracy Strategies were based on direct instruction and emphasized direct teaching and questioning of the whole class, individuals or groups of students. This meant that during the beginning and ending of lessons there was a strong focus on interactive whole-class teaching, which was regarded as especially helpful for reviewing, reflecting and consolidating teaching points and discussing work carried out in the lesson to check students' understanding (Muijs and Reynolds 2000). Factors that are considered important in direct instruction are: directing learning, which includes sharing learning goals/ objectives with students; instructing, demonstrating, explaining and illustrating; questioning and discussing; consolidating; evaluating students' responses; and summarizing and reviewing learning, particularly in closing a lesson.

The primacy of teacher effects and the relative effectiveness of teacher variables

The prime focus of early teacher effectiveness research was to investigate the effect of the teacher on student outcomes. In doing so, teacher effectiveness research largely ignored contextual variables in the school such as community and the education system. However, it was recognized that teachers work in schools and that their practice may be influenced by conditions within the school, which in turn could affect their teacher effectiveness. In addition, the school may have a direct impact on pupil outcomes. Moreover, the debate on the impacts of socio-economic factors on learning outcomes and concerns about equity led to the rise of school effectiveness research (Sammons 2007).

Though school-level factors affecting pupil outcomes have been identified in a number of studies (Levine and Lezotte 1990; Cotton 1995; Sammons et al. 1995; Scheerens and Bosker 1997; Marzano 2003), the research evidence on school effectiveness suggests that while schools can make a difference to student achievement, the most substantial portion of that difference may be attributed to teachers (Scheerens et al. 1989; Tymms 1993; Creemers 1994; Hill and Rowe 1996, 1998; Sammons et al. 1997; Sanders 1998, 2000; Nye et al. 2004; Konstantopoulos 2007; Muñoz and Chang 2007; Creemers and Kyriakides 2008; Kyriakides and Creemers 2008a, 2008b). This point is illustrated by Sanders (1998: 27):

> Of all the contextual variables that have been studied to date (indicators of socio-economic status, class size, student variability within classrooms, etc.), the single largest factor affecting academic growth of populations of students is differences in the effectiveness of individual classroom teachers. Also, the effects of teachers appeared to be cumulative. At the extreme, a high-high-high sequence [of three-year teacher effects of fifth-grade pupils] resulted in more than a 50 percentile point higher score in 5th-grade maths achievement than the low-low-low sequence . . . As the level of teacher effectiveness increased, students of lower achievement were the first to benefit, and only teachers of the highest effectiveness generally were effective with all students.

Studies carried out by Mortimore et al. (1988) at primary schools in England found similar cumulative effects. Also, a meta-analysis synthesizing over 800 studies relating to the influences on achievement in school-aged students further confirmed the role of the teacher, and classroom factors, as being of greater influence on pupils' outcomes than other school factors. As part of the meta-analysis a list was created of 138 variables affecting student achievement, and in the top 30, 19 variables related to teachers or teaching with an effect size above 0.5. To see the top 30 and the full list see Darling-Hammond (2000).

It was argued by some that as subject departments are the immediate working context of teachers, individual departments may have a greater impact on teachers' effectiveness than schools (Ainley 1994; Luyten 1994; Witziers 1994; Harris et al. 1995; Sammons et al. 1997). Results suggest departments have a strong impact on teachers; however the results also show variation from year to year.

Measurement challenge

Classroom observation has been one of the major methods of enquiry in teacher effectiveness research (often in conjunction with analyses of students' educational outcomes). However, developing valid and reliable instruments for observation has proved a challenge. This is illustrated by Mortimore *et al.* (1988) who pointed out in a study of primary teachers that using classroom observation to try to characterize 'teacher styles' (such as traditional or progressive) was an unhelpful dichotomy. Their research showed that the variance in teachers' observed behaviours *within* styles was far greater than the variance *between* styles. Rather, they argued that teachers varied in more particular ways in relation to specific features of observed practice along a continuum and that the division of teachers into those exhibiting a given style was too simplistic and unhelpful. The need to develop reliable observation instruments has been a focus for comparative and international research. This was stimulated by the International School Effectiveness Research Project (Reynolds 2006) which showed few agreed international constructs for measuring teaching effectiveness. As such, the need was recognized to develop a classroom observation instrument that would measure some agreed teacher effectiveness constructs (Darling-Hammond *et al.* 2010).

A study conducted by Muijs and Reynolds in England in 2000 used The Mathematics Enhancement Classroom Observation Record (MECORS), which was a modified version of an earlier instrument by Schaffer *et al.* (1991 in Meehan *et al.* 2004) and had been previously validated in the USA. Using the MECORS instrument a seven-factor model of effective teaching behaviours was identified. Moreover, the study showed that whole-class teaching creates the conditions for effective teaching to occur rather than directly affecting pupil progress. Muijs and Reynolds also found that effective teachers tend to be effective in most or all aspects because they found strong correlations among different dimensions of teaching observed.

A large-scale longitudinal study investigating the impact of pre-school and primary school on children's developmental outcomes in England (Sammons *et al.* 2006, 2007) used both the Instructional Environment Observation (IEO) Scale by Stipek (1999) as well as the Classroom Observation System for Fifth Grade (COS-5), designed by the National Institute of Child Health and Human Development (NICHD 2001). The motivation for choosing these instruments was that they were devised relatively recently for the primary age group, covering a wider range of pupil and teacher behaviours and offering the opportunity to facilitate comparison with research in other contexts.

The International School Effectiveness Research Project (ISERP) by Reynolds *et al.* (2002) provides the most extensive results on teacher and school effects in different countries using the same instruments. The Vergilio Teacher Behaviour Inventory (VTBI) (Teddlie *et al.* 1990; Virgilio *et al.* 1991) and the QAIT instrument (Quality of instruction, Appropriate level of interaction, Incentive, and Time), which is an updated version of Special Strategies Observation Systems (SSOS) by Schaffer *et al.* (1994), were used to measure teacher effectiveness. The use of multiple measures, as well as employing both quantitative and qualitative measures for triangulation, helped to enrich the findings of the study. The study showed that classroom management, classroom climate and teaching/instruction were the three factors that had statistically significant positive impacts on student academic outcomes in the USA, the UK and Norway. The project also stimulated research efforts to create an instrument for teacher observation and feedback with a broad external validity that could be used in a range of different countries, leading to the ISTOF (International Instrument for Teacher Observation and Feedback) project. Practitioners, education advisers/inspectors and researchers were consulted on what constitutes effective teaching and this complemented teacher effectiveness research which was used to generate the different components of the ISTOF instrument (Teddlie *et al.* 2006).

The original ISTOF scale was made up of 45 items and seven theoretical components. The items were descriptive statements specifying a particular teacher behaviour and were grouped together representing a total of 21 indicators of certain dimensions of teaching behaviours. Counting the occurrence of the specific teaching behaviours is not required, though – the rating is expected to be based on the observed relative frequency of the behaviours without passing judgement on whether an observed behaviour was 'good' or 'poor'.

Through a collaboration of the English and Dutch inspectorates, another classroom observation protocol, The Lesson Observation Form for Evaluating the Quality of Teaching (QoT) was developed (Van de Grift *et al.* 2004; Van der Grift 2007). The evaluative categories were based on both findings from teacher effectiveness research as well as inspectors' experiences of effective teaching. Like ISTOF, QoT is intended to study generic teacher behaviours in the classroom. Van de Grift explains that: 'the standards and indicators must be observable in (almost) each lesson such that the instrument could be used every time in classrooms in an inspection visit' (2007: 128). Instead of focusing on frequency, teachers are assessed based on the perceived effectiveness of their behaviour. A study in England and the Netherlands (Van de Grift *et al.* 2004), as well as a later study in England, the Netherlands, Flanders and Lower Saxony (Van de Grift 2007) confirmed the internal consistency, inter-rater reliability and validity of the model. The QoT model, similar to the original Dutch model, consists of a list of 26 indicators, which in turn cover nine criteria for evaluating the quality of teaching (Van de Grift *et al.* 2004).

Each indicator is supplemented with examples of teaching behaviours considered as good practice to help the observers make their judgements. Only when all good practice examples are observed by the raters can they give a score indicating more strengths than weaknesses. One way in which the model differed from the Dutch original was its inclusion of an overall grade for teaching to reflect an overall judgement of the lesson quality, which was a distinctive characteristic of the English inspection model. It was expected that the correlation analysis would indicate which teacher behaviours have the greatest association with the global judgement of teacher effectiveness and eventually a set of indicators suitable for an international comparative analysis of characteristics of effective teaching would be developed.

Both the ISTOF (a behavioural instrument) and the QoT (an evaluative instrument) models were chosen to be used in our Effective Classroom Practice (ECP) project in England (Day *et al.* 2008; Sammons and Ko 2008) in order to see whether teachers showed the characteristics of effective practice that international instruments suggest are important. As we show in later chapters, these instruments provided valuable sources of data which were complemented by detailed qualitative field notes (Kington *et al.* 2011).

Pianta and Hamre developed the Classroom Assessment Scoring System (CLASS) (2009a, 2009b), a tool for observing teachers which also aims to provide feedback intended to help improve teachers' interactions and relationships with students. It represents a development of the COS system discussed above. By observing student-teacher interaction and providing feedback on this, it is claimed that the CLASS instrument can help teachers improve their practice and as a result improve student outcomes. The instrument covers three key domains – emotional supports, classroom organization and instructional supports. In addition to the three main domains, more specific dimensions of classroom interactions viewed as important to students' academic and/or social development are also described.

The manuals for observation are very detailed and each dimension and behavioural indicator is very clearly described. Moreover, the observers' interpretations of behaviour in relation to culture and background are considered as well. The observers' judgements of the relative value of a teacher's behaviour are central to the CLASS instrument. They are trained to look for children's cues, teacher responses and the children's subsequent behaviours. The Center for Advanced Study of Teaching and Learning of the University of Virginia offers further information on the application of the CLASS instrument at different levels of education as well as providing links to academic papers.

Summary

This chapter has provided a brief overview of the way teacher effectiveness and teacher effects can be defined and measured, and explored some of the different sources of evidence that can be used to investigate these topics. Defining teacher effectiveness can be based on student outcomes of various kinds (typically academic outcomes have received most focus but similar approaches can be used with other measures of outcome including academic self-concept and student engagement). It is important that data are used appropriately however. Though value-added scores can be very useful in assessing student progress and provide some guide to teacher effectiveness, in our view such estimates are not reliable enough to evaluate teachers, for example in making high-stakes decisions about pay, remediation or removal of teachers. No one source of evidence is sufficient, because observations also have their limitations, as do student reports. For making better judgements about teacher effectiveness and to support teacher self-evaluation and inform professional development we recommend a triangulated approach including using attainment data wisely (e.g. value-added measures of student outcomes can provide a guide to progress in particular classes and departments). Different observations of classroom practice (both systematic and qualitative) also have a role to play, especially when conducted as part of a formative process involving feedback. In addition, measures of teachers' subject knowledge can also be illuminating. Student ratings of their classroom experiences can also provide valuable additional evidence and are an important way to involve students in their learning. No one source is sufficient in itself but analyses of various sources of evidence through research can shed light on effective classroom practice and in the ECP project we sought to use several different approaches to gather evidence that would provide a broader focus and enable us to deepen our understanding of teachers and teaching and the features of their classroom practice that help us to illuminate the concepts of effective teaching and effective teachers.

References

Ainley, J. (1994) Curriculum areas in secondary schools: differences in student response, paper presented at the International Congress for School Effectiveness and School Improvement, Melbourne, Australia.

Baker, A.M. (1986) Validity of Palestinian university students' responses in evaluating their instructors, *Assessment & Evaluation in Higher Education*, 11(1): 70–75.

Ball, D.L. and Rowan, B. (2004) Introduction: measuring instruction, *Elementary School Journal*, 105(1): 3–10.

Barber, M. and Mourshed, M. (2007) *How the World's Best-performing School Systems Come Out on Top*. New York: McKinsey & Company.

Bennett, N. (1976) *Teaching Styles and Pupil Progress*. London: Open Books.

Bloom, B. (1976) *Human Characteristics and School Learning*. New York: McGraw-Hill.

Brophy, J. and Good, T. (1986) Teacher behaviour and student achievement, in M. Wittrock (ed.) *Handbook of Research on Teaching*, 3rd edn, pp. 328–75. New York: Macmillan.

Camburn, E. and Barnes, C.A. (2004) Assessing the validity of a language arts log through triangulation, *Elementary School Journal*, 105, 49–74.

Campbell, J., Kyriakides, L., Muijs, D. and Robinson, W. (2004) *Assessing Teacher Effectiveness: Developing a Differentiated Model*. Abingdon: Routledge Falmer.

Cheng, Y.C. (1995) *Function and Effectiveness of Education*, 3rd edn. Hong Kong: Wide Angle Press.

Cheng, Y.C. and Tsui, K.T. (1996) Total teacher effectiveness: new conception and improvement, *International Journal of Educational Management*, 10(6): 7–17.

Clark, C. and Peterson, P. (1986) Teachers' thought processes, in M. Wittrock (ed.) *Handbook of Research on Teaching*, 3rd edn, pp. 255–96). New York: Macmillan.

Cotton, K. (1995) *Effective Schooling Practices: A Research Synthesis 1995 Upda*te. Portland, OR: Northwest Regional Educational Laboratory.

Creemers, B.P.M. (1994) *The Effective Classroom*. London: Cassell.

Creemers, B.P.M. (1999) The effective teacher: what changes and remains, *Asia-Pacific Journal of Teacher Education and Development*, 2: 51–64.

Creemers, B.P.M. and Kyriakides, L. (2008) *The Dynamics of Educational Effectiveness*. New York: Routledge.

Darling-Hammond, L. (2000) Teacher quality and student achievement: a review of state policy evidence, *Education Policy Analysis Archives*, 8(1).

Darling-Hammond, L., Dieckmann, J., Haertel, E., Lotan, R., Newton, X., Philipose, S., Spang, E., Thomas, E. and Williamson, P. (2010) Studying teacher effectiveness: the challenges of developing valid measures, in G. Walford, E. Tucker and M. Viswanathan (eds) *The Sage Handbook of Measurement*. Los Angeles, CA: Sage.

Day, C., Stobart, G., Sammons, P. and Kington, A. (2006) Variations in the work and lives of teachers: relative and relational effectiveness, *Teachers and Teaching: Theory and Practice*, 12(1): 169–92.

Day C., Sammons, P., Stobart, G., Kington, A. and Gu, Q. (2007) *Teachers Matter*. Maidenhead: Open University Press.

Day, C., Sammons, P., Kington, A. and Regan, E. (2008) *Effective Classroom Practice (ECP): A Mixed Method Study of Influences and Outcomes*. Swindon: ESRC.

DfES (Department of Education and Skills) (2002) *Organizing the daily mathematics lesson in Mixed Reception/Year 1 Classes*. London: Department of Education and Employment.

Follman, J. (1992) Secondary school students' ratings of teacher effectiveness, *The High School Journal*, 75(1): 168–78.

Follman, J. (1995) Elementary public school pupil rating of teacher effectiveness, *Child Study Journal*, 25(1): 57–78.

Gage, M. (1978) *The Scientific Basis of the Art of Teaching*. New York: Columbia University Teacher College Press.

Galton, M., Simon, B. and Croll, P. (1980) *Inside the Primary Classroom*. London: Routledge & Kegan Paul.

Glass, G.V. (1977) Integrating findings: the meta-analysis of research, *Review of Research in Education*, 47(5): 351–79.

Good, T.L., Biddle, B J. and Brophy, J.E. (1983) *Teacher Effectiveness: Research Findings and Policy Implications*. Washington, DC: Dingle Associates, Inc.

Gray, J. (2000) *Causing Concern but Improving: A Review of Schools' Experiences on Special Measures*. London: Department for Education and Employment.

Hanushek, E.A., and Rivkin. S.G. (2006) Teacher quality, in E.A. Hanushek and F. Welch (eds) *Handbook of the Economics of Education*, Vol. 1, pp. 1051–78. Amsterdam: North-Holland.

Harris, A., Jamieson, I. and Russ, J. (1995) A study of effective departments in secondary schools, *School Organisation*, 15(3): 283–9.

Hattie, J. (2009) *Visible Learning: A Synthesis of Over 800 Meta-analyses Relating to Achievement*. Abingdon: Routledge.

Hill, H., Kapitula, L. and Umland, K. (2011) A validity argument approach to evaluating teacher value added scores, *American Educational Research Journal*, 48(3):794–31.

Hill, P. and Rowe, K. (1996) Multilevel modelling in school effectiveness research, *School Effectiveness and School Improvement*, 7(1): 1–34.

Hill, P. and Rowe, K. (1998) Modelling student progress in studies of educational effectiveness, *School Effectiveness and School Improvement*, 9(3): 310–33.

Jin, L. and Cortazzi, M. (1998) Dimensions of dialogue: large classes in China, *International Journal of Educational Research*, 29: 739–61.

Joyce, B., Weil, M. and Calhoun, E. (2005) *Models of Teaching*, 7th edn, Boston, MA: Allyn & Bacon.

Joyce, B., Calhoun, E. and Hopkins, D. (2008) *Models of Learning, Tools for Teaching*, 3rd edn. Maidenhead: Open University Press.

Kington, A., Sammons, P., Day, C. and Regan, E. (2011) Stories and statistics: describing a mixed methods study of effective classroom practice, *Journal of Mixed Methods Research*, 5(2): 103–25.

Ko, J. and Sammons, P. with Bakkum, L. (2013) *Effective Teaching: A Review of Research and Evidence*. Reading: CfBT Education Trust.

Konstantopoulos, S. (2007) *How Long do Teacher Effects Persist?* Bonn: Institute for the Study of Labor (IZA).

Kyriacou, C. (2007) *Effective Teaching in Schools – Theory and Prac*tice. Cheltenham: Nelson Thornes.

Kyriakides, L. (2005) Drawing from teacher effectiveness research and research into teacher interpersonal behaviour to establish a teacher evaluation system: a study on the use of student ratings to evaluate teacher behavior, *Journal of Classroom Interaction*, 40(2): 44–66.

Kyriakides, L. and Creemers, B.P. (2008a) Using a multidimensional approach to measure the impact of classroom-level factors upon student achievement: a study testing the validity of the dynamic model, *School Effectiveness and School Improvement*, 19(2): 183–205.

Kyriakides, L. and Creemers, B.P. (2008b) A longitudinal study on the stability over time of school and teacher effects on student outcomes, *Oxford Review of Education*, 34(5): 521–45.

Levine, D. and Lezotte, L. (1990) *Unusually Effective Schools: A Review and Analysis of Research and Practice*. Madison, WI: National Center for Effective Schools Research and Development.

Light, R. and Smith, P. (1971) Accumulating evidence: procedures for resolving contradictions among different studies, *Harvard Educational Review*, 41(4): 429–71.

Luyten, H. (1994) Stability of school effects in Dutch secondary education: the impact of variance across subjects and years, *International Journal of Educational Research*, 2(2): 197–216.

Marsh, H.W. (1982) SEEQ: a reliable, valid, and useful instrument for collecting students' evaluations of university teaching: dimensionality, reliability, validity, potential biases, and utility, *British Journal of Educational Psychology*, 52: 77–95.

Marsh, H.W. (1984) Students' evaluations of university teaching: dimensionality, reliability, validity, potential biases, and utility, *Journal of Educational Psychology*, 76(5): 707–54.

Marsh, H.W. (1987) Students' evaluations of university teaching: research findings, methodological issues, and directions for future research, *International Journal of Educational Research*, 11(3): 253–388.

Marsh, H.W. (2007) Students' evaluations of university teaching: a multidimensional perspective, in R.P. Perry and J.C. Smart (eds) *The Scholarship of Teaching and Learning in Higher Education: An Evidence-based Perspective*, pp. 319–84. New York: Springer.

Marsh, H.W. and Bailey, M. (1993) Multidimensional students' evaluations of teaching effectiveness: a profile analysis, *Journal of Higher Education*, 64: 1–18.

Marsh, H.W. and Cheng, J.H.S. (2008) *NSS: Dimensionality, multilevel structure, and differentiation at the level of university and discipline*, retrieved from http://www. heacademy.ac.uk/resources/detail/ourwork/research/NSS_herb_marsh.

Marsh, H.W. and Hocevar, D. (1991) The multidimensionality of students' evaluations of teaching effectiveness: the generality of factor structures across academic discipline, instructor level, and course level, *Teaching and Teacher Education*, 7: 9–18.

Marzano, R. (2003) *What Works in Schools: Translating Research into Action*. Alexandria, VA: ASCD.

Matthews, P. and Sammons, P. (2004) *Improvement Through Inspection: An Evaluation of the Impact of Ofsted's Work*. London: Ofsted/Institute of Education.

Matthews, P. and Sammons, P. (2005) Survival of the weakest: the differential improvement of schools causing concern in England, *London Review of Education*, 3(2): 159–76.

McBer, H. (2000) *Research into Teacher Effectiveness: A Model of Teacher Effectiveness.* London: DfEE.

Medley, D.M. (1982) Teacher effectiveness, in H. Mitzel (ed.), *Encyclopedia of Educational Research*, 5th edn, pp. 1841–51. New York: Free Press.

Meehan, M.L., Cowley, K.S., Finch, N., Chadwick, K., Ermolov, L.D. and Riffle, J.S. (2004) *Special Strategies Observation System – Revised: A Useful Tool for Educational Research and Evaluation.* Charleston, WV: AEL.

Mortimore, P., Sammons, P., Stoll, L., Lewis, D. and Ecob, R. (1988) *School Matters: The Junior Years.* Wells: Open Books.

Moses, I. (1986) Self and student evaluation of academic staff, *Assessment & Evaluation in Higher Education*, 11(1): 76–8.

Muijs, D. and Reynolds, D. (2000) School effectiveness and teacher effectiveness in mathematics: some preliminary findings from the evaluation of the Mathematics Enhancement Programme (Primary), *School Effectiveness and School Improvement*, 11(3): 273–303.

Muijs, D. and Reynolds, D. (2005) *Effective Teaching: Evidence and Practice*, 2nd edn. London: Sage.

Muñoz, M. and Chang, F. (2007) The elusive relationship between teacher characteristics and student academic growth: a longitudinal multilevel model for change, *Journal of Personnel Evaluation in Education*, 20: 147–64.

Murray, H.G. (1997) Does evaluation of teaching lead to improvement of teaching? *International Journal for Academic Development*, 2(1): 8–23.

NICHD (2001) *Fifth Grade School Observation Procedures Manual: NICHD Study of Early Child Care and Youth Development.* Rockville, MD: National Institute of Child Health and Human Development.

Nye, B., Konstantopoulos, S. and Hedges, L.V. (2004) How large are teacher effects? *Educational Evaluation and Policy Analysis*, 26(3): 237–57.

Ofsted (Office for Standards in Education) (1994) *Primary Matters: A Discussion on Teaching and Learning in Primary Schools.* London: Ofsted.

Ofsted (Office for Standards in Education) (1999) *Primary Education 1994–98: A Review of Primary Schools in England.* London: Ofsted.

Ofsted (Office for Standards in Education) (2009) *The Annual Report of Her Majesty's Chief Inspector of Education, Children's Services and Skills 2008/09.* London: Ofsted, retrieved from www.ofsted.gov.uk/publications/annualreport0809.

Opdenakke, M-C. and Van Damme, J. (2006) Teacher characteristics and teaching styles as effectiveness enhancing factors of classroom practice, *Teaching and Teacher Education*, 22(1): 1–21.

Patrick, J. and Smart, R.M. (1998) An empirical evaluation of teacher effectiveness: the emergence of three critical factors, *Assessment and Evaluation in Higher Education*, 23(2): 165–8.

Philpott, J. (2009) *Captivating Your Class: Effective Teaching Skills.* London: Continuum.

Pianta, R.C. and Hamre, B.K. (2009a) Conceptualization, measurement, and improvement of classroom processes: standardized observation can leverage capacity, *Educational Researcher*, 38: 109–19.

Pianta, R.C. and Hamre, B.K. (2009b) A lot of students and their teachers need support: using a common framework to observe teacher practices might help, *Educational Researcher*, 38(7): 546–8.

Porter, A. and Brophy, J. (1988) Synthesis of research on good teaching: insights from the work of the Institute for Research on Teaching, *Educational Leadership*, 46: 74–85.

Pratt, D., Kelly, M. and Wong, W. (1999) Chinese conceptions of effective teaching in Hong Kong: towards culturally sensitive evaluation of teaching, *International Journal of Lifelong Education*, 18(4): 241–58.

Ramsden, P. (1991) A performance indicator of teaching quality in higher education: the course experience questionnaire, *Studies in Higher Education*, 16(2): 129–50.

Reynolds, D. (2006) World-class schools: some methodological and substantive findings and implications of the International School Effectiveness Research Project (ISERP), *Educational Research and Evaluation*, 12(6): 535–60.

Reynolds, D., Creemers, B., Stringfield, S., Teddlie, C. and Schaffer, G. (eds) (2002) *World Class Schools: International Perspectives on School Effectiveness*. London: RoutledgeFalmer.

Rosenshine, B. (1971) *Teaching Behaviours and Student Achievement*. London: NFER.

Rowe, K. (2006) Effective teaching practices for students with and without learning difficulties: issues and implications, *Australian Journal of Learning Disabilities*, 11(3): 99–115.

Sammons, P. (1996) Complexities in the judgement of school effectiveness, *Educational Research and Evaluation*, 2(2): 113–49.

Sammons, P. (2007) *School Effectiveness and Equity: Making Connections. A review of school effectiveness and improvement research and its implications for practitioners and policy makers*. Reading: CfBT.

Sammons, P. (2008) Zero tolerance of failure and New Labour approaches to school improvement in England, *Oxford Review of Education*, 34(6): 651–64.

Sammons, P. and Ko, J. (2008) *Using Systematic Classroom Observation Schedules to Investigate Effective Teaching: Overview of Quantitative Findings*. An Effective Classroom Practice project report. Swindon: ESRC.

Sammons, P., Hillman, J. and Mortimore, P. (1995) *Key Characteristics of Effective Schools: A Review of School Effectiveness Research*. London: Ofsted.

Sammons, P., Thomas, S. and Mortimore, P. (1997) *Forging Links: Effective Schools and Effective Departments*. London: Sage.

Sammons, P., Taggart, B., Siraj-Blatchford, I., Sylva, K., Melhuish, E. and Barreau, S. (2006) *The Effective Pre-school and Primary Education 3–11 project (EPPE 3-11). Summary report – variations in teacher and pupil behaviours in Year 5 classes*. London: DfES/Institute of Education, University of London.

Sammons, P., Day, C., Kington, A., Gu, Q., Stobart, G. and Smees, R. (2007) Exploring variations in teachers' work, lives and their effects on pupils: key findings and implications from a longitudinal mixed methods study, *British Educational Research Journal*, 33(5): 681–701.

Sammons, P., Sylva, K., Melhuish, E.C., Siraj-Blatchford, I., Taggart, B., Smees, R., Draghici, D. and Toth, K. (2011a) *Effective Pre-school, Primary and Secondary Education 3–14 Project (EPPSE 3–14): Influences on Students' Dispositions in Key Stage 3: Exploring Enjoyment of School, Popularity, Anxiety, Citizenship*

Values and Academic Self-Concept in Year 9. London: Institute of Education, University of London/DFE.

Sammons, P., Sylva, K., Melhuish, E.C., Siraj-Blatchford, I., Taggart, B., Smees, R., Draghici, D. and Toth, K. (2011b) *Effective Pre-school, Primary and Secondary Education 3–14 Project (EPPSE 3–14): Students' Reports of Their Experiences of School in Year 9*. London: Institute of Education, University of London/DFE.

Sanders, W. (1998) Value added assessment, *School Administrator*, 11(3): 24–7.

Sanders, W. (2000) Value added assessment from student achievement data: opportunities and hurdles, *Journal of Personnel Evaluation in Education*, 14(4): 329–39.

Schaffer, E., Nesselrodt, P. and Stringfield, S. (1991) The groundings of an observational instrument: the teacher behaviour – student learning research base of the special strategies observation system, Kaohsiung, Taiwan, International Research Workshop, 26–7 September, Kaohsiung Normal University.

Schaffer, E., Nesselrodt, P. and Stringfield, S. (1994) The contribution of classroom observation to school effectiveness research, in B. Creemers, P. Nesselrodt, E. Schaffer, S. Stringfield and C. Teddlie (eds) *Advances in School Effectiveness Research and Practice*, pp. 133–50. Oxford: Pergamon Press.

Scheerens, J. (2004) *Review of School and Instructional Effectiveness Research*, retrieved from http://unesdoc.unesco.org/images/0014/001466/146695e.pdf.

Scheerens, J. (2008) *Review of Research on School and Instructional Effectiveness*. Enschede, Netherlands: University of Twente.

Scheerens, J. and Bosker, R. (1997) *The Foundation of Educational Effectiveness*. Oxford: Pergamon.

Scheerens, J., Vermeulen, C.J. and Pelgrum, W.J. (1989) Generalizibility of instructional and school effectiveness indicators across nations, *International Journal of Educational Research*, 13(7): 789–800.

Shirbagi, N. (2007) Are students' evaluations of teaching valid? Evidence from an Iranian higher education institution, *Bulletin of Education & Research*, 29(2): 21–32.

Siraj-Blatchford, I., Shepard, D-L., Melhuish, E., Taggart, B., Sammons, P. and Sylva. K. (2011) *Effective Primary Pedagogical Strategies in English and Mathematics in Key Stage 2: a study of Year 5 classroom practice from the EPPSE 3-6 longitudinal study*, research report DFE-RR129, Institute of Education, Birkbeck (University of London) and University of Oxford, retrieved from: http://dera.ioe.ac.uk/3876/1/3876_DFE-RR129.pdf.

Slavin, R. (2010) Effective programmes in reading and mathematics: lessons from the best evidence encyclopaedia, keynote speech at the second meeting of the European Association for Research on Learning and Instruction (EARLI) special interest group on Educational Effectiveness: Models, Methods and Applications, Leuven, Belgium.

Stipek, D. (1999) *Instructional Environment Observation Scale*. Los Angeles: University of California: MacArthur Pathways through Middle Childhood Network.

Stufflebeam, D. and Shinkfield, A. (1995) *Teacher Evaluation: Guide to Effective Practice*. Norwell: Kluwer.

Teddlie, C., Virgilio, I. and Oescher, J. (1990) Development and validation of the Virgilio Teacher Behavior Inventory, *Educational and Psychological Measurement*, 50(2): 421–30.

Teddlie, C., Creemers, B., Kyriakides, L., Muijs, D. and Yu, F. (2006) The international system for teacher observation and feedback: evolution of an international study of teacher effectiveness construct, *Educational Research and Evaluation*, 12(6): 561–82.

Tymms, P.B. (1993) Accountability – can it be fair? *Oxford Review of Education*, 19(3): 291–9.

Van de Grift, W. (2007) Quality of teaching in four European countries: a review of the literature and application of an assessment instrument, *Educational Research*, 49(2): 127–52.

Van de Grift, W., Matthews, P., Tabak, l. and de Rijcke, F. (2004) *Comparative Research into the Inspection of Teaching in England and the Netherlands*. London: Ofsted.

Virgilio, I., Teddlie, C. and Oescher, J. (1991) Variance and context differences in teaching at differentially effective schools, *School Effectiveness and School Improvement*, 2(2): 152–68.

Walberg, H.J. (1986) Syntheses of research on teaching, in M. Wittrock (ed.) *Handbook of Research on Teaching*, 3rd edn, pp. 570–602. New York: Macmillan.

Wittrock, M. (ed.) (1986) *Handbook of Research on Teaching*, 3rd edn. New York: Macmillan.

Witziers, B. (1994) Coordination in secondary schools and its implications for student achievement, paper presented at the Annual Conference of the AERA, 4–8 April, New Orleans.

Worrell, F.C. and Kuterbach, L.D. (2001) The use of student ratings of teacher behaviors with academically talented high school students, *The Journal of Secondary Gifted Education*, 14: 236–47.

Wragg, E. (1984) *Classroom Teaching Skills*. London: Croom Helm.

3 Studying effective classroom practice

Introduction

This chapter will outline the integrated mixed methods design of the Effective Classroom Practice (ECP) project. Focusing on two distinct fields of research – teacher effectiveness and effective practice – the project had three broad aims:

1 To describe, analyse and explain the variation in primary and secondary school teachers' classroom behaviours and practice, focusing on English and mathematics teaching.
2 To explore typical and more effective classroom practice of teachers in Years 2, 6 and 9, across different school contexts, professional life phases and ages in relation to professional, situated, and/or personal factors, which are perceived to affect observed practice over time.
3 To draw out implications from the findings of (1) and (2) above for policy-makers concerned with raising standards for schools and for teacher development.

It is important to note at this point that the research was not trying to identify whether particular teachers were effective, rather to explore the practices, strategies and methods used in classrooms by effective practitioners (where effectiveness indicators had already been developed to aid sampling).

Developing an approach for the study of classroom practice

At the time of this project, there was a need for research in the UK that examined more closely the links between effectiveness at the school level and the ways in which it can promote and support effective teaching within individual classrooms, particularly since the impact of classroom-level effectiveness has been shown to influence practice more directly than whole-school effectiveness (Scheerens 1992; Creemers 1994; Muijs and Reynolds 2000; Teddlie and Liu 2008). This has continued to be an area of interest to policy-makers as indicated by two large-scale studies, funded by the government: the Effective Provision of Pre-School Education project (Sammons *et al.* 2005; Siraj-Blatchford *et al.* 2008; Sylva *et al.* 2010) and the

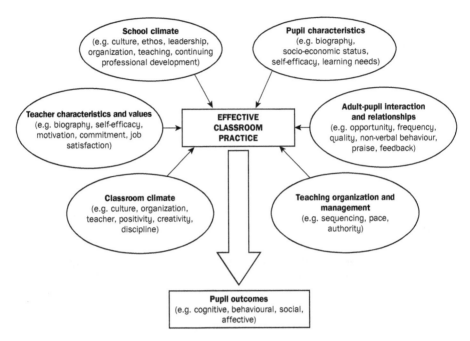

Figure 3.1   Initial model of factors contributing to effective classroom practice.

aforementioned Variations in Teachers' Work, Lives and their Effects on Pupils (VITAE) project (Day *et al.* 2006a, 2007). Both these projects focused on aspects of effectiveness and utilized mixed method designs.

Having examined the relevant literature, a set of guiding questions was developed by the team, which formed the basis of an initial conceptualization for the development of a research design. However, at this stage, the concepts were kept sufficiently broad in order that, as the research advanced, a process of progressive focusing could be applied (e.g. Strauss and Corbin 1998). Figure 3.1 illustrates this conceptualization.

The questions the study sought to address were the following:

1   What are the factors that influence typical and more effective teachers' classroom practices?
2   What are the relationships between typical and more effective teachers' perceived effectiveness and their classroom practice and organization?
3   What are the similarities and differences in the factors that influence classroom practice in different school phases and subjects?
4   What are the relationships between observed classroom practice and policy, school context, teacher professional life phase and professional identity?
5   What are the implications of this for key stakeholders who are involved in raising standards in schools?

To examine the complexities of effective classroom practice, the study developed a holistic design to integrate method types in all phases of the project simultaneously while illustrating the interdependence of alternative methods (e.g. Caracelli and Greene 1997; Day *et al.* 2007; Sammons *et al.* 2007; Day *et al.* 2008). This enabled a research-informed account and explanation of the relationships between teachers' backgrounds, contexts, interactions and experiences over time and their classroom practice. The design included an observational component (van de Grift *et al.* 2004; Teddlie *et al.* 2006) to provide a deeper understanding of the specific classroom contexts under investigation than could be gained solely through the collection of participants' perceptions (e.g. Hammersley 1990).

Design decisions

Increasingly, mixed methods approaches have gained favour as an alternative to reliance on either a qualitative or quantitative orientation (Lincoln and Guba 2000; Johnson and Onwuegbuzie 2004; Sammons 2010; Teddlie and Sammons 2010). Unlike the pragmatic stance advocated by Tashakkori and Teddlie (2003), the starting point for this project was the conceptualization of the problem as an *a priori* to establishing a design that was fit for purpose and, like the VITAE research, it demonstrated ways in which mixed methods research may create new and synergistic understandings through conceptualization, data integration and research dialogue (Day *et al.* 2008). The demands of this project led to the development of an integrated, holistic approach involving the combination of a range of research techniques, including those traditionally associated with both 'quantitative' and 'qualitative" paradigms. In this way, the study was able to explore the broad and complex set of research questions without the constraints associated with using a single method or technique. Rather, it allowed further insight and understanding of the factors that influence effectiveness and the relationships between (a) observed practice; (b) teacher, head teacher and pupil perceptions; and (c) the analytical lenses of teachers' professional life phase and teachers' identity. So, while teacher case studies were the prime focus of the study, these involved three main sources of evidence: interviews (semi-structured and repertory grid), questionnaire surveys and observations of classroom practice (both quantitative and qualitative). The project sought first to develop a distinctive theoretical position and then to translate this into the project design using (a) a combination of qualitative and quantitative approaches and (b) an integration of these approaches in relation to the conceptualization of research questions, data collection, data analysis and data interpretation.

To avoid qualitative (stories) and quantitative (statistical) elements of the research being designed and conducted separately, combined only at the stage of interpreting findings, this study sought to integrate the various forms of data in an ongoing and interactive way (Tashakkori and Teddlie 1998; Creswell 2003). In fact, the process of integration began at the point of developing the research questions and continued through sampling, data collection, analysis and reporting. The more detailed and holistic combination of approaches also allowed data, investigator and methods triangulation (Denzin 1978), and provided greater mapping, analysis, interpretation and comprehension of the research area (Tashakkori and Teddlie 2003). A plethora of mixed method designs exist, which has prompted researchers to devise typologies (Tashakkori and Teddlie 1998, 2003; Creswell 2003; Onwuegbuzie and Johnson 2004; Leech and Onwuegbuzie 2009) indicating the varying levels of qualitative and quantitative contribution and/or sequencing within a specific design. Since 'the actual diversity in mixed methods studies is far greater than any typology can adequately encompass' (Maxwell and Loomis 2003: 244), this project's design most closely resembles a fully mixed, concurrent, equal status design (Tashakkori and Teddlie 1998; Leech and Onwuegbuzie 2009). This was necessary to gather the range of information needed to address all the complex and potentially interrelated issues and concerns and to provide a detailed, holistic and methodologically robust, rigorous account of effective classroom practice. However, in addition to this design, there were also partial elements that worked sequentially within each of the phases of data collection in which the findings from one method were elaborated and expanded through another method (e.g. factors identified via teacher questionnaire explored in pre- and post-observation interviews). The design also allowed for data collected by one method to feed into more than one subsequent research instrument, examining the focus of the study from different perspectives (e.g. first round of teacher interviews, interviews with school leaders and a pupil questionnaire – see Figure 3.2). Consequently, it amounts to a fully mixed, concurrent, multiphase, equal status, triangulation design.

Sampling and recruitment of participants

The original sampling involved the team identifying two purposive subsamples of teachers from the VITAE database (Day *et al.* 2006b): those whose pupils had consistently achieved above the expected level for their classes and those whose pupils had consistently achieved as expected. The two subsamples were based on an examination of three key characteristics: (a) the individual teacher profiles and cameos created as a result of the VITAE research; (b) teachers' relative effectiveness (as defined by their pupil value-added data over three years); and (c) pupil attitudinal data. The overall sample was also chosen to represent a range of career phases and age groups, teacher identities and socio-economic contexts (measured from high through to low quartiles based on free school meal (FSM) indicator).

The sample consisted of 81 teachers in two groups – 26 (32 per cent) were chosen based on results of an earlier study, VITAE (Day *et al.* 2007), after analysis of existing data on pupil outcomes (pupil views and value-added attainment data) as being typical or more effective. In addition, another 55 (68 per cent) participants were newly recruited for the ECP study. These newly recruited teachers were drawn from an ongoing study of Leadership and Pupil Outcomes funded by the Department for Children, Schools and Families (DCSF) (Day *et al.* 2007). It was anticipated that they might be more likely to show behaviours associated with academic effectiveness, because they were purposively selected from schools identified as academically highly improved/more effective using national assessment and examination data for three years 2003–5 (Gu *et al.* 2008). The teachers selected were also identified by head teachers and, in secondary schools, by heads of departments, as particularly effective teachers in these improved/effective schools (see Figure 3.3).

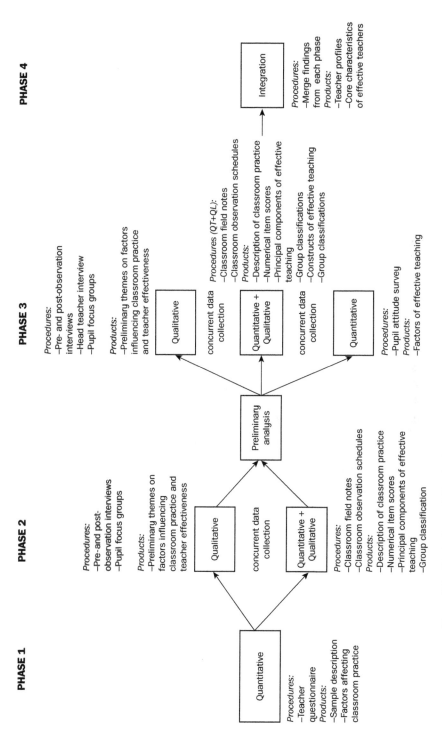

Figure 3.2 Illustration of fully mixed, concurrent, multiphase, equal status design.

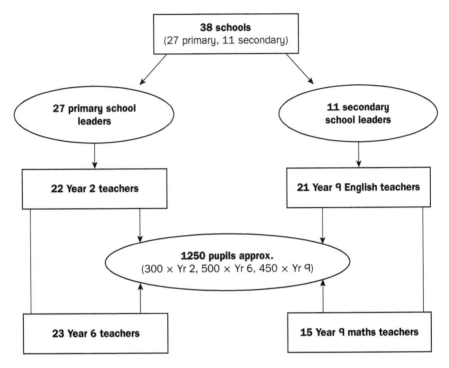

Figure 3.3 Illustration of sampling design.

As part of the school selection criteria, consideration was also given to the numbers of pupils on the school roll, in order to provide, as far as possible, a representative number of small, medium and large schools. In addition to the school profile, the teacher sample was selected to ensure representation in the following categories: age, experience, gender, phase, subject specialization, length of service and career phase. The teachers were located in schools that represented a range of geographical locations (urban, suburban, rural) and socio-economic status (high to low disadvantage, see Table 3.1).

Table 3.1 Summary of teacher demographics

School phase	Years of experience					Year groups/subjects		Gender	
	0–3	4–7	8–15	16–23	24 +				
Primary	2	13	11	7	12	Year 2	22	Male	1
								Female	21
						Year 6	23	Male	9
								Female	14
Secondary	7	14	7	1	7	Year 9 maths	15	Male	11
								Female	4
						Year 9 English	21	Male	6
								Female	15

The numbers of teachers in the primary and secondary samples were not equal: 45 (55.6 per cent) in the former and 36 (44.4 per cent) in the latter since the primary sample covered Years 2 and 6 and it was desirable to have reasonable numbers in both years for comparison. The gender balance for primary school teachers (25 per cent male, 75 per cent female) overrepresented men compared with the national profile (12 per cent male, 88 per cent female). However, the sample of secondary school teachers (50 per cent male, 50 per cent female) was more representative of the national profile (45 per cent male, 55 per cent female). In terms of teaching experience, about one-third of the teachers (N = 27) had four to seven years of experience, whereas about a quarter (N = 18) had taught for eight to fifteen years and another quarter (N = 19) for 24 years or more.

Motivation and commitment levels

The vast majority (N = 64, 86.5 per cent) of teachers in the study indicated that their current motivation as a teacher was either high or very high, with only one teacher indicating that his motivation was low and nobody giving the lowest response rating (very low). Similarly, teachers' self-reported commitment was extremely high in the sample, and more teachers (N = 34, 45.9 per cent) claimed that their commitment was very high than was found for the percentage reporting very high current motivation (N = 22, 29.7 per cent, see Figure 3.4). For this sample there was no indication of any significant association between self-reported motivation and commitment and the number of posts or the number of years in teaching. There was, as might be expected, a significant positive association (rho = 0.61) between teachers' self-reported motivation and satisfaction and between motivation and commitment (rho = 0.57).

Hours worked and stress level

The number of hours the teachers reported they worked per week during the term gives an indication of workload. Over half indicated they worked 52 or more hours a week in term time. A little over a quarter (29 per cent) reported high or very high stress levels compared with 20 per cent reporting low or very low stress (see Figure 3.5).

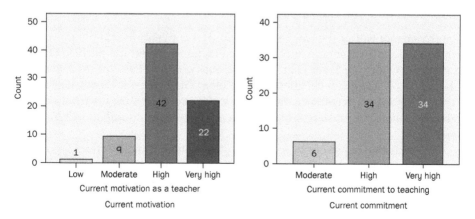

Figure 3.4   Teachers' self-reported motivation and commitment levels.

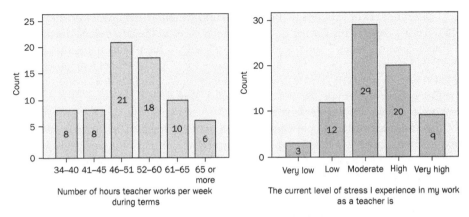

Figure 3.5   Hours the teachers worked per week and stress level.

Hours of reported work were only moderately but significantly correlated with levels of reported stress while the association with current commitment to teaching was positive but weaker and that with current motivation interestingly was non-significant. In addition, there was a moderate but significant negative association (rho = −0.30) between teachers' reported stress and their motivation levels and between stress and job satisfaction (rho = −0.34).

There were no statistically significant associations between the level of social disadvantage of school context (measured by the percentage of pupils eligible for FSM) and teachers' self-reported motivation, commitment, job satisfaction or stress levels for this sample. However, there was a weak but significant and positive association between teachers feeling they could make a difference to pupil learning and the level of disadvantage of intake. Interestingly, in this sample of typical to more effective teachers those in more disadvantaged schools were more likely to feel they could make a difference to pupil learning (rho = 0.24) but were somewhat less likely to report they could get parents involved in school activities (rho = −0.24).

Educational level and teaching experience

Approximately half of the teachers (N = 38, 51.4 per cent) listed only one qualification. The most common educational qualification among the participants was a degree (N = 60, 81.1 per cent), while about two-fifths (N = 31, 41.9 per cent) also had a postgraduate certificate or diploma. The highest level of qualification reported by the participants in the sample was a masters. Of the ten teachers (12.4 per cent) who had a masters degree, 5 also possessed a postgraduate certificate or diploma.

The distribution pattern of the length of time in teaching (i.e. teaching experience) was similar to that of age distribution. Out of the 74 teachers who returned a questionnaire, about 30 per cent (N = 27) had four to seven years of experience, while about 25 per cent (N = 18) had taught for eight to fifteen years and another 25 per cent (N =19) for 24 years or more. As shown in Figure 3.6, primary teachers were in general slightly more experienced than the secondary teachers in this sample.

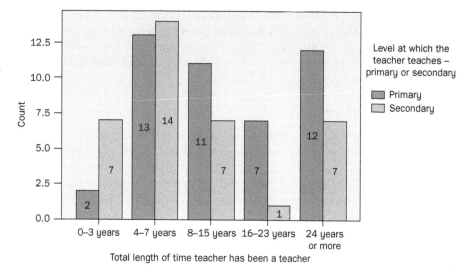

Figure 3.6   Teachers' educational level and teaching experience.

Ethical considerations in the study of teachers, head teachers and pupils

The development of the research design was influenced by a number of ethical considerations. The team developed a code of conduct, which adhered to ethical guidelines developed by professional bodies, such as the British Educational Research Association (BERA 2011).

Welfare of participants and informed consent

Prior to any data collection, all head teachers and participating teachers were visited by a member of the research team and informed of the aims of the study, including the level of commitment involved. They were then asked if they still wished to participate. It was accepted that individual teachers or schools had the right to withdraw from the study at any point during the research, without the need to give a reason. Access and consent was carefully negotiated between researcher and members of staff and, in the case of data collection with pupils, the consent of both parent(s) and the child was sought. As with the teachers, permission was also obtained from pupils to digitally record interviews at the beginning of each session. It was also explained to the pupils that they could leave the study at any time without having to give a reason.

Confidentiality and anonymity

All participants were assured of confidentiality and anonymity to ensure that neither individuals nor institutions could be identified. This was important in the building of relationships and rapport and encouraged open, honest discussion while allowing for the reporting of contentious issues. Head teachers were also informed that they would not have access to data (or data interpretation) regarding individual teachers and that pupil survey data would only be given (on request) to class teachers, aggregated to the class level. In accordance with the principle of anonymity, unique identification codes were used for all research participants to protect their identities and ensure 'non-traceability'.

Instrument development

The relationship between the qualitative and quantitative research elements in this mixed methods study required the combination of interviews with data collected via questionnaire surveys and observation protocols. The instruments, the majority of which were developed by the team and designed to respond to the research questions, were innovative in several ways (see Table 3.2). First, different data

Table 3.2   Connecting research questions and methods

Research aim	Method of data collection
1 What are the factors which influence *typical* and *more effective* teachers' classroom practices in primary and secondary schools?	Teacher questionnaire Pre-observation interview Classroom observation Post-observation interview Pupil survey Pupil focus group interview Existing VITAE data sets
2 What are the relationships between *typical* and *more effective* teachers' perceived effectiveness and their classroom practice and organization?	Pre-observation interview Classroom observation Post-observation interview School leader interview Existing VITAE data sets
3 What are the similarities and differences in the factors that influence classroom practice in different school phases and subjects?	Teacher questionnaire Pre-observation interview Classroom observation Post-observation interview School leader interview Pupil survey Pupil focus group interview Existing VITAE data sets
4 What are the implications of this for key stakeholders who are involved in raising standards in schools?	Pre-observation interview Post-observation interview School leader interview
5 What are the relationships between observed classroom practice and school context in different school and teacher career phases?	Teacher questionnaire Pre-observation interview Classroom observation Post-observation interview School leader interview Pupil survey Pupil focus group interview Existing VITAE data sets

sources were linked together, both descriptive, interpretative stories and statistical summaries. Second, collaborative and participatory methods were used in shaping these accounts, working with individual teachers and head teachers to share interpretations of the data generated. In addition, the team was offered the unique opportunity to test the applicability (and score reliability and validity) of two new observational instruments for the study of classroom practice:

1 The International System of Teacher Observation and Feedback (ISTOF) (Teddlie *et al.* 2006).
2 Quality of Teaching (QoT) (van de Grift *et al.* 2004).

Piloting

The first stage of the piloting process involved researchers watching videoed lessons to enable them to practise and refine the detailed field notes to be taken and to train in the use of the observation schedules. This training was given to gain inter- and intra-judge reliability (Tashakkori and Teddlie 1998). This was followed by preliminary piloting of observation, interview and survey instruments in two primary and two secondary schools, after which the team met to discuss issues that had arisen. Having made revisions to all relevant instruments, a further stage of piloting was conducted in four primary and two secondary schools. This stage of piloting was conducted in pairs to seek agreement (for the observational tools) between sites for individual researchers, as well as between researchers for a single site. Piloting of instruments was carried out with the same group of teachers before each round of school-based fieldwork, which ensured continuity of questions between visits. In addition, other teachers were also involved who had not been involved in the piloting of the previous round (content validity, construct validity, internal consistency). Where there were differences in an instrument relating to age, piloting was conducted with a sample from each age group to ensure suitability of the instrument.

Data collection

We provide a brief outline of each of the methods adopted and instruments designed for the purposes of this research. As already mentioned, the teacher participants were the primary unit of investigation; however, the perceptions of the head teachers and pupils associated with each teacher were also collected and their influences on effective classroom practice considered.

Teachers

Questionnaire survey

The initial questionnaire was administered to all teachers involved in the study and was delivered to participant teachers during an initial visit to the schools, along with a stamped, addressed envelope for their return. The response rate was high, with a total of 91 per cent (N = 74) of teachers completing and returning the questionnaire. The survey was carried out for three main reasons:

1   To identify key characteristics (or attributes) of each teacher involved in the study in terms of their age, years in teaching, school phase, roles and responsibilities and so on.

2   To establish, in conjunction with the literature, key factors thought to affect and influence teachers' classroom practice.

3   To initiate the development of an empirically based framework for the development of further research instruments, as well as a continuously progressive framework for the analysis of teachers' effective classroom practice.

The questionnaire survey design was informed by the initial review of relevant literature and examination of a number of instruments used in a variety of earlier surveys. The instrument drew on previous classroom effectiveness research literature (e.g. Teddlie and Reynolds 2000; Sammons *et al.* 2004) and focused on a number of aspects of classroom practice, resources and class composition. In addition, its aim was to collect background details regarding years of teaching in current school, additional responsibilities and so on.

Classroom observation protocols

The strength of the study was in its mixed methods design with the actual observation of classroom practice the principal part of the research design. The qualitative component comprised rich descriptive field notes to describe the lesson, which included detail on the structure, organization and flow of the lesson; nature of lesson activities; interaction; classroom climate; and comments on the teachers' persona. The first of the systematic observation instruments used in the field was the ISTOF, derived from reviews of school and teacher effectiveness research and expert opinion from a range of countries (using the Delfic method). The ISTOF observation schedule explored assessment and evaluation, differentiation and inclusion, clarity of instruction, instructional skills, promotion of active learning and development of meta-cognitive skills, classroom climate and classroom management (Teddlie *et al.* 2006). The second observation instrument, QoT, was developed in collaboration between different inspection systems (Dutch and UK) and was also based on expert opinion, in the form of professional judgement (van de Grift *et al.* 2004). In addition to items included on the first round schedule (ISTOF), it also included items such as teacher knowledge, teacher professionalism and reflectivity, and principles of constructivism in teaching. Both these instruments required the individual researcher to rate specific elements of the observed lesson. This activity was carried out immediately after the observation had taken place rather than during the lesson in order that the researcher could focus on the activity and make judgements based on their experience of the whole lesson.

Pre- and post-observation interviews

A pre-observation interview with teachers was conducted in Phases 2 and 3 of school-based fieldwork. These interviews explored issues such as planning, differentiation and inclusion, classroom management, teaching skills, assessment and role as classroom teacher. They comprised a series of generic questions drawn from classroom effectiveness research literature (e.g. Muijs *et al.* 2005) along-side a set of questions designed for the project, based on the longitudinal data already collected during VITAE. This instrument was used in conjunction with a post-observation interview, which allowed the in-depth probing of issues, this time relating to the observed teaching session and its purposes, as well as following up important data strands empirically grounded in the VITAE data, such as teacher effectiveness, leadership issues, teacher identity, professional life phase and teacher efficacy. The interview also provided teachers with an opportunity to reflect on their role in the classroom. This interview schedule was used in Phase 2 data collection only. For Round 2, it was replaced by a repertory grid interview (discussed below). However, questions that had gleaned data most relevant to the aims of the study (e.g. teacher identity, professional life phase, motivation and commitment) were included in a revised and extended pre-observation interview schedule.

Repertory grid interview

In Phase 3, the post-observation interview was replaced by a technique commonly used within repertory grid interviewing (see Fransella *et al.* 2003; Jankowicz 2004 for more details). The aim of this technique was to provide data triangulation through exploring personal constructs related to teaching. Unlike the pre- and post-observation interviews, which were semi-structured in design, the repertory grid interview is a far more participatory technique, necessitating teachers to make decisions about how they feel with regard to certain predetermined elements (see Figure 3.7) and enhancing the quality of the process by facilitating the exploration of conflicting viewpoints and (underlying) claims with regard to effective teaching. Teachers were presented with preselected dyadic combinations of these elements (in the example, 'You as a teacher now – effective' and 'Experienced teacher') and asked to say what was common about them in terms of their classroom practice. The response given by the teacher ('classroom experience') provided the explicit construct, which the teacher wrote onto the grid. They were then asked which, of the remaining three elements, was least like those two in that respect. For example, Figure 3.7 shows the 'Beginning teacher' element being identified as different because of a 'lack of classroom experience'. This formed the implicit construct and was also written onto the grid. A total of ten constructs were elicited for each teacher in this way.

School leaders

A semi-structured interview was conducted with school leaders. In the majority of cases, this was carried out with the head teacher, although in some cases the head of department participated. The main purpose of this interview was to gather a further perspective on the practice and effectiveness of participating teachers and the role of school leadership. The instrument was designed to collect information relating to pupil intake, behaviour, parental involvement and school culture, in addition to data relating to the participating teachers, their classroom practices, relationships with pupils, professional development needs and effectiveness.

If the elements presented to the teacher are *'you as a teacher now'* and *'an experienced teacher'*, it might be said that classroom experience is a common factor that would enhance the effectiveness of you and the experienced teacher. The term classroom experience would be taken as the explicit pole of the construct. When asked to identify a third element, if the teacher chose *'the beginning teacher'*, and said the difference was lack of experience to draw on, this would be the opposite, or implicit, pole of the construct.

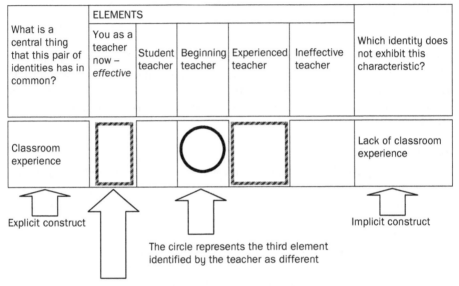

The striped boxes represent the elements presented as a dyadic pair to the teacher

Figure 3.7 An example of construct elicitation, identification and scoring using repertory grid.

Pupils

Pupil attitudinal questionnaire survey

There were three versions of the questionnaire survey (Year 2, Year 6 and Year 9). Although many of the items were similar across questionnaires, they were worded according to the age of the pupils. There were also a number of more complex items on the questionnaires for older pupils that did not appear on the Year 2 questionnaire. The pupil attitudinal questionnaire was conducted with approximately 30 pupils in each class or teaching group involved in the study. The numbers of pupil, class and school returns are shown in Table 3.3. Items on the questionnaire were organized into sections relating to 'My school', 'My teacher', 'My classroom' and 'About you in this class' items. The purpose of the pupil questionnaire was to gather information about pupils' perceptions of different aspects of their classroom experiences, including their attitudes towards their school and views of teaching. It also provided further measures of classroom practice.

The team also took the opportunity to talk to small groups of pupils in focus group interviews (approximately six to eight) after each of the classroom observation sessions in Phases 2 and 3. The focus group interview centred on pupils' experiences and perceptions of the observed lesson.

Table 3.3 Pupil questionnaire data returns

	Number of pupils	Number of classes	Number of schools
Year 2	302	13	12
Year 6	509	23	20
Year 9 English	226	10	5
Year 9 Maths	221	10	6

Analysis of data

Turning to the analysis of the data, we consider this in three parts: qualitative sources, quantitative sources and mixed methods sources. Although described separately, this in no way detracts from the interactive nature of these strands. In fact, each source maintained a dialogue with the others, with stories adding meaning and individuality to the statistics, and the statistics identifying patterns and contributing generalizability (to the whole ECP sample) to the stories.

Qualitative sources

The pre- and post-observation interviews were digitally recorded, transcribed and subsequently saved as anonymized, uniquely identified files onto a centralized database. The research team collectively developed an initial coding system, based on the interview schedule, to develop organizational themes for the analysis. This coding system was gradually developed using a grounded approach to the coding (e.g. Strauss and Corbin 1998). Coding was carried out using NVivo, a qualitative analysis software package, through which themes were developed for further investigation (Bazeley 2007).

Quantitative sources

Teacher questionnaire data

The data from each teacher questionnaire were entered into SPSS where descriptive statistics for the teacher population were generated. Principal component analysis was used to reduce the data from each questionnaire into a number of robust and meaningful underlying factors. Scores for these values were then analysed by school context, teacher professional life phase and teacher gender.

Pupil questionnaire data

The data from each pupil questionnaire were entered into SPSS. To investigate whether individual questionnaire items could be drawn together to form underlying factors, principal component analyses were run on the data from each year group. The factors produced can be seen as indicators of the school and classroom environment and can be linked to analyses of the teachers' effective classroom practice based on both the observation and interview data.

Mixed methods sources

Observation data

Data collected via two systematic observation schedules were subject to a range of descriptive and exploratory analysis in SPSS. Measures tested related to contexts (e.g. subject or sector differences and the FSM band) and teacher characteristics (e.g. gender or total number of years in teaching). The QoT schedule differed from the ISTOF by inclusion of an overall grade for teaching to reflect an overall judgement of lesson quality, which allowed a correlation analysis on the indicators and overall grade. Data reduction was conducted using exploratory factor analysis (principal component varimax rotated) followed by confirmatory factor analysis, using the LISREL program, to explore underlying structures and dimensions and identify the main factors of effective practice in the two instruments, and their relationship (Sammons and Ko 2008). The field notes were typed up, noting each five-minute segment of time and various types of activity (e.g. opening, main body and closure of the lesson, interactions, critical incidents). These field notes were then coded further, classified and tagged to link with the numeric observation records.

Repertory grid data

The repertory grid interviews were analysed in two parts. First, as each of the interviews was digitally recorded, a proportion of these were transcribed and a content analysis carried out on the process by which the constructs were elicited. This was not conducted on all the interview data as some teachers did not discuss the constructs or their reasoning behind them in a suitable amount of detail. The grids also yielded valuable statistical data. To conduct an analysis of the ratings contained in the grids, it was necessary to categorize the constructs contained in the grids (more than 600) into 'themes'.[1] The categorization process was done by the researchers involved in the actual construct elicitation interviews with participants. At the end of the categorization process, some 18 themes had been identified and these were expressed as bipolar constructs by eliciting the opposite poles to the themes (see Table 3.4). A new standard repertory grid (or group grid) was then designed using the original elements and the new bipolar construct themes. Ratings from the original grids were then inserted into the new standard grid, where there was a 'match' between a construct used in the original grid and the new standard grid.

As part of a participant validation process, sheets containing the 18 construct themes were sent out to those who had completed the original repertory grids, as well as to the head teachers of the schools in which the participants worked. Each participant was asked to rank (1–18) the list of constructs in order of priority to them. The response rate for this activity was moderate, with a total of 25 (31 per cent) teachers and 24 (63 per cent) head teachers returning the ranking sheets. Mean rankings were calculated for various groups. Asking participants to rank order the constructs provided useful information as it compels participants to choose between competing issues all or most of which are probably important to them. Such rank order data can help when trying to understand a group of people and why they make the choices they do. Finally, data from the actual repertory grids were also analysed using a specially designed analysis package. Mean ratings, standard errors and t-tests between the mean ratings of the subgroups in the demographic variables were carried out.

Combining stories and statistics

Now we move on to describe the analytical approach that was adopted for the project, which had four main strands: the analysis of quantitative observation and survey data to identify underlying dimensions of effective classroom practice, the use of NVivo to analyse qualitative interviews and detailed observation field notes, the development of analytical matrices at the teacher level, and the creation of individual teacher profiles.

Dimensions of effective classroom practice

These dimensions (discussed in Chapters 4 and 6) were developed in two ways. The first was through the analysis of pupil questionnaire data, which produced underlying factors that could be used as indicators of effective practice from the pupils' perspectives. The second approach was via the analysis of systematic observation data, which revealed a number of major underlying dimensions in teachers' practices. The teachers generally scored highly on most of these dimensions, supporting the conclusion that these were key features of more effective practice. Dimensions identified by both these methods were subsequently used as additional attributes in NVivo.

NVivo

The results of the independent analyses were combined at the interpretation stage of the research using NVivo, although each data set remained analytically separate from each other. NVivo provided a robust analytical tool in the synthesis and integration of descriptive and statistical strands through the use of key attributes at teacher, school and pupil group levels (Bazeley 2007). These attributes were developed primarily from the initial teacher questionnaire and included the characteristics of the school in which the teacher works, professional life phase, post of responsibility and gender. In the same way, value-added indicators of academic effectiveness and measures based on pupils' views were also added to NVivo. Following analysis of teachers' observational and pupil questionnaire data, a number of summary measures were added to the NVivo database in the form of further attributes, which were used to explore the data for the teachers in the sample (see Figure 3.8). For instance, an attribute labelled typically effective/more effective was derived from an examination of school value-added data over a three-year period prior to the project, as well as pupil attitudinal scores, combined with overall scores for individual teachers calculated from the classroom observation instruments. This attribute was used to explore the qualitative interview and observation data. Qualitative data, such as identity scenario, were 'quantitized' and also added to the databases as variables by which the data could be explored. Analyses of interview and other data in NVivo helped produce groupings of typically and more effective teachers. Basic statistical techniques were then adopted to explore the frequencies of different aspects of teaching behaviours, practice and contextual features, such as classroom resources, organization and teacher-pupil interactions.

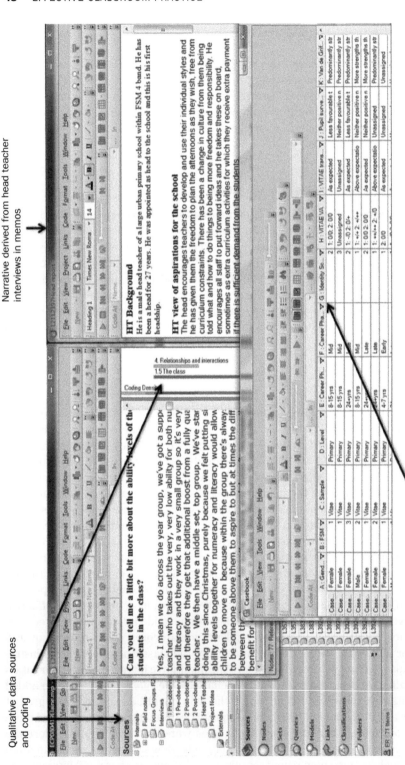

Figure 3.8 An illustration of data integration using NVivo.

Analytical matrices

The next stage involved the construction of analytical matrices (Miles and Huberman 1994) to combine attributes from the quantitative components with the qualitative data to enable the researchers to explore key strands. Further analysis was carried out that combined the separate data sets into one overall database, prior to various analytical techniques being applied. As part of this process of analytical integration, qualitative data were 'quantitized' and quantitative data were 'qualitized' where necessary (Tashakkori and Teddlie 1998: 126). Each matrix was constructed independently of others, reducing the risk of unintentional bias by the researcher.

The areas on which the integrated analysis focused were professional identity and professional life phase. Each of these areas provided a unique lens (developed through the original VITAE study) through which to explore factors contributing to effective classroom practice. Numerical data and text were imported into the matrices for every teacher involved in the study. In this way, the quality of teaching was associated with qualitative and quantitative data, the former locating the teaching in personal, situational and professional contexts, and the latter locating teaching in behaviours and pupils' socio-economic contexts. Bringing these two lenses together in these ways is unique in 'effectiveness' classroom research.

Narrative teacher profiles

Throughout the analytical process, individual narrative profiles were constructed for teachers. Each profile included data from the interviews, questionnaires, observations, repertory grids and used scores from instruments to create profiles of each teacher. Combining qualitative and quantitative measures, these profiles were a key outcome of the mixed methods strategy and formed a foundation for further analysis (see Box 3.1).

Box 3.1   Excerpt from a narrative profile

Michael (above expected VA data; most +ve pupil views; predominantly strong) Michael is a Year 9 maths teacher. He teaches in a large, high socio-economic status, specialist science secondary school with 967 pupils on roll. The school is located in a fairly affluent, suburban area with little ethnic diversity. Michael is 51 years old and has been teaching for more than 28 years, all in this school. He is an assistant head and advanced skills teacher within the school and typically works up to 60 hours per week. He reports a high level of motivation, commitment and job satisfaction, but is starting to consider retirement now that his children have left home. Michael has very high expectations of the pupils and feels well supported in the school.

The use of narrative is believed to be 'the primary scheme by which human existence is rendered meaningful' (Polkinghorne 1988: 1). When teachers talk about their lives as teachers a narrative structure exists (Butt *et al.* 1992) and is usually considered to be located within the qualitative paradigm (Gudmundsdottir 2001) where the participants assign meaning to their experiences through the stories they tell. In this project, the researchers generated narrative stories about what they saw in the classrooms they observed, the teachers and head teachers generated their stories in the before and after interviews, and the surveys and systematic observation instruments tell their own story of teacher effectiveness from the perspective of researchers, teachers and students. The teacher profiles offer an integrated approach to the generation of narratives and the representation of mixed methods research (see Elliott 2005).

The narrative profiles had three main analytical purposes. First, it was possible to examine and explore similarities and differences between teachers in relation to their effectiveness (i.e. more and typically effective). Second, it allowed interrogation of the data in terms of their professional life phase or professional identity. These theoretical groups were then analysed to explicate the features of each group that made each of them similar to each other and the features that made each group distinctive from one another. Finally, the profiles were shown to the individual teachers during the final round of interviews as a means of validating (or not validating) researcher interpretation of results and teachers had the opportunity to comment on their own profile and indicate whether they agreed with the interpretation of their professional life trajectory and identity. In this way, the qualitative and quantitative analyses fed into each other and contributed to the development of models and theories regarding the linkages between different factors that have an impact on teachers' effective classroom practice. The design of the study allowed for the analysis of the effects of factors at two levels: pupil factors (class composition, intake, etc.) and individual teacher factors (motivation, gender, age, etc.). These techniques enabled the researchers to 'genuinely integrate' the data and write up the research in a way that both components were 'mutually illuminating' (Bryman 2007: 8).

Summary

The research design described in this chapter and employed in this study addresses many of the issues raised regarding mixed methods research (Bryman 2007) in general. As will be illustrated throughout this volume, the multi-stage design of the research process allowed a 'mixing' from initial conceptualization of the project, to multiple-staged data collection and analysis. The design also exemplifies effective strategies for integration at different stages of the research process such as using Bazeley's (2007) techniques for combining quantitative and qualitative data as attributes within NVivo, and it is this that has provided the analysis and interpretation presented in the following chapters that explore teacher perceptions and constructs, dimensions of classroom practice and the views of the pupils themselves.

Notes

1. Good lesson organization, understanding the needs of individual children, having enthusiasm for teaching, having good pedagogical knowledge, having high

levels of motivation and commitment, good behaviour/discipline management, good collegiality within the school, having a variety of teaching strategies, being an effective teacher, having confidence in the classroom, being open to new ideas, having well-developed subject/curriculum knowledge, having many years of teaching experience, good classroom management skills, ability to be flexible/adapt practice, having positive relationships with pupils, having a sense of vocation and planning lessons thoroughly.

References

Bazeley, P. (2007) *Qualitative Data Analysis with Nvivo*. Thousand Oaks, CA: Sage.

BERA (British Educational Research Association) (2011) *Revised Ethical Guidelines for Educational research*, London: BERA, www.bera.ac.uk/publications/Ethical%20 Guidelines.

Bryman, A., (2007) Barriers to integrating quantitative and qualitative research, *Journal of Mixed Methods Research*, 1: 1–18.

Butt, R., Raymond, D., McCue, G. and Yamagishi, L. (1992) Collaborative autobiography and the teacher's voice, in I. Goodson (ed.), *Studying Teachers' Lives*, pp. 51–8. New York: Teachers College Press.

Caracelli, V.J. and Greene, J.C. (1997) Crafting mixed-method evaluation designs, in J.C. Greene and V.J. Caracelli (eds) *Advances in Mixed-method Evaluation: The Challenges and Benefits of Integrating Diverse Paradigms*, pp. 19–32. San Francisco, CA: Jossey-Bass.

Creemers, B.P.M. (1994) *The Effective Classroom*. London: Cassell.

Creswell, J.W. (2003) *Research Design. Qualitative, Quantitative and Mixed Methods Approaches*. Thousand Oak, CA: Sage.

Day, C.W., Sammons, P., Kington, A., Gu, Q. and Stobart, G. (2006a) Methodological synergy in a national project: the VITAE Story, *Evaluation and Research in Education*, 19(2): 102–25.

Day, C.W., Stobart, G., Sammons, P., Kington, A., Gu, Q., Smees, R. and Mujtaba, T. (2006b) *Variations in Teachers' Work, Lives and Effectiveness. Final Report for the VITAE Project*. London: DfES.

Day, C.W., Sammons, P., Stobart, G., Kington, A. and Gu, Q. (2007) *Teachers Matter*. Maidenhead: McGraw-Hill.

Day, C.W., Sammons, P. and Gu, Q. (2008) Combining qualitative and quantitative methodologies in research on teachers' lives, work, and effectiveness: from integration to synergy, *Educational Researcher*, 37(6): 330–42.

Denzin, N.K. (1978) *The Research Act: A Theoretical Introduction to Sociological Methods*. New York: Praeger.

Elliott, J. (2005) *Using Narrative in Social Research: Qualitative and Quantitative Approaches*. Thousand Oaks, CA: Sage.

Fransella, F., Bell, R. and Bannister, D. (2003) *A Manual for Repertory Grid Technique*. Chichester: John Wiley & Sons.

Gu, Q., Sammons, P. and Mehta, P. (2008) Leadership characteristics and practices in schools with different effectiveness and improvement profiles, *School Leadership and Management*, 28(1): 43–63

Gudmundsdottir, S. (2001) Narrative research on school practice, in V. Richardson (ed.) *Fourth Handbook for Research on Teaching*, pp. 226–40. New York: Macmillan.

Hammersley, M. (1990) What's wrong with ethnography? The myth of theoretical description, *Sociology*, 24: 597–615.

Jankowicz, D. (2004) *The Easy Guide to Repertory Grids*. Oxford: John Wiley & Sons.

Johnson, R.B., and Onwuegbuzie, A.J. (2004) Mixed methods research: a research paradigm whose time has come, *Educational Researcher*, 33(7): 14–26.

Leech, N.L. and Onwuegbuzie, A.J. (2009) A typology of mixed methods research designs. Quality & quantity, *International Journal of Methodology*, 43: 265–75.

Lincoln, Y.S. and Guba, E. G. (2000) Paradigmatic controversies, contradictions, and emerging confluences, in N.K. Denzin and Y.S. Lincoln (eds) *Handbook of Qualitative Research*, 2nd edn, pp. 163–88. Thousand Oaks, CA: Sage.

Maxwell, J.A. and Loomis, D.M. (2003) Mixed methods design: an alternative approach, in A. Taskakko and C. Teddl (eds) *Handbook of Mixed Methods in Social and Behavioural Research*, pp. 214–72. Thousand Oaks, CA: Sage.

Miles, M. and Huberman, M. (1994) *Qualitative Data Analysis: An Expanded Sourcebook*. Thousand Oaks, CA: Sage.

Muijs, D., Campbell, J., Kyriakides, L. and Robinson, W. (2005) Making the case for differentiated teacher effectiveness: an overview of research in four key areas, *School Effectiveness and School Improvement: An International Journal of Research, Policy and Practice*, 16(1): 51–70.

Muijs, R.D. and Reynolds, D. (2000) School effectiveness and teacher effectiveness: some preliminary findings from the evaluation of the Mathematics Enhancement Programme, *School Effectiveness and School Improvement*, 11(3): 273–303.

Onwuegbuzie, A. and Johnson, R.B. (2004) Mixed research, in R.B. Johnson and L.B. Christensen (eds) *Educational Research: Quantitative, Qualitative, and Mixed Approaches*, 2nd edn, pp. 408–31. Needham Heights, MA: Allyn & Bacon.

Polkinghorne, D.E. (1988) *Narrative Knowing and Human Sciences*. New York: State University of New York Press.

Sammons, P. (2010) The contribution of mixed methods to recent research on educational effectiveness, in A. Tashakkori and C. Teddlie (eds) *Handbook of Mixed Methods Research*, 2nd edn. London: Sage.

Sammons, P. and Ko, J. (2008) *Using Systematic Classroom Observation Schedules to Investigate Effective Teaching: Overview of Quantitative Findings, Effective Classroom Practice (ECP)*, ESRC Project Report, Ref. no. RES-000-23-1564.

Sammons, P., Elliot, K., Wellcome, W., Taggart, B. and Levacic, R. (2004) England: a country report, in H. Doöbert, E. Klieme and W. Sroka (eds) *Conditions of School Performance in Seven Countries – A Quest for Understanding the International Variation of PISA Results*, pp. 65–149. Berlin: Waxmann Publishing Co.

Sammons, P., Siraj-Blatchford, I., Sylva, K., Melhuish, E., Taggart, B. and Elliot, L. (2005) Investigating the effects of pre-school provision: using mixed methods in the EPPE research, *International Journal of Social Research Methodology, Theory & Practice*, special issue on mixed methods in educational research, 8(3): 207–24.

Sammons, P., Day, C.W., Kington, A., Gu, Q., Stobart, G. and Smees, R. (2007) Exploring variations in teachers' work, lives and their effects on pupils: key findings and implications from a longitudinal mixed methods study, *British Educational Research Journal*, 33(5): 681–701.

Scheerens, J. (1992) *Effective Schooling: Research, Theory and Practice*. London: Cassell.

Siraj-Blatchford, I., Taggart, B., Sylva, K., Sammons, P. and Melhuish, E. (2008) Towards the transformation of practice in early childhood education: the effective provision of pre-school education (EPPE) project, *Cambridge Journal of Education*, 38(1): March: 23–36.

Strauss, A. and Corbin, J. (1998) *Basics of Qualitative Research*. Thousands Oak, CA: Sage.

Sylva, K., Melhuish, E., Sammons, P., Siraj-Blatchford, I. and Taggart, B. (eds) (2010) *Early Childhood Matters: Evidence from the Effective Pre-school and Primary Education Project*. Oxford: Routledge.

Tashakkori, A. and Teddlie, C. (1998) *Mixed Methodology: Combining Qualitative and Quantitative Approaches. Applied Social Research Methods Series (Vol. 46)*, Thousand Oak, CA: Sage.

Tashakkori, A. and Teddlie, C. (eds) (2003) *Handbook of Mixed Methods in Social & Behavioral Research*. Thousand Oaks, CA: Sage.

Teddlie, C. and Liu, S. (2008) Examining teacher effectiveness within differentially effective primary schools in the People's Republic of China, *School Effectiveness and School Improvement*, 19(4): 387–407.

Teddlie, C. and Reynolds D. (eds) (2000) *The International Handbook of School Effectiveness Research*, pp. 55–133. London: Falmer Press.

Teddlie, C., Creemers, B., Kyriakides, L., Muijs, D. and Yu, F. (2006) The International System for Teacher Observation and Feedback: evolution of an international study of teacher effectiveness constructs, *Educational Research and Evaluation*, 12(6): 561–82.

Teddlie, C. and Sammons, P. (2010) Applications of mixed methods to the field of educational effectiveness research, in B.P.M Creemers, L. Kyriakiand and P., Sammons (eds) *Methodological Advances in Educational Effectiveness Research*. London: Routledge.

van de Grift, W., Matthews, P., Tabak, l. and de Rijcke, F. (2004) *Comparative Research into the Inspection of Teaching in England and the Netherlands*, HMI 2251. London: Ofsted.

PART 2

4 Exploring effective teaching: learning from classroom observation

Introduction

This chapter begins with a brief summary of teacher effectiveness research and inspection evidence on the characteristics of effective practice is given to contextualize the findings and provide a rationale for the choice of two systematic observation instruments to be used in the quantitative component of the concurrent mixed methods design of the Effective Classroom Practice (ECP) research. The chapter then discusses analyses of the observed variation in practices found in the sample and identifies items where there was either little or alternatively greater variation among teachers. It then identifies a number of models summarizing the underlying dimensions (factors) of teacher behaviour measured by the two observation instruments and draws a comparison. This chapter also uses some qualitative cameos to illustrate and illuminate the results obtained from the quantitative observations. The concluding section summarizes key findings and their implications.

Teacher effectiveness research and inspection evidence

Teacher effectiveness research

Muijs and Reynolds (2005) have highlighted the lack of a strong research base on teacher effectiveness in the UK which they partly attribute to a cultural belief that teaching is an art not a science, the lack of a tradition of studying learning and instruction within educational psychology in the UK, and the dislike of making comparisons of performance between individual teachers. Elsewhere, educational effectiveness researchers have sought to study and explore a range of actual behaviours of teachers in classrooms, observing individual lessons and linking the behaviours observed to data about student outcomes, such as scores on standardized tests. Early teacher effectiveness researchers in the USA, who studied teacher behaviours using classroom observation instruments, gradually started to find patterns which indicated that more effective teachers (a concept of relative effectiveness defined by value-added approaches as teachers whose students made stronger gains on standardized achievement tests) tended to actively teach the whole class, spending significantly more time than ineffective teachers explicitly lecturing, demonstrating or interacting with the class as a whole. As well as actively teaching the whole class for more of the time, effective teachers were found to be characterized by a number of observed behaviours.

Despite the lack of a strong teacher effectiveness tradition, some British studies have investigated classroom practice and pupil outcomes. Classic examples include the ORACLE study (Galton and Croll 1980; Galton and Simon 1980; Galton 1995) and School Matters (Mortimore *et al.* 1988). The ORACLE research indicated that teachers identified as 'Class Enquirers' generated the greatest gains for pupils in the areas of mathematics and language, whereas pupils in classes of teachers identified as operating a highly individualized approach, termed 'Individual Monitors', made least progress. The Class Enquirers group of teachers were observed to utilize significantly more time in whole-class interactive teaching than the Individual Monitors (Croll 1996). Further analyses showed an association between progress and non-individualized interaction. The ORACLE study found that whole-class interaction was positively associated with high levels of pupil time on task. The later PACE study of primary schools investigated the impact of major educational reforms such as the introduction of curriculum and National Curriculum changes (Pollard *et al.* 1994). This also reported high levels of whole-class interaction associated with greater pupil task engagement.

Mortimore *et al.* (1988) studied primary school effects using an educational effectiveness design including information on children, their classrooms and teachers and their primary schools, following children aged seven to eleven years. The research showed that teachers were spending much more time communicating with individual children than they were doing whole-class teaching or facilitating collaborative group work. At classroom level the effective teacher characteristics identified were:

- teacher responsibility for ordering activities during the day for pupils, i.e. structured teaching;
- pupils having some responsibility for their work and independence within these sessions;
- a limited focus covering only one curriculum area at a time;
- high levels of teacher interaction with the whole class;
- providing ample, challenging work;
- high levels of pupil involvement in tasks;
- a positive atmosphere in the classroom;
- greater use of praise and encouragement.

Teachers who spent more time interacting with individual pupils tended to focus on routine, i.e. non-work, matters and made less use of higher-order questioning, or work-related feedback while teachers who interacted more with the whole class made relatively more use of higher-order communication and work-related feedback. Mortimore *et al.* (1988) concluded that the key classroom factors contributing to effective outcomes were structured sessions, intellectually challenging teaching, a work-oriented environment, communication between teacher and pupils and a limited focus within the sessions.

More recent research in the USA in elementary schools has drawn attention to the independent contribution to the prediction of achievement growth of students across first, third and fifth grade classrooms of the quality of teacher-child interactions and the quantity of exposure to instructional activities, but also to their interactive effects (Pianta *et al.* 2008). Their review found that for first graders 'teachers' focus on concepts and provision of feedback have an even stronger positive effect for students whose parents have low levels of education themselves' (Pianta *et al.* 2008: 4). It concludes that 'there is accumulating evidence that teachers' instructional interactions with children have the greatest value for student performance when they are focused, direct, intentional and characterized by feedback loops involving student performance'. In addition it is noted that 'The value of intentional, focused interaction and feedback is not limited to reading but appears to be a key component in other skill domains that may extend to cognition and higher order thinking' (Pianta *et al.* 2008: 4). These conclusions are in accord with those of van der Werf (2006) who reviewed evidence concerning more recent constructivist teaching approaches with alternatives such as direct instruction, using empirical data from the Netherlands. She argues that there is little evidence of positive effects of constructivist approaches on student attainment whereas, in contrast, she concludes that direct instruction emphasizing learning as an active process is a more effective strategy for raising attainment, especially for lower ability students and those from disadvantaged backgrounds.

Quantitative research on 125 primary schools in England conducted in 2005–6 as part of the Effective Pre-School and Primary Project (EPPE 3-11) adopted two US observational protocols to explore variation in teachers observed practice in Year 5 classes (Sammons *et al.* 2008). These were the Instructional Observation Schedule (Stipek 1999) and the Classroom Observation Schedule Grade 5 (NICHD 2001). The study indicated that there was significant variation in teachers' observed classroom practices and revealed the existence of a number of underlying dimensions. Higher quality was found to be significantly associated with the use of a plenary session in literacy and numeracy lessons, although only half the sample studied were found to use a plenary.

The authors summarized the findings that explored the relationship between children's progress and social behavioural outcomes (measured over four years) and classroom practice in terms of 'What Matters in the Classroom' as follows:

- The observations reveal considerable differences in teachers' and children's behaviours and classroom practices indicating significant variation in the quality of children's educational experiences during Year 5. We found that teachers can be classified into different groups in terms of overall teaching quality, and that observed Year 5 overall teaching quality is a significant predictor of better cognitive progress from Year 1 to Year 5 in both reading and maths.
- Quality of pedagogy in Year 5 (richness of instructional method, a positive climate, productive use of instructional time, the use of evaluative feedback, teacher sensitivity and lack of teacher detachment) was found to be

a significant predictor of progress in maths, but not in reading. It was also important for children's progress in terms of reducing hyperactivity, and promoting pro-social behaviour and self-regulation.

- Classroom attention and control was related to better progress in maths and better development in self-regulation. Child positivity (which involved child-teacher relationships, children's co-operative skills and their self-reliance) was related to better progress in reading.
- High levels of observed classroom disorganization in Year 5 (related to teachers' organization and the behavioural climate of the classroom) were predictors of poorer progress in both reading and maths and increased hyperactivity (Sammons *et al.* 2008: 2).
- The EPPE results on primary Year 5 teachers indicated that global measures of overall teacher quality could predict variations in pupils' academic progress in both reading and mathematics (effect Sizes 0.35–7) but in addition teachers varied in more specific features of practice and these tended to relate to social behavioural as well as academic outcomes. In particular, pupils showed poorer developmental progress in several aspects of social behaviour in schools where teachers' classroom practice scored more highly on the negative factor disorganization.

Inspection evidence

In England inspection evidence has also been used to study teaching quality and to comment on teacher effectiveness, especially since 1993 after the creation of Ofsted and the introduction of regular and high-stakes inspection with publication of schools' reports. Although such evidence is not based on process product research directly linked to data on pupil outcomes (in contrast to the teacher effectiveness research tradition) it relies on professional judgement and experience and many of the findings are in accord with the results of educational effectiveness research. The HMCI annual report has provided a regular and detailed commentary on standards of teaching in England and specific reports on teaching different subjects have received widespread attention during the period 1993 to 2007 (the most recent inspection framework draws on the *Every Child Matters* agenda and involves much less detailed focus on teaching). A number of general teacher/teaching factors associated with positive outcomes for pupils were identified in *Primary Matters* (Ofsted 1995) and these provide a good indication of the aspects of effective teaching considered relevant by the inspection model of teaching quality. They include:

- good subject knowledge;
- good questioning skills;
- an emphasis upon instruction;
- a balance of grouping strategies;
- clear objectives;
- good time management;
- effective planning;
- good classroom organization;
- effective use of other adults in the classroom.

Later, the development of the National Literacy and Numeracy Strategies evolved drawing on research and inspection evidence and had a major impact on practice and teachers' perceptions of what characterized effective primary practice in England, as did the Key Stage 3 Strategy in lower secondary school. Evaluations of the strategies noted positive relationships with improvements in the quality of teaching in terms of inspection data (Ofsted 2005), as well as links with improved pupil outcomes in national assessment outcomes and in international comparisons (PIRLS and TIMSS), although, as with most educational and social research, it is not possible to draw causal connections between such improvements and the introduction of the strategies, nor to separate their influence from that of other initiatives intended to raise attainment.

Commenting on the Literacy and Numeracy Strategies, Webb and Vulliamy (2007) note that teachers generally perceived them to have played an important role that had improved primary practice in England considerably, but found from interviews that there were objections to their perceived prescriptive nature:

> In general the Strategies were viewed very positively because they promoted continuity of teaching and learning in literacy and numeracy across all English schools, gave a structure and learning objectives for lessons, helped pupil understanding and provided ideas and resources for teachers – particularly important for those lacking specialist knowledge in English and/or mathematics. Despite their support for the Strategies, teachers were highly critical of the government for imposing them 'in such a way that "You don't have to do it, it is an option, but woe betide anybody who doesn't!"'. The Strategies were viewed as another expression of the government's lack of trust in the teaching profession and a public declaration that teachers lacked expertise in teaching basic subjects which further lowered morale and reduced teacher self-confidence.
>
> (Webb and Vulliamy 2007: 567–8)

Choosing systematic classroom observation instruments for the ECP research

The use of systematic observations is intended to allow for comparisons of teachers in terms of certain predetermined and agreed categories of behaviour and practice and originated in the teacher effectiveness field of inquiry (Muijs and Reynolds 2005). Muijs and Reynolds note the difference between value-oriented instruments that require a value judgement from the observer compared with behavioural instruments that are designed to look at the occurrence, or not, of specific behaviours without passing global judgements on whether the observed behaviour was deemed to be either a 'good' or a 'poor' feature of practice. This is related to the distinction between high and low inference measures. They argue that teacher effectiveness research has tended to focus on mathematics and reading, and on primary classes, thus the generalizability of the findings to other subjects or activities and to the secondary sector requires further study.

The International System for Teacher Observation and Feedback

Teddlie *et al.* (2006) suggest that successful international comparative research will depend on the development of internationally valid instruments, particularly teacher effectiveness protocols. The International System for Teacher Observation and Feedback (ISTOF) was developed based on a review of research on effective teaching and using an iterative, multiple step, internet-based, modified 'Delphi' technique involving teams from 21 participating country experts (researchers, practitioners and education advisers/inspectors) whose opinions about what constitutes effective teaching were used to help generate the components in the instrument. The ISTOF schedule has been in the process of development since 2006 as part of a collaborative, cross-national research initiative by the Methodology of Research in Effectiveness (MORE) group of the International Congress for School Effectiveness and Improvement (ICSEI). The scale was intended to be an observation protocol for measuring teacher effectiveness in lessons with a broad ecological validity for a variety of country and cultural settings. The ECP team was asked to contribute to the international pilot phase of the ISTOF project and chose to use the ISTOF schedule as one of the two instruments in the study to enable its applicability to the English context to be explored.

The ISTOF scale consists of 45 items, with two to three items representing one indicator and two to three indicators forming one component, making up 21 indicators and seven components in total:

- component 1: assessment and evaluation;
- component 2: differentiation and inclusion;
- component 3: clarity of instruction;
- component 4: instructional skills;
- component 5: promoting active learning and developing meta-cognitive skills;
- component 6: classroom climate;
- component 7: classroom management.

For each item, participants were rated on a 5-point Likert type scale with values ranging from five for the highest or 'strongly agree' to one for the lowest or 'strongly disagree'. Thus, a higher value indicate that more of the behaviour described by the item has been observed. There is a 'NA' (not applicable, unable to observe) response option to indicate a condition in which the item might not be relevant/observable in some classroom settings. The pilot instrument ISTOF guidance indicated that field researchers would be likely to mark 'NA' for around 5–10 per cent of the items.

Out of the 45 items in the ISTOF scale, a total of 16 had higher levels (above 17 per cent) of missing values. Moreover, six items have more than 30 per cent missing values. The majority relate to component five of the schedule, 'Promoting active learning and meta-cognitive skills', suggesting that field researchers found this area of teacher behaviour the most difficult to make judgements about. Since the significant proportion of missing data has implications for the subsequent quantitative analyses and interpretations, the missing data were imputed using appropriate techniques.

Lesson Observation Form for Evaluating the Quality of Teaching

In addition, the ECP team chose an additional instrument based on an international collaboration between two national inspectorates (senior inspectors from Ofsted) in England and Dutch inspectorate equivalents). The Lesson Observation Form for Evaluating the Quality of Teaching (QoT) is intended to utilize professional judgement and has a deliberate high inference evaluative framework based on professional judgements.

Inspection has a high profile in evaluating schools and the quality of teaching and learning in England and therefore an inspection-based instrument might be expected to provide an additional source of relevant evidence to contribute to understandings of what constitutes effective classroom practice in the English context and to what extent current classroom practice in a sample of effective classroom teachers fits with inspection-based concepts of 'good practice'. The team also sought to explore the utility of the QoT instrument for use in lower secondary classes as it had been developed in the primary sector originally.

A series of collaborative comparative studies on the instruments used by the inspectors in England and the Netherlands had been conducted by Her Majesty's Inspectorate and the Dutch Inspectorate and contributed to an evaluation of the Impact of Ofsted (Matthews and Sammons 2004). The Dutch Inspectorate focused on investigating the quality and consistency of inspectors' judgements, methods of working and the instruments used by both inspectorates. The QoT GRIFT schedule was developed on the basis of an original instrument used by the Dutch Inspectorate for lesson observation. Its high degree of standardization and structuring reflects the Dutch approach to inspection that has a rather more detailed focus than that used by Ofsted in England. The collaborative research was intended to serve two purposes: to test the reliability and consistency of inspectors' judgements when the same instrument was used by both English and Dutch inspectors and to compare the quality of teaching strategies in English and Dutch primary schools. The reliability and validity of the QoT schedule to identify the quality difference in the teacher strategies in both countries are reported in van de Grift et al. (2004). The authors found good evidence to support the instrument as a measure of teacher quality in terms of reliability and validity of judgements made.

The QoT instrument comprises a detailed checklist of indicators, covering nine criteria for evaluating the quality of teaching. According to van de Grift et al. (2004), the original Dutch instrument only had 23 indicators and seven criteria. It differed from its Dutch predecessor schedule in its inclusion of an overall grade for teaching to reflect an overall judgement of the lesson quality, which was a distinctive characteristic of the English Ofsted approach. The advantage of such an inclusion is that it allows a correlation analysis to be performed on the Dutch indicators and the overall grade. It was expected that the correlation analysis would indicate which teacher behaviours have the greatest association with the global judgement of teacher effectiveness and might identify a set of robust indicators suitable for an international comparative analysis of characteristics of effective teaching. In other words, despite its origin as a professional instrument aimed at lesson observation by inspectors, the QoT schedule shared similar aims to ISTOF in its development.

The ECP team decided to adopt the QoT as an additional observational schedule in the ECP research for comparison with the ISTOF teacher effectiveness research-based instrument and trial its use in both primary and lower secondary classes. ISTOF and QoT are also similar in some features of their structures. The criteria used to evaluate teaching quality in the QoT instrument are broadly comparable with the seven theoretical components of ISTOF. The areas covered by the nine criteria, followed by final judgement of overall quality of teaching, are:

- safe and orderly school climate;
- stimulating learning climate;
- clear objectives;
- clear instruction;
- activating pupils;
- adaptation of teaching;
- teaching learning strategies;
- effective classroom organization;
- effective classroom layout;
- final judgement of overall quality of teaching.

Each component or criterion is supported by two to four indicators in both scales. The two scales differ in their relative degree of standardization and depth of hierarchical structure. In QoT, teaching behaviours are described only as examples to help inspectors to judge the teacher's relative strength or weakness on each indicator, but teaching behaviours were conceptualized and formalized as specific items for evaluation in ISTOF. In other words, indicators are the targets for evaluation, and teaching behaviours are references to support evaluations in the QoT instrument, while specific teaching behaviours are the targets for evaluation and indicators act as labels for grouping-related teaching behaviours in ISTOF. These are important distinctions in purpose and measurement properties.

Another distinction between the two instruments lies in their rating scales for evaluation. In ISTOF, a 5-point Likert scale was used to indicate how often the teacher behaviours were seen, while in QoT, a 4-point Likert scale was used to indicate the inspector's assessment of the overall relative strength or relative weakness of classroom practice seen in regard to the indicator of interest. For example, a value of 1 indicates the relative quality of teaching was predominantly weak, 2 for more weaknesses than strengths, 3 for more strengths than weaknesses and 4 for predominantly strong. Field researchers were instructed to give a score of 3 only when all practice examples were observed. Although relative strength (as used in QoT) and relative frequency (as used in ISTOF) of a particular teaching behaviour are related, they are conceptually and practically very different types of measure.

Field researchers were supplied with descriptions of some behaviour related to each indicators as practice examples. The QoT instrument seemed to be more straightforward to use as the number of indicators was smaller than the number of items in the ISTOF schedule. Overall, there were 11 teachers (cases) without lesson observations in which QoT was the target instrument. Among the remaining 70 valid cases, there were eight indicators with missing values, six with only one or two missing values (Indicators 2.1, 2.3, 3.1, 3.2, 7.3 and 8.1). The other two indicators with 16 (23 per cent) missing values were Indicator 7.1, 'The teacher ensures that the teaching materials are oriented towards transfer' and Indicator 7.2, 'The teacher stimulates the use of control activities'. Both indicators are linked to the teaching learning strategies criteria and they may not be something that teachers would normally do in every lesson, and this might partly explain why there were more missing values for these items.

Training field researchers to use the systematic observation schedules

Training was given to all members of the research team, in order to gain inter- and intra-judge reliability (Tashakkori and Teddlie 1998). This was achieved through a two-stage process:

- Using video footage from classrooms, each researcher observed a series of recorded lessons in appropriate age phase settings.
- Researchers conducted paired observations in actual classrooms prior to, and during, the piloting phase of the study.

In each instance, the observation schedules were completed after the observation and subsequently the judgements were compared by the researchers themselves, as well as an independent researcher who had not been present for the observation.

Generally speaking, field researchers reported that it was easier to use the QoT schedule in the ECP study. It may be that the process of making higher inference judgements on strengths and weaknesses based on their impression of the presence and strength of some related behaviour(s) when they evaluated on the QoT indicators was somewhat easier than making judgements about the extent to which a specific category of behaviour was seen. Moreover, in England, which has a strong inspection-based culture in evaluating schools, this may have been an activity which was seen as more familiar to staff who would be aware of current notions of 'good practice'. Finally, another feature of the QoT scale compared with the ISTOF scale is its lack of neutral and NA options.

Objectives of the quantitative analyses of classroom observation data

The main aim of the ECP quantitative analyses was to explore the extent of variations in teachers' observed classroom practice for a purposive sample of relatively effective teachers in English primary and secondary schools. The objectives were:

- To examine the utility of the ISTOF and QoT instruments in the English context in identifying various features of effective classroom practices.
- To examine the relationships between features of teachers' observed practices measured by the two instruments.
- To explore variations in observed practices between primary and lower secondary teachers and identify the key underlying dimensions of practice.
- To explore variations in observed practice between English and mathematics teachers in the secondary school sample.

- To explore variations in observed practice according to school context (in terms of level of social disadvantage measured by the percentage of pupils eligible for the free school meals (FSM) indicator).
- To investigate the relationships between variations in observed practice and teachers' self-reported commitment, motivation and stress levels.
- To investigate any relationships between pupils' views and experiences (derived from surveys) and variations in teachers' observed classroom practice.
- To produce different groupings of teachers according to overall and specific features of their observed classroom practice to incorporate into teachers' individual profiles (in terms of whether teachers were relatively above, typical or below the sample average in specific aspects).

Evidence from analysis of the systematic observation schedules to investigated effective classroom practice

Exploring variation between teachers in the ratings made on ISTOF items

The first main characteristic of the rating scores was the high mean score and small standard deviation for most of the items. Except for Item 20, 'The teacher uses different, appropriate instructional strategies for different groups of students', all items had a mean above 3. Moreover, in total, 33 of the 45 items (73.3 per cent) had means above 4; and 14 items (31.1 per cent) means above 4.5. For the majority of items, the standard deviation (60 per cent) was below 1. High means and small standard deviations contribute to the second main characteristic of the distributions of the current data set – many negatively skewed distributions with high positive kurtosis values. However, these main characteristics might be expected due to the ECP's focus on typical and relatively more effective teachers who may be more likely to be homogenous in many aspects of their teaching practices. A negatively skewed distribution means that the majority of teachers received higher ratings because they showed more of the particular teaching behaviour described by an item during the lesson observed by a field researcher. The higher the skewness value is, the more the teacher sample were given scores from the higher rating points. A distribution with a high peak (i.e. a high kurtosis value) means that the variations in the sample were small. The higher the peak is and the narrower the base of a distribution curve is, the smaller the variation among the teachers in regard to the particular teaching behaviour (item) concerned.

However, two items showed a different pattern. Item 12, 'The teacher asks students to identify the reasons why specific activities take place in the lesson' and Item 20, 'The teacher uses different, appropriate instructional strategies for different groups of students'. Overall, about three-quarters of the items (i.e. 33 items) had a skewness value exceeding 1 standard deviation. Most of the negatively skewed distributions also had a prominent peak shape as is shown for Item 34, 'The teacher's instruction is interactive with lots of questions and answers', and Item 32, 'The teacher shows respect for the students in both his or her behaviour and use of language'. Thirty-three items (73.3 per cent) had a positive kurtosis value exceeding

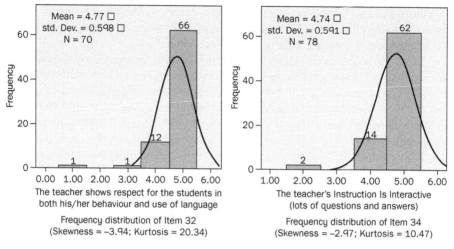

Figure 4.1 Two ISTOF items on which teachers were rated most favourably (the most extreme skewed distribution patterns).

1 standard deviation suggesting that most teachers in the sample showed strong similarities in their observed practice in these areas.

Figure 4.1 shows the two most extreme negatively skewed distribution patterns with a high kurtosis, because almost all teachers in the sample were given high scores for these aspects of behaviour indicating that teachers showed a lot of respect for their students and teaching was highly interactive.

By contrast there was more variation in ratings for Item 4, 'The teacher explains how assignments are aligned to the learning goals of the lesson', and Item 15, 'The teacher provides sufficient wait time and response strategies to involve all types of learner'. Some teachers were rated less highly in these areas.

Exploring variation between teachers in the ratings made on the QoT items

Like the ISTOF items, most of the QoT indicators had high means and small standard deviations. Eighteen indicators had a mean above 3.6 and, for 22, standard deviations were below 1. High means and small standard deviations produced many negatively skewed distributions and high positive kurtosis values. Again, these main characteristics were to be expected because most participants were recruited as typical or above effectiveness. The data showed an even stronger predominance of the strengths of the teachers in the sample, because all the QoT indicators had negatively skewed distributions. Twenty-two (84.6 per cent) of the 26 GRIFT Indicators had a skewness value exceeding 1 standard deviation, 19 of which (73.1 per cent) were significantly negatively skewed.

In terms of the overall judgement of teaching quality 54 (77.1) of the 70 teachers in the QoT observation group were given the highest rating ('predominantly strong'), 12 (17.1 per cent) 'strengths outweigh weaknesses' and only 4 (5.7 per cent) 'more weaknesses than strengths'. None received the lowest rating ('predominantly weak'). These results provide broad support for the sampling strategy adopted (that sought to identify typical and more effective teachers). Despite the overall judgement there was evidence of some variation in practice among the sample of teachers in terms of scores on other indicators in the schedule.

Despite a higher percentage of negatively skewed distributions in the data, the skewness and kurtosis values of QoT indicators were not as high as those of the ISTOF items. For example, Indicator 1.3, 'Supports the self-confidence of pupils' had the highest skewness at –2.92 and kurtosis at 8.25. The other indicators with extreme skewness and kurtosis values included Indicator 1.4, 'Shows respect for the pupils in behaviour and language', Indicator 9.1, 'Ensures the classroom layout supports the pupil activities', and Indicator 9.2, 'The teaching environment is educational and contemporary'.

The data also showed that the number of teachers who were rated as predominantly weak or having more weaknesses than strengths need not be very high to obtain reduced skewness and kurtosis values. In Figure 4.2, for example, the skewness and kurtosis for Indicator 2.1 was moderate when only five teachers were rated as having more weaknesses than strengths, and this was also the case for Indicator 2.3 when 10 teachers were rated as weak.

Only four QoT indicators did not have negatively skewed distribution (i.e. did not show very high ratings on the positive end of the scale): 'Adapts the instruction to the relevant differences between pupils' (Indicator 6.1), 'Adapts the assignments and processing to the relevant difference between pupils' (Indicator 6.2), 'Ensures that the teaching materials are oriented towards transfer' (Indicator 7.1) and 'Stimulates the use of control activities' (Indicator 7.2).

Figure 4.3 shows that Indicator 6.1 is the only QoT indicator to possess a bimodal distribution. The results showed that catering for individual pupil differences in class was a feature in which there was a greater variation in this teacher sample. In all, 14 (20 per cent) teachers were rated as predominately weak and four teachers were identified as having more weaknesses than strengths in this area. Nonetheless, about three-quarters of the teachers were rated as particularly strong or had more strengths than weaknesses in the judgement of catering for individual differences in their class. In other words, the majority of teachers were rated as strong in

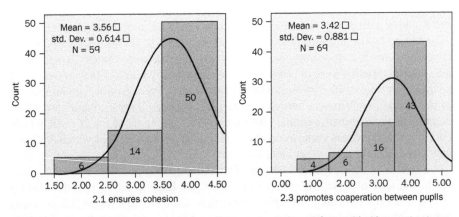

Figure 4.2 Two QoT indicators on which teachers were rated most favourably (the most extreme skewed distribution patterns).

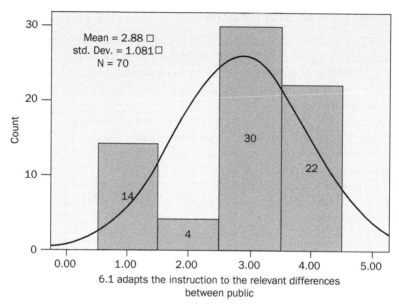

Figure 4.3   A QoT indicator on adapting instruction to meet different pupils' needs, showing a bimodal distribution.

this area. It should be noted that some teachers may intend all students to cover the same work rather than seeking to differentiate their practice, particularly where mixed-ability classes are not in use.

Exploring underlying dimensions of effective practice

Both the QoT and ISTOF instruments utilized a theoretically driven underlying structure that sought to measure features of classroom organization and teacher behaviour associated with the notion of 'effective 'practice (ISTOF) and 'quality' of teaching (QoT). One of the aims of the ECP research was to explore the utility of the instruments to study teachers in English primary and the middle years of secondary school and to establish whether the empirical observation data supported the theoretical underpinnings of the two instruments. In addition, the study sought to establish the extent to which teachers would be identified as relatively more effective on both instruments (in other words whether teachers rated highly on one would also be likely to be rated highly on the other).

In order to conduct these comparisons missing data were imputed and initial exploratory factor analyses (EFA) based on principal components analysis (varimax rotated) were conducted prior to the use of confirmatory factor analysis (CFA) on both data sets. The use of CFA is recommended to test and refine theoretical models by identifying latent variables. It should be noted that the relatively small teacher sample size had implications for the use of CFA. These analyses are summarized and the results for the two instruments compared.

A CFA model based on ISTOF indicators

An initial EFA model was obtained using principal components extraction with varimax rotation by SPSS DATA REDUCTION as the hypothetical CFA model for testing in LISREL. A final five-factor model (shown in Table 4.1) was obtained with acceptable fit indices and good reliability, after deleting the three indicators with the lowest EFA loadings.[1]

Most of the ISTOF indicators have relatively strong loadings in the five factor CFA solution, ranging from 0.60 to 0.93. Accordingly, the explanatory powers of these indicators are quite strong as indicated in their square multiple correlations. The only exception is Indicator 4.2. (the teacher possesses good questioning skills) which has a lower loading at 0.45. Moreover, the overall internal consistency of the total scale measured by Cronbach's Alpha at 0.83 is higher than those of the individual factors, with the exception of factor 3, Responsiveness to Students' needs. This

Table 4.1   The ISTOF indicators that formed a five-factor model

Factor Name	Ind. No.	Indicator Name	Factor loading	Square multiple correlation	Reliability Cronbach's alpha
Structured lessons that maximize learning and involvement (ECP core)	2.1	The teacher creates an environment in which all students are involved	0.69	0.48	0.80
	3.3	Lessons are well structured	0.93	0.56	
	4.1	The teacher is able to engage students	0.81	0.66	
	6.3	The teacher interacts with all students	0.70	0.49	
	6.4	The teacher communicates high expectations	0.71	0.50	
	7.1	Learning is maximized	0.62	0.39	
High-quality communication and interaction (ECP skilled)	1.1	The teacher gives explicit detailed and constructive feedback	0.60	0.36	0.55
	3.1	The teacher shows good communication skills	0.52	0.67	
	4.2	The teacher possesses good questioning skills	0.45	0.20	
	6.1	All students are valued	0.92	0.85	
Responsiveness to students needs (ECP advanced)	2.2	The teacher takes full account of student differences	0.82	0.68	0.84
	4.3	The teacher uses various teaching methods and strategies	0.87	0.77	
Active learning	5.2	The teacher gives students opportunities to be active learners	0.72	0.52	0.71
	5.3	The teacher fosters critical thinking in students	0.86	0.74	
Purposive learning	1.2	Assessment is aligned with goals and objectives	0.69	0.40	0.54
	3.2	Clear explanation of purpose	0.63	0.48	
N = 79		Total			0.83

Table 4.2 The QoT indicators that formed a six-factor model

Factor Name	Ind. No.	Indicator content	Factor loading	Square multiple correlation	Reliability cronbach's alpha
Supportive and stimulating lesson climate	1.1	ensures a relaxed atmosphere	0.94	0.89	0.87
	1.2	promotes mutual respect	0.9	0.8	
	1.3	supports the self-confidence of pupils	0.98	0.95	
	2.1	ensures cohesion	0.91	0.83	
	2.2	stimulates the independence of pupils	0.82	0.67	
	2.3	promotes cooperation between pupils	0.66	0.43	
	2.4	there is good individual involvement by the pupils	0.86	0.74	
Proactive lesson management	5.1	involves all pupils in the lesson	0.91	0.83	0.88
	8.1	gives a well-structured lesson	0.91	0.83	
	8.2	ensures the orderly progression of the lesson	0.93	0.86	
	8.3	uses learning time efficiently	0.91	0.82	
Well-organized lessons with clear objectives	3.1	clarifies the lesson objectives at the start of the lesson	0.45	0.2	0.73
	3.2	evaluates whether the objectives have been achieved at the end of the lesson	0.56	0.31	
	4.1	gives clear instructions and explanations	1	1	
	4.2	gives clear explanations of the learning materials and the assignments	0.87	0.76	
	4.3	gives feedback to pupils	0.96	0.93	
Effective classroom layout	9.1	ensures the classroom layout supports the pupil activities	0.96	0.92	0.79
	9.2	the teaching environment is educational and contempory	0.81	0.65	
Adapation of teaching	6.1	adapts the instruction to the relevant differences between pupils	0.92	0.84	0.90
	6.2	adapts the assignments and processing to the relevant difference between pupils	0.96	0.92	
Teaching learning strategies	7.1	ensures that the teaching materials are oriented towards transfer	0.63	0.39	0.69
	7.2	stimulates the use of control activities	0.76	0.57	
	7.3	provides interactive instruction and activities	0.99	0.98	
		Total			0.91

suggests that the total ISTOF instruments works fairly well as a scale providing a global measure of teaching effectiveness with the ECP teacher sample.

A CFA model based on QoT indicators

The goodness of fit of the six-factor EFA model was tested in LISREL and a CFA model as shown in Figure 3.1 was obtained after deletion of three indicators and some re-specifications of indicators. The model showed strong empirical support with excellent fit indices and reasonably good reliability test results.[2]

The structure of the CFA factors proved to be fairly close to those of the original criteria proposed in the QoT schedule . For example, the last three factors, Effective classroom layout, Adaptation of teaching, and Teaching learning strategies, were respectively identical to Criteria 9, 6, and 7 of the QoT schedule. However, the CFA solution led to the deletion of Indicators 5.2, 1.4 and 4.1 and linked Indicators 2.3 and 2.4 into the first factor, Supportive and stimulating lesson climate. The resulting main factor is thus a combination of the first two criteria of the QoT schedule, namely Safe and orderly climate and Stimulating learning climate. Similarly, analyses led to the removal of Indicators 7.3 and 8.1 and the addition of Indicators 4.1 and 4.3 to form the third factor, Well-organized lessons with clear objectives was thus formed by indicators relating to the criteria Clear objectives and Clear instruction only. The deletion of Indicators 2.4 and 8.4 did not change the coherence of Factor Proactive lesson management much as it still seemed to indicate that the effective lesson management is closely associated with enhanced pupil involvement.

In general, the intra-scale factor correlations for ISTOF were not strong as those for the QoT, only the first two factors, (i) Structured lessons that maximize learning and involvement and (ii) High-quality communication and interaction, were significantly correlated with each other (rho = 0.49) and with most other factors. The fifth factor, Purposive learning, was only significantly correlated with the first two factors. In contrast, the factors of the QoT scale were all significantly correlated with one another. Their correlations were also somewhat stronger, ranging from 0.3 to 0.75. The strongest association was between Proactive lesson management and Well organized lessons with clear objectives (rho = 0.75) followed by Proactive lesson management and Supportive lesson climate (rho = 0.63).

The field researchers' overall judgement of the quality of teaching made at the end of the QoT observation was significantly correlated with all the individual QoT factors. The factor Proactive lesson management appeared to contribute most to the field researchers' overall judgement with a strong positive correlation (rho = 0.8).

Overall, the results of the quantitative analyses of the two sets of systematic observation data suggest that the ISTOF and the QoT instruments measure rather different aspects of teaching behaviour (one focusing on observed frequencies of behaviour, the other on judgements of strengths and weaknesses). In addition, it is likely that teachers probably vary in their observed behaviour over time. Because the two instruments were used in two different terms, the study of consistency across these two instruments is confounded by the time factor. Further research using both of the two scales at a common time point and rating the same teachers on several occasions over a set period of time would be needed to investigate the extent of correspondence in more depth.

Differentiated versus generic models of teacher effectiveness

Campbell *et al.* (2004) proposed a differentiated model for investigating teacher effectiveness, which was further elaborated by Creemers and Kyriakides (2008) into a dynamic model of educational effectiveness. This refers to multiple factors of effectiveness that operate at student, classroom, school and context levels. Campbell *et al.* (2004) argued that multiple factors in various dimensions may affect a teacher's effectiveness. For example, they made a distinction between teacher effectiveness observed with time stability (such as over different lessons or periods of an academic year) and that observed with subject consistency (such as across various subjects or across diverse areas within a subject). In the ECP study, teachers in the sample were observed for two observations in different terms and with different observation schedules. Any consistent practices observed in the teachers on the two instruments across the two observation occasions would imply some time stability and subject consistency for the secondary sample and at the least some time stability for the primary sample.

In comparing the two instruments, we note that there are certain similarities in content. For example, both schedules seek to measure classroom climate, classroom management, instructional qualities and student involvement/response. In other words, when the relationships between features of teachers' observed practices measured by the two instruments are explored, positive correlations might be expected in some of the CFA factors of the two instruments, especially in these three emphasized areas.

The ECP research approach has been used to explore variations in teachers' observed behaviour in relation to two possible sources of influence: the school sector (between primary and secondary) and school contexts (as measured by the percentage FSM indicator). Some sector differences (primary and secondary) and contextual differences (by level of social disadvantage of the school's pupil intake) have been identified which indicate that effective teachers' practice may be affected by and/or responsive to these differences in context (see Sammons and Ko 2008 for details). Nonetheless in most respects the differences were not strong, which provides support for the view that effective teachers share many common features.

The most important assumption of the differentiated model proposed by Campbell *et al.* (2004) is that teacher effectiveness should not be viewed as a generic concept. They argue against the assumption that effective teachers are likely to be effective with all students, in all contexts, in all aspects of teaching, and so on. A model based on a generic concept of teacher effectiveness, they claim, is too simple. It would tend to identify a general set of characteristics that define the effective teachers and might ignore the possibility that teachers may have a range of strengths and weaknesses in their teaching practices and that their behaviour may change over time. The distribution patterns of the factor scores of the various CFA models of the two scales used provides a degree of support for their arguments because it is clear that there is variation across teachers in the sample although this is greater in some areas measured than in others.

Nonetheless, the high scores identified for this purposive sample of primary and secondary teachers on a number of the underlying factors and on particular items also provide quite a lot of support for the generic view of overall effectiveness and enabled the research to identify some key features of effective practice.

Cameos of practice

In addition to the use of the two international observation instruments, researchers' qualitative field notes were used to collect more detailed information about teachers' behaviours and pupils' responses. These notes were analysed to produce cameos of practice.

The selected examples of teaching cameos that follow illustrate examples from the observed lessons of effective teaching approaches identified also in the quantitative data. These analyses of the field notes and the extracts reported here show that these more effective teachers were able to create supportive and positive classroom climates in well-organized lessons, using both starters and plenaries. In most cases the lesson objectives were made clear, and explained from the beginning, and typically were returned to in the plenary sessions to round up the lesson and enhance pupil learning. The teachers showed high levels of teacher-pupil interaction and engagement with the pupils on purposive learning tasks where the assessment is aligned to the learning objectives set out at the beginning. Knowledge of pupils' specific learning needs was also evident both in the variety of teaching methods employed but also in the use of differentiated tasks for individual and small groups of students. These teachers made extensive use of questioning strategies, giving explicit feedback and praise and revealing that pupils' contributions are valued in their lessons. These effective and highly effective teachers set high expectations for learners, engaged in high levels of teacher-pupil interaction and led engaging, active and creative lessons, often with humour.

Our cameos include both primary and secondary school teachers and males and females to illustrate what effective classroom practice looks and feels like in the classroom context.

John, highly effective Year 6 teacher

John, a 55-year-old Year 6 late-career stage teacher, has numerous roles including deputy head, subject coordinator and key-stage manager in a medium-sized school with high numbers of FSM (3). He reports that he has high efficacy and commitment, with high motivation, job satisfaction and stress, and consequently, work dimensions dominate his life somewhat.

In a mathematics lesson with 33 students designed to see the use of maths in real life, John sets clear objectives and values all students' contributions. He begins with a mental arithmetic starter game of 15 questions called 'Who Wants to be a Mathionaire?', like the TV show, before using the interactive whiteboard, small group work and whole-class teaching in a well-managed, structured and active lesson. The classroom climate is supportive and positive, as John demonstrates that he is an enthusiastic teacher who relates well to the children. John sets high expectations, and gives clear and precise instructions in his lesson, and his communication style is positive. It is a very interactive and fast-paced lesson and he uses lots of questions which results in high pupil involvement and engagement through small group and pair work.

John's Year 6 maths lesson: everyday maths

Lesson objectives are displayed on the white board on the right-hand side:

- Attempt to become mathionnaire.
- To use partitioning when multiplying more difficult numbers.
- To see the link between multiplication and division.
- To solve 'real life' problems using a calculator.

John asks the students how they feel about the lesson before they begin. 'Do you think we can achieve that?' Students respond enthusiastically: 'Yes.' John: 'Good, I have enthusiasm, positivity.' John calls out the questions in the 'Who Wants to be a Mathionnaire?' quiz. Students discuss the work in pairs and with John in whole-class work. There are lots of question and answering techniques used . . . Students use the program called Mathswiz on IWB in pairs . . . two pupils stand at the front on the right-hand side. John explains the problem and asks students how they should work it out, then asks them to complete the working out. One student completes it on interactive whiteboard, others do so on a PC . . .

John is aware that a student has missed some lessons and completes a revision segment to help her catch up. John: 'I need a favour.' He tells the class that he wants to revise work so that Daniella can rejoin the work . . . All students are grouped, differentiated, for maths. 'Ok, before we go to our maths group, you need to know what you need, pens, pencils . . . quickly, quietly, sensibly.' Students move into their maths groups – squares, triangles.

John is very enthusiastic and appreciative of the work that the students complete in the lesson. He is very positive and encouraging and uses lots of praise throughout the entire lesson, praising students who answer individually and the class as whole class.

John: 'Have we got any mathionaires, ones that got them all right?' Students raise their hands. John: 'Well done the mathionnaires. How many were one or two questions short of mathionnaire?' Students raise hands. John: 'Well done . . . You've shown me up, [John tears up target] I thought you'd get 11, you got 13/14 . . . Excellent again that group, thought you'd get 12.' John speaks to the final group: 'Beaten my estimate, I had you down for 13. You excelled yourself, well done.' John moves to Daniella on the table at the top right-hand side. John praises her work: 'Considering you were off earlier in the week that was brilliant.'

Chloe, effective Year 2 teacher

Chloe is an early-career Year 2 teacher in her mid-twenties in a large school with a high numbers of FSM (4) and high proportions of students with English as an additional language (EAL). She reports that she has high motivation, job satisfaction and stress, with high commitment working between 61–5 hours per week. Her identity is in balance (Scenario 1).

In a well-managed lesson on story-writing aimed at students producing their own retelling of a big book story, Chloe changes the pace and focus of the lesson frequently, moving between speaking and listening, writing, review, pair work and whole-class work. She monitors progress and process throughout and gives one-to-one assistance to the students who need it. The lesson is very interactive, with lots of questions. Chloe is very good humoured but firm and the students respond very well to it, they are relaxed and participate in a very full way in all parts of the lesson, although they appear to need constant behaviour reminders. Consequently, relationships are good and pupils are engaged in the lesson's activities and respond enthusiastically to the praise given by Chloe.

Chloe's Year 2 literacy lesson: story-telling

Chloe introduces the book and talks through the genre, looking at the introduction and the first three characters, and pulls out the use of descriptive language and time connectives, and builds up a word bank that students can put into meaningful sentences since the class is predominately children for whom English is a second language. There are lots of questions used throughout the lesson. Chloe checks that the students understand some of the key terms. Chloe points to the title and the class read it together. 'What type of book is this?'

Student response: 'Fiction.' Chloe: 'What does "legend" mean?' After several student responses, Chloe summarizes and reviews the responses using a dramatic voice. The class continue to read the story aloud together and intermittently she asks questions to check for understanding of words and comprehension of the story narrative. Chloe: '"Took the lead in the race", what does that mean?' Several students respond to the questions. Chloe praises the students for their responses and continues through several rounds of reading and questioning. 'What word could we use to describe the rat now?' Chloe: 'He's a bit selfish' . . . 'Should he really be feeling proud?'. . . 'The first year of the zodiac goes to? . . . And the second? . . . Can anyone from 2G remember who came third?' . . . 'OK let's find out.' Students respond 'tiger', when they see the picture of the tiger on the next page of the book . . . 'What made you say tiger? . . . What's on this page? How is that an interesting word . . . is it an interesting word or a necessary word? It's a necessary word, it's necessary for the sentence to make sense . . . It's giving you information about how they are feeling, well done!'

Chloe is aware of the individual needs of her students and the activities are differentiated by ability. She gives individual learning and instruction to students on the blue table. She also questions one student to try to get him started on the writing activity. 'I want you to think, say, write.' Chloe chats to the student about the progress of his work, telling him that he will need to write some more if he doesn't want to finish it in golden time. As the students continue to write the beginning of the story, Chloe circulates the room, checks work and gives one-to-one assistance to the students who need it.

Peter, highly effective Year 9 English teacher

Peter is a young teacher (under 30) who has just started his career and is teaching in a large, challenging school (FSM 4). His motivation and job satisfaction are high, his commitment is very high (he works more than 60 hours per week), but he feels that the professional dimension of his identity dominates (Scenario 2). His pupils (an all-girls class) have very positive views of him. In his lesson on the function of pronouns Peter demonstrates high levels of teacher interaction with the pupils and a high level of pupil response. He used scaffolding techniques and praise extensively in the observed lessons which resulted in a high level of pupil engagement. Peter's style focuses on interactions with students, relationships and the use of humour ('Don't call out in future or I'll staple your lips together!') and shows good behaviour and good teacher-pupil relationships where he uses pupils' ideas and opinions in the lesson.

Peter's Year 9 English lesson: to explore the function of pronouns

Peter has prepared the whiteboard with the name of the book and author, date and the learning objective of the lesson which the students can see as they enter the room. Today's lesson will explore the function of pronouns, the analysis of the sentence and word level features of an extract from the text. Peter greets the students with a friendly 'hello' as they enter the room. When most have arrived he tells them to take off their jackets, sit down and take down the details from the board. He explains the purpose of the lesson and how it relates to previous work they have completed. He manages potential behaviour issues positively, talking to one student by asking her nicely if she would mind sitting on the other side of the desk and reminding students of his expectations: 'I'm looking around the room and I can see about six girls who are taking down notes.' The students are very quiet in the class, and listen, answering questions while taking down details from the whiteboard . . .

Peter tells students they are now at Level 6 and then instructs the class to summarize the replies to the question and answer session in the box with the hand-out. All students quietly complete the task while Peter circulates room to check work . . . *Whole-group instruction* – Peter comments on work saying that he thinks they have all grasped the work and asks them to take out their planner and gives them homework due in Monday 11 December. He writes the homework on the whiteboard: 'Write a continuation of the extract analysed in class. Annotate the word, text and sentence level features in your extract.' He explains the homework task and asks students to listen carefully as he acknowledges that it is a big piece of homework.

Marion, effective Year 9 maths teacher

Marion is a late-career Year 9 maths teacher in her early fifties in a challenging school with high proportions of FSM (4). She has maintained high commitment to teaching (working almost 50 hours per week) and her identity is in balance. Her pupils (a low ability set group of 16 girls, many with English as a second language) have very positive views of her. Marion demonstrates high levels of teacher interaction with the pupils and high pupil response. She uses lots of scaffolding techniques and praise in her lessons which results in a high level of pupil engagement and a focus on interactions, relationships and humour. Her lessons are supportive and well organized, with learning objectives clearly displayed. She uses a combination of didactic and interactive techniques in her plenaries. Good pupil behaviour and good teacher-pupil relationships were observed in her lessons and she likes to use pupil ideas and opinions in her approach to learning.

Marion's Year 9 maths lesson: function machines and inverse function machines

Marion's lesson recaps on how to use function machines and inverse functions in order apply a different approach to solving equations. The lesson has been planned to support a SATs mock exam next week and is the second maths lesson she has had with this group today. The lesson objectives are on the whiteboard: 'To be able to use function machines to solve equations'. She begins by reviewing what the students already know through a series of questions beginning with, 'Who can tell me what a function machine is?' before she summarizes the topic. The students raise their hands to reply and the teacher responds with 'Well done' or 'You're not listening to me' to encourage students to focus on what questions she is asking them. Marion then gets the students to develop a function machine. She directs the girls to turn to page 43 in their books and explains the task, which is to use the inverse to solve problems, and explains what the first and second questions require. She instructs the students to record the title and objectives and to complete questions 1 and 2 as quickly as possible, reminding them that they did great work that morning . . .

A student questions her to make sure she was clear in the task and two other students ask for pencils. Marion manages the lesson climate and pace well, and responds to the needs of the girls as they arise. 'If you find it takes too long to draw the machines, draw them as boxes so that you don't spend all of your time drawing the machines.' The students work silently and independently on the two questions. Marion checks that a student knows what she has to do and prompts her through the task. The student seems very pleased with herself when she gets the answer right, and nods her head and smiles. Marion then moves to the top-left table to check the students' work. Students freely ask questions in the class and Marion explains in a calm way.

Marion helps students with questions and says, 'Well done' when students answer correctly. 'You're just doing the inverse, the opposite, so what's the opposite of multiply? . . . Good, well done.' She has a good relationship with the students and uses humour when a student speaks to her and she misunderstands . . . Marion uses the whiteboard and writes a question to use as a plenary. The students continue to complete their tasks quietly. She ends the lesson praising the students' hard work. 'There, you've done it . . . that's it, now you're going to solve the equation in the same way . . .'

Summary

The observation data we analysed here suggests that effective teachers in the sample are effective in all 'core' aspects of teaching practices, and observation findings provide support for the view that there is an overall (or generic) concept of teacher effectiveness. The classroom factors found to be important in the definition of effective teachers were largely focused upon innovative pedagogical approaches related to level of teacher challenge to pupils, creativity and flexibility, positive relationships, praise and feedback, climate for learning, learning styles and organizational techniques. This confirms findings from previous research, for example, by Fraser (1989) and McBer (2000). The findings also concur with those of Mortimore et al. (1988) who found that the key classroom factors of effective teachers included communication involving high levels of interaction, the facilitation of pupil responsibility and independence, providing challenging work, a positive classroom environment and high levels of praise and encouragement.

The results reveal that this sample of effective and highly effective teachers scored highly in terms of the following factors related to judgements of the quality of teaching from the QoT schedule (where ratings imply predominant strengths) – supportive lesson climate, proactive lesson management, well-organized lesson with clear objectives, and environmental and teacher support.

From the ISTOF observations that explored frequency of observed behaviours it was also found that the sample scored very highly in terms of the following factors: clear and coherent lesson in a supportive learning climate, engaging students with assignments and activities, positive classroom management, purposive learning, and quality questioning and feedback for students. These various features can be seen as necessary and key characteristics of effective or high-quality teaching across different sectors, subjects and contexts.

There was greater variation within the teacher sample in other areas observed, particularly in relation to the use of differentiation of work and instructional strategies for different groups of students related to the ISTOF factor 'Teacher strategies with respect to teacher expectations'. There was also notable variation in the 'Responsiveness to student needs' and the 'Active learning' factors. Similarly, in the QoT schedule the factor 'Adaptation of teaching' showed greater variation, as did the factor 'Teaching learning strategies'. These again involved adaptation of teaching approaches or work to meet students' perceived needs. The analyses showed that secondary teachers tended to obtain lower scores on these factors. This may relate to differences in organization such as greater use of setting in Year 9 than in primary schools where mixed-ability classes are more prevalent and therefore there may be greater diversity in approaches. Also in primary schools, a teacher tends to work with the same class and therefore will have greater knowledge of individual pupil needs.

Interestingly, teachers in schools in more disadvantaged contexts (higher FSM) showed lower scores on these factors. It may be that such approaches are found to be less appropriate in such contexts and this may reflect the findings of earlier teacher effectiveness studies that conclude that low socio-economic status and/or low ability students tend to benefit more from approaches linked to the concept of interactive direct instruction (van de Werf 2006).

The quantitative component of the ECP research enabled the research to investigate in detail the variation in observed practice using two different instruments and to test notions of effective practice identified by research-informed expert opinion and from inspectors' professional judgements. The qualitative analyses reveal that there is considerable variation in the ways in which these are enacted. In addition, qualitative data provide support for a differentiated concept of teacher effectiveness. This suggests that effective and highly effective teachers can show both strengths and weaknesses in different aspects of their teaching practices and might vary in their effectiveness over time, in different lessons and for different pupil groups.

The quantitative classroom observation evidence was supplemented by the use of qualitative field notes. These were analysed and used to create teacher cameos. Examples of these are shown in this chapter to illuminate and enrich the quantitative findings further and provide a feel for the way teachers acted in their classrooms and responded to their classes. The teachers who participated in the ECP project utilized classroom-level approaches to ensure the learning experience catered for pupils with a variety of learning approaches, combining verbal, visual, aural and kinaesthetic styles where appropriate, and for the learning needs of both groups and individual pupils. The classroom practice of these teachers not only illustrates unique pedagogical practices, but also demonstrates innovation through modification and adaptation.

Notes

1. Satorra-Bentler χ^2 = 120.34, df = 94, p = 0.035, RMSEA = 0.060, CFI = 0.98, IFI = 0.98, SRMR = 0.086. The Cronbach's alpha of the whole model was 0.827.

2. Satorra-Bentler $\chi^2 = 221.05$, df = 215, p = 0.37, RMSEA = 0.020, CFI = 1.00, IFI = 1.00, SRMR = 0.12. The Cronbach's alpha was 0.91 for the whole scale and 0.69 to 0.90 for its subscales.

REFERENCES

Campbell, J., Kyriakides, L., Muijs, D. and Robinson, W. (2004) *Assessing Teacher Effectiveness: A Differentiated Model*, London: RoutledgeFalmer.

Creemers, B. and Kyriakides, L. (2008) *The Dynamics of Educational, Effectiveness*. London: Routledge.

Croll, P. (1996) Teacher-pupil interaction in the classroom, in P. Croll and N. Hastings (eds) *Effective Primary Teaching*. London: David Fulton.

Fraser, B.J. (1989) Twenty years of classroom climate research, *Journal of Curriculum Studies*, 21(4): 307–27.

Galton, M. (1995) *Crisis in the Primary Classroom*. London: David Fulton.

Galton, M. and Croll, P. (1980) Pupil progress in basic skills, in M. Galton and B.Simon (eds) *Progress and Performance in the Primary Classroom*. London: Routledge & Kegan Paul.

Galton, M. and Simon, B. (1980) *Progress and Performance in the Primary Classroom*. London: Routledge & Kegan Paul.

Matthews, P. and Sammons, P. (2004) *Improvement Through Inspection: An Evaluation of the Impact of Ofsted's Work*. London: Ofsted/Institute of Education.

McBer, H. (2000) *Research into Teacher Effectiveness: A Model of Teacher Effectiveness*. London: DfEE.

Mortimore, P., Sammons, P., Stoll, L., Lewis, D. and Ecob, R. (1988) *School Matters*. Wells: Open Books.

Muijs, D. and Reynolds, D. (2005) *Effective Teaching: Evidence and Practice*. London: Sage.

NICHD (2001) *Fifth Grade School Observation Procedures Manual, NICHD Study of Early Child Care and Youth Development*. Rockville, MD: developed by R. Pianta.

Ofsted (1995) *Primary Matters*. London: HMSO.

Ofsted (2005) *The Primary National Strategy: An Evaluation of its Impact in Primary Schools 2004/05*. London: Ofsted.

Pianta, R., Belsky, J., Vandergrift, N., Houts, R. and Morrison, F. (2008) Classroom effects on children's achievement trajectories in elementary school, *American Educational Research Journal*, 45(2): 365–97.

Pollard, A., Broadfoot, P., Croll, P., Osborne, M. and Abbott, D. (1994) *Changing English Primary Schools?* London: Cassell.

Sammons, P. and Ko, J. (2008) *Using Systematic Classroom Observation Schedules to Investigate Effective Teaching: Overview of Quantitative Findings*. An Effective Classroom Practice project report. Swindon: ESRC.

Sammons, P. Sylva, K., Melhuish, E., Siraj-Blatchford, I., Taggart, B., Barreau, S. and Grabbe, Y. (2008) *Effective Pre-school and Primary Education 3-11 Project (EPPE 3-11): The Influence of School and Teaching Quality on Children's Progress in Primary School, Research Report DCSF-RR028*. London: Institute of Education, University of London.

Stipek, D. (1999) *Instructional Environment Observation Scale. University of California: MacArthur Pathways through Middle Childhood Network*. Berkeley, CA: University of California, MacArthur Pathways through Middle Childhood Network.

Tashakkori, A. and Teddlie, C. (1998) *Mixed Methodology: Combining Qualitative and Quantitative Approaches*. Thousand Oaks, CA: Sage.

Teddlie, C., Creemers, B., Kyriakides, L., Muijs, D. and Yu, F. (2006) The International System for Teacher Observation and Feedback: evolution of an international study of teacher effectiveness constructs, *Educational Research and Evaluation*, 12(6): 561–82.

van de Grift, W., Matthews, P., Tabak, I. and de Rijcke, F. (2004) *Comparative Research into the Inspection of Teaching in England and the Netherlands, A Contribution to the Ofsted Impact Project and the Publication Improvement through Inspection*, HMI 2251. London: Ofsted.

van der Werf, G. (2006) General and differential effects of constructivist teaching, keynote presentation, Annual Conference of the International Congress for School Effectiveness and Improvement, Florida, January.

Webb, R. and Vulliamy, G. (2007) Changing classroom practice at Key Stage 2: the impact of New Labour's national strategies, *Oxford Review of Education*, 33(5): 561–80.

5 Being an effective practitioner: learning from teachers' accounts and perceptions

Introduction

In this chapter we build on the discussions of what we observed from teachers' practice, by exploring what it means to be an effective practitioner according to the accounts and perceptions of teachers themselves. The interview data supports the findings of the observations in terms of the need for supportive lesson climates and proactive lesson management. These effective teachers talked about the importance of coherent, well-organized lesson plans with clear objectives, where students are engaged with the activities. Some of the key themes to emerge from the interviews were the importance of positive classroom management and providing feedback to students, both as a means of achieving learning objectives and as a way to support positive relationships. In this chapter we are able to dig a little deeper into how teachers understand effectiveness, how it is built on their motivation and professional development, and the ways they communicate expectations with students and plan flexible and creative lessons.

The main driver of variation in student learning is the quality of the teachers (Barber and Mourshed 2007). Therefore, what it means to be an effective practitioner is a vital area of research. Indeed, Hattie (2009) claims that teacher characteristics have a larger effect size on student learning than the school, the home or the curriculum. So it is important to know what qualities make a good teacher. It is argued that it is non-cognitive skills that are essential in effective classroom practice, and we need to understand what those are in order to select the best teachers to the profession (Barber and Mourshed 2007).

Day *et al.* (2011) found that teachers identified as effective practitioners promoted the personal, psychological and social growth of students, and a study by Kington (2009) found that teachers value 'caring' as an important attribute of effective practice. Earlier studies (e.g. Lortie 1975; Placek and Dodds 1988) indicate that good teachers place students at the centre of their practice, focusing on classroom climate and positive student-teacher interaction. This finding supports research into highly effective teaching (Abbott-Chapman *et al.* 1990) that indicates that not only must teachers perceive themselves as effective, but they must be seen as effective by their students, based on the level of their interpersonal skills rather than management or content expertise.

The literature discussed in Chapter 2 suggests that effective practitioners are motivated and have good subject knowledge, which corresponds to our finding that effective teachers have high job satisfaction and value learning and professional development. Communicating high expectations, being clear about instructional goals and planning enriching lessons, which are adapted to student needs, were all areas where our findings were aligned to existing literature on effective practice.

The findings here are drawn from themes emerging from interviews triangulated with repertory grid data. In this sense, statistical data were reinforced by in-depth qualitative data. The pre-observation interview explored issues such as planning, differentiation and inclusion, classroom management, teaching skills, assessment and role as classroom teacher, while the post-observation instrument allowed the in-depth probing of issues relating to aspects of the observed teaching session as well as exploring teacher effectiveness, leadership issues, teacher identity, professional life phase and teacher efficacy.

The findings here have been divided into two main sections. The first discusses the characteristics of effective practitioners. We found that all the effective teachers in the study were highly motivated and enjoyed their work; this meant they had high levels of job satisfaction. In addition, many effective teachers derived job satisfaction from a desire to learn and develop their professional skills; they attended training, researched their subject knowledge and were interested in succession planning. Their feelings of self-efficacy fed into their identity and their enjoyment of the job.

The second section considers what effective practitioners do. Four strongly correlated constructs emerged from both the interviews and the repertory grid data: these practitioners build strong student-teacher relationships, they give positive praise and feedback to their students, they have high expectations and communicate this clearly and consistently with learners, and finally, they teach creative, flexible and student-led classes, which acknowledge different learning styles and ability levels. In this chapter, through exploring who they are and what they do, we aim to move towards a deeper understanding of what it means to be an effective practitioner.

Effective practitioner characteristics

Effective practitioners are committed and motivated by doing a job they love, seeing their students progress and interacting with learners. Good teachers are also good learners, and we found that effective practitioners are interested in learning more about their subject and developing their professional skills. They learn from life and school experiences and endeavour to manage a balance between life and work by keeping on top of new ideas and continually advancing their knowledge and understanding. Box 5.1 gives an illustration of an effective primary practitioner, who comments on the development of her confidence and the support she has received from the school, and how this fed into her sense of effectiveness and her commitment.

Box 5.1   Julia – an illustration of an effective primary practitioner

(Measures of effectiveness: 'Above expected value-added data'; 'Most positive pupil views')

Julia is 27 years old and is a Year 6 teacher who works in a medium-sized school that has a high proportion of free school meals (FSM) (band 3). She is in the early stages of her teaching career, having been teaching for between four and seven years. Since coming to her current school after her NQT year, Julia has seen her *confidence* continue to grow. She works in a *'great school'* where people support each other and share good practice. Staff *collegiality* has had a positive impact on her *sense of effectiveness*. She also enjoys support from the head teacher and said that this was a major contributory factor to her *sustained commitment*. She has *good relationships with pupils* which motivate her to be a good teacher and her results have improved. Julia has experienced a considerable *increase in her self-efficacy* and feelings of being an effective teacher:

> I am more confident in my teaching. I am more confident in my classroom control. I am also more comfortable so I am more able to plan amendments to the lessons as we go through and to improve it while we are in there, adapt to what they need on that particular day.

> (Teacher interview)

She is a *highly creative* teacher and uses a *high level of interaction and questioning* in her lessons. She has a *strong sense of self* in her classroom and has *consistent and firm behaviour management* strategies in place. She demonstrates a *high level of teacher involvement* and consequently, *pupils are highly involved and engaged* in the lesson. The creativity of this teacher shines in how she *combines role play, models and information and communications technology (ICT)* in unusual, imaginative and novel ways. She is very *positive in her interactions* with her students, while *maintaining authority and control*.

Enjoyment and job satisfaction

Teachers referred to a strong sense of motivation, commitment, self-efficacy and well-being with regard to their effectiveness. These factors confirmed findings from previous research, for example, Day *et al.* (2007), who reported that teacher identity, resilience and belief in themselves to do the job were vital to being a successful and effective practitioner. This supports other studies in the areas of teacher self-efficacy (Brouwers and Tomic 2000), commitment (Day *et al.* 2005; Zembylas 2003) and well-being (Kelly and Colquhoun 2003). Klassen and Tze (2014) also found that self-efficacy has a medium to large effect on teacher performance.

The majority of teachers, 90 per cent, talked about having a high level of motivation and commitment and enjoying the challenges and high standards expected from the job. Enjoyment was a key feature, with 93 per cent of the primary and 83 per cent of secondary teachers discussing this. Both groups of teachers talked about enjoyment and feeling fortunate to have a job they love:

> I suppose it's because I get a real buzz from it. You know, I really enjoy it. And also because there's such a positive feedback when the children say . . .

> hum, you know 'I get it now!' . . . The way they respond 'Oh I get it!', you know or when they're willing to read out their work to the rest of the class. That sort of thing, I invite that.
>
> (Diane, Year 6 teacher, FSM 4)

High job satisfaction came from the enjoyment they derived from their work and this made them feel motivated and committed. For almost 90 per cent of the primary teachers and two-thirds of the secondary teachers their main motivation was the desire to do their best for the students, get the best out of them and see their progress. While they recognized that motivation levels could go up and down they were also clear that each cohort of children deserved to get the best out of them as teachers, and they commented that if they let their commitment slip, that would have repercussions for their students:

> I'm still as committed to the job as I ever was, just because I think I owe it to the children to be as committed, irrespective of motivation or levels, each one of those children deserves to get the best out of me.
>
> (Benjamin, Year 6 teacher, FSM 3)

However, it was not only that they felt that there might be negative consequences for their students if they lowered their commitment and motivation, they also saw it as a virtuous circle, whereby by putting their all into the job, the students made more progress and these teachers gained pleasure from this, which impacted on their sense of self-efficacy:

> It is motivating for you to see the children making progress and you look back in their books and see where they were in the beginning of the year and where they were at the end, that's really rewarding to see the progress that they're making and to have them responding and I guess things like parents evenings, when you share the work of the children and the parents are really pleased with the progress and things, that's very rewarding. And staff will comment if they see something or a display or something, they'll just say to each other 'well that's really nice' and those things are motivating.
>
> (Amy, Year 2 teacher, FSM 2)

Clearly, a number of factors impact on teachers' levels of motivation and commitment. The Variations in Teachers' Work, Lives and their Effects on Pupils (VITAE) project (Day *et al.* 2007, 2008) suggests that school leadership, professional development and support from colleagues can be important in sustaining teachers' professional identities, their job satisfaction, commitment to teaching, resilience and perceived effectiveness. Indeed, opportunities and environments where teachers were given opportunities for learning and developing were closely related to their levels of job satisfaction, and this was another prominent theme to emerge from our data.

Learning and development for success

Many teachers commented on their interest in learning and constantly developing themselves, through peer learning or training. Of course, the school environment and support from the school leadership have a huge impact on the professional development opportunities for teachers. As Day *et al.* (2011) found, enhancing teacher quality through both internal and external continuing professional development is an important feature of successful school leadership. Effective teachers engage with these opportunities and value their own learning, which feeds not only into their effectiveness, but also into their sense of efficacy, which in turn impacts on their motivation.

More than two-thirds of the primary teachers and over 80 per cent of the secondary teachers talked about the importance of well-structured continuing professional development, both through formal training, and also through personal research and development, as contributing to their effectiveness. This interest in learning came through from teachers in each of the three career phases; this will be discussed in more detail in Chapter 8. Examples of teachers' personal interests in learning came through strongly in the interview data, with teachers reporting on taking sabbaticals for postgraduate courses in diverse areas such as outdoor education, which enabled them to bring new ideas back to the school and directly see them impact on their own teaching and on that of their students' learning. Teachers discussed the benefits of attending external training, as well as training internal to the school, such as regular twilight sessions and learning from other colleagues. This was equally true in primary and secondary schools:

> I think it's the . . . the CPD programme's really important that the twilight sessions and the training sessions are there. He's always arranging things and always letting the TLR [teaching and learning representative] and subject leaders arrange things for staff to deliver to other staff. So you've got the staff given the confidence to actually lead something but then you've got other staff who wouldn't come up and say "I need help in this, this, and this" who then become more willing to take the help.
>
> (Graham, Year 6 teacher, FSM 3)

> We have every Thursday as a training session and we're all involved in taking part in that training and we lead that training every Thursday. We lead research and development groups every Monday and one of my roles on the leadership team is to make sure that everything we do comes back to thinking about teaching and learning. Because there is a danger in management that you start to run the whole thing like a business and start treating children just as commodities and making profits and we forget about the teaching and learning.
>
> (Michael, Year 9 maths teacher, FSM 1)

Many teachers observed that when they did not feel confident with a subject they would research it to ensure they are always competent with the subject matter. Over two-thirds of the secondary teachers who talked about personal development also talked about the importance of having good subject knowledge and almost half of the primary teachers who commented on professional learning and development talked about doing background reading or research as part of their practice. Having good subject knowledge and taking an interest in learning more, particularly in areas that they were less confident in, was an important feature of these effective practitioners.

The learning was collaborative as well as individual, and teachers talked about learning taking place through observations and sharing ideas with colleagues. Teachers felt that where the school supported and facilitated this, it had an impact on their personal effectiveness:

> We're encouraged to go and watch each other's lessons and there's been a heads of department forum introduced this year, where they all get together, and I think last time they watched a video, you know good practice, and discussed that. So there is . . . and you obviously have inset days where you have courses – so it's quite a lot I suppose.
>
> (Sheila, Year 9 maths teacher, FSM 1)

Technology was a specific area where learning and development was important, with its constant changes often requiring new skills. This challenge was identified by more than a third of primary teachers and one-in-ten secondary teachers, who acknowledged the growing importance of ICT in the classroom, and their own understanding of it as a means of teaching effectively:

> I'll use overhead projectors and stuff easily, take the folders and that sort of thing, and the subjects I'm teaching at the moment, the French . . . I've put stuff onto interactive whiteboards, websites and BBC stuff for teachers to log onto as follow-ons from what I've been doing, which sort of moves the effectiveness from that teaching back into the classrooms.
>
> (Carol, Year 2 teacher, FSM 1).

Professional development and a supportive environment for teacher learning also corresponded to school-level opportunities for succession planning. For half of the primary teachers and nearly a third of the secondary teachers, promotions and succession planning fed into their sense of self-efficacy and job satisfaction. This is another area identified by Day *et al.* (2011) as an important dimension of successful school leadership. Effective teachers are often ambitious, but equally, the leadership can impact on their levels of motivation through strategic succession planning. Many effective teachers noted that a recent promotion had increased their levels of motivation and commitment:

> It's gone up. I've got a lot of ambition since I've been made Key Stage 1 coordinator. I didn't, there was a time when I was quite happy being a class teacher and I put 100 per cent in my job but I didn't really want to go any further. When I got this Key Stage 1 position I think it was the fact that the school believed in me because I had to go for an interview with other outside candidates as well so that was quite a push for me because it made me feel that I could do this. And I am motivated, I'm ready to move on from this school, I'd like to go for an assistant head job or deputy head sort of post and I feel my time here's probably coming to an end very soon but I've got the motivation to go out there and get it.
>
> (Bridget, Year 2 teacher, FSM 3).

Box 5.2 gives another illustration of an effective practitioner, this time at secondary level, who noted the importance of professional challenges and succession planning for her feelings of commitment and self-efficacy.

Box 5.2   Vanessa: an illustration of an effective secondary practitioner

---

(Measures of effectiveness: 'Above expected value-added data'; 'positive pupil views')

Vanessa, aged 42, is a Year 9 English teacher and has been teaching for 10 years. She teaches in a school with a rich cultural mix of pupils. A very high percentage (48 per cent) speak English as an additional language and the percentage of pupils eligible for FSM is high (FSM 4).

She was primarily attracted to teaching because she wanted to 'work with children' (teacher interview) and wanted to try new approaches in the teaching of English so that more children had access to it. Vanessa feels that her level of *commitment and self-efficacy remain high*. She enjoys the facilities and resources that the school offers, and has developed 'social' relationships with many other members of staff.

Vanessa feels that she had a lot of *support* from the senior management team, especially in relation to initial behaviour issues and recalls how colleagues helped her to settle in when she first started at the school. In spite of these early problems with the wide range of abilities in her class and some children demonstrating very disruptive behaviour, her *relationship with pupils has improved* and is now strong. In addition to this, her class has benefited from the support of a learning support assistant (LSA). The impact of having an additional adult in the classroom has made lessons a lot easier and substantially *increased her effectiveness*, especially in terms of *planning and preparation*. Her level of *motivation is increasing* and her pupils were achieving results that were *much higher than expected*.

Vanessa is still seeking *professional challenges* and recently decided to apply for advanced skills teacher (AST) status. She is keen to progress into middle management and feels that she is being given the opportunities to further her training.

Teachers' experience was also mentioned by many as playing a key role in their effectiveness. This included having many years of experience within the school, or conversely, life experience outside the school. Many agreed that a varied experience of teaching facilitated effectiveness, and being able to learn from experience and mistakes provided opportunities to improve practice. Almost three-quarters of the primary teachers and half of the secondary teachers claimed that their experience made them more effective:

> I still enjoy what I'm doing; I feel very confident, I think, about my own abilities because I know I'm experienced and I know nobody wants to have a Year 6 class because they keep telling me that there's only me can do it, nobody wants it. And I think it's experience, I think there's so much to the Year 6 primary.

> (Catherine, Year 6 teacher, FSM 1)

All of these features feed into feelings of self-efficacy through building up teachers' professional knowledge and practice. They develop confidence and commitment and this in turn fosters effectiveness. In the next section we discuss how effective teachers talked about their practice and look at the key dimensions that contributed to their effectiveness.

Effective practice

The classroom factors identified through the repertory grid data found to be important in the definition of effective practice were largely focused upon innovative pedagogical approaches related to the level of teacher expectations of students, creativity and flexibility, positive relationships, and praise and feedback. The interviews confirmed these factors, with teachers highlighting the relationships they formed with students as a key dimension to their effectiveness. This related to how they gave praise and feedback and their expectations of their students. These factors were interrelated and supported each other in creating an atmosphere of success for the students.

Moreover, the interview data are in line with the literature in that teachers valued the importance of planning well-organized lessons with clear objectives, in which they enriched the content and adapted the lessons to students' needs (Ofsted 2002; Campbell et al. 2004; Rowe 2006). In particular, many effective practitioners discussed the need for lessons to be student-led and to cater to a range of learning styles. Positive feedback and communicating high expectations was another area in which our data strongly correlates with the literature (Teddlie et al. 2006; Sammons 2007).

Indeed, these factors also related to teacher-student relationships. Again our results correlate with the literature, demonstrating that building strong relationships with students is an important feature of effective teaching. For example, according to Hattie (2009), the effect size of teacher-student relationships and teacher expectations on teacher variance in student achievement by far outweigh teacher training and subject matter knowledge. Indeed, teacher relatedness with students is one of the most important factors affecting student engagement (Klassen et al. 2012).

Building strong relationships

The importance of building positive relationships with students was the strongest aspect of perceptions of effectiveness from the interviews. From the repertory grid data the ability to build and sustain good relationships with students was an issue that emerged from the vast majority of teachers (96 per cent) as contributing to their effectiveness. A number of factors influenced this; for example, getting to know the students well, establishing good rapport and interaction, using humour, listening to what the students had to say and communicating effectively with them. Relationships needed to be based on fairness, consistency and support.

Similarly, from the interview data, we found that making connections with the students, trust, knowing the students well, humour and rapport, student enjoyment, caring, listening, fairness and respect were all essential aspects of forming good relationships with students and this clearly impacted on effectiveness. Some teachers said that authority came before friendship, while others said that friendship with students was important, albeit within clearly established boundaries. Perhaps the most common features were being firm and fair and having a connection with students through personal characteristics: 'My main strength as a teacher is my personality . . . And the relationship I build with the children. That's the most important thing about being a teacher' (Daniel, Year 6 teacher, FSM 1).

Indeed, teacher personality as a key indicator of effectiveness has received more research attention in recent years. We found that trust was an important element of relationship-building and all teachers used terms associated with the building and sustaining of trust in the classroom, particularly enabling the students to trust the teacher and therefore feel safe, and also modelling relationships to help students relate to one another. This was also affected by how well teachers knew their students. Well over two-thirds of the primary teachers mentioned the importance of knowing the children well in order to be effective, and this included knowing something about them as people, as well as knowing their capabilities. Teachers hoped students felt comfortable to come to them with problems and valued a deeper dimension to the relationship than purely academic knowledge:

> I think I do get to know each child quite well as fast as I can because I really want to find out where I can get them to and I try and find them as interesting things as possible. So there's no point in us writing a story about something that they won't get to be excited about . . . I do try to work with each child.
>
> (Sally, Year 6 teacher, FSM 2)

Nearly three-quarters of the secondary teachers described the process of getting to know students as important to sustaining relationships; they discussed establishing good rapport and generating two-way understanding, helping students to feel more confident and comfortable in class: 'Just time and teaching them and getting to know them, really. By the end of the year you know a class much better than at the start so you know how they respond to you and vice versa really' (Hayley, Year 9 English teacher, FSM 3).

Three-quarters of secondary and 85 per cent of primary teachers talked about fun, enjoyment and humour as important elements of their relationship with their students and as a means of more effective teaching. Some noted how 'having a laugh' with students can help form a positive relationship. This tended to be accompanied by an acknowledgement of the need for boundaries within this fun relationship:

> I think that as I just said, I'm firm but fair. I will have a laugh and a joke with them when need be. They know that I'm not afraid of making a fool of myself, I suppose, in front of them. For example, somebody asked me a question and I just wanted to collapse in a heap and cry because I couldn't believe they'd asked me that question, and, you know, I can do that – I can pretend to collapse in a heap and cry in front of them. So I think the fact that I'm prepared to do that sort of thing, but they still know that I'll give them tools to learn, I think helps to get to the positive position that we're in.
>
> (Kelly, Year 9 maths teacher, FSM 3)

Indeed, firm but fair was a common mantra. Fairness was perceived to be an essential element of the relationship between teachers and students. Consistency and fairness were specifically mentioned by more than half the teachers as key features of building a positive relationship with the students: 'I'm straight in the eye sort of thing, if I say something, that's exactly what I mean so there's no messing about so they know exactly where they stand and I like to think I'm very fair' (Amanda, Year 6 teacher, FSM 4). In maintaining a balance within building relationships with students, respect was a fundamental dimension. Respect was defined in terms of setting the disciplinary environment and forming appropriate relationships. Over half of the teachers emphasized the role of two-way respect between students and teachers and talked about earning students' respect and encouraging respect among students. The most important aspect was that there should be an environment of mutual respect between teacher and students in the classroom:

> They respect me, and I respect them and the relationships are very good I think. The relationships between the children themselves, they respect each other and they try and they're very polite, they're very helpful to each other.
> (Audrey, Year 2 teacher, FSM 4)

> Respect for your class and respect from them is really important. There isn't any hope without it.
> (Keith, Year 9 English teacher, FSM 3)

Tied into the notion of respect was the *style* of the relationship that teachers developed with their students. One in three talked about being a friend to the students. Of these, 16 per cent also mentioned that this friendship must be balanced by the idea that they are still a figure of authority. This balance between being friendly and the students knowing where the line is drawn also relates to the setting of rules and boundaries for behaviour. One in five of the primary teachers felt that it was important to be seen as a figure of authority, and that this was more important than being friends with the students, although many liked the idea that they could be both. A quarter of the primary teachers also felt that to build a friendship they should let the students see them as a person rather than just a teacher. This variation to some extent reflects the importance of teachers having their own style and being true to their own way of being, and again we see the importance of personality on effectiveness:

> I'd just say it was like, I'd like to see me as a human being really, not someone who just stands up and shouts and then disappears into the staff room. I try to find a balance in chatting to staff and chatting to them, you know, I'll have my lunch in the classroom and just talk with different people. Wander outside every now and then when it's playtime and they come up to you, I just want them to see me as a human person, you know.
> (Robin, Year 6 teacher, FSM 2)

There was less variation with secondary teachers, with 83 per cent talking about the need to be an authority figure to the students more than a friend. There was far less emphasis on the notion of friendship. Indeed, this was consistently deemed less important than retaining a position of authority; this possibly reflects the different environment at secondary school, and having different groups of students through-out the day. Where there is less time to nurture strong relationships with students, the element of authority is perhaps more important. However, they did see a place for friendship alongside this:

> You're there to be looked up to in a kind of way. You are the authority in that room and have to maintain control. You can't be a friend all the time, it doesn't work and they get confused.
>
> (Laura, Year 9 English teacher, FSM 4)

For both primary and secondary teachers, there was also a caring dimension to their relationships with students. Almost a third of secondary teachers discussed the importance of listening to the views of their students and how this impacted on form-ing relationships and the way this in turn influenced their effectiveness. Similarly, a third of the primary teachers saw their role as caring and supportive, a relation-ship in which the children feel comfortable asking things of the teacher and where the teacher provides a role of dispelling any worries the children may have. This was even seen as a maternal relationship in some cases. Listening and communica-tion were important aspects of building relationships within a caring and supportive environment where students felt comfortable and supported in asking questions and giving their ideas and opinions. One in three of primary teachers commented on how important it is to listen to the students in order to build meaningful relationships:

> The children know they can come and talk to us about anything. I think they appreciate the fact that it's not just standing there telling them and they listen and that's it, it's a team thing.
>
> (Graham, Year 6 teacher, FSM 3)

Building strong relationships with students was also tied to other aspects of their effective practice. Communication with students, and particularly giving posi-tive praise and feedback, significantly contributed to the relationships formed. How-ever, feedback was also an important dimension of effective practice in its own right. Again there was evidence of the role of non-cognitive skills as teachers emphasized the importance of knowing students well and adapting praise and feedback to indi-vidual student needs.

Giving positive praise and feedback

Unsurprisingly, all the teachers saw the importance of praise and feedback, which served a number of purposes. We found that most of these effective teachers, 91 per cent, identified praise and feedback as a means of building relationships with students. In the interviews the teachers were asked to expand on the ways they gave praise and feedback in their classes. It was clear that strong relationships gave more meaning to praise and feedback, and equally, that well-directed praise and feedback helped nurture those relationships:

> Oodles of praise, golden time I always try to go all out and give them the things they want to do and take time to sit down and make sure I'm playing

with them, establishing that relationship with them so it's actually mean-ingful when I say 'that's brilliant' they get that feeling, because I've worked hard to try to build that relationship with them . . . And we try to word things in a very positive way, kind of 'I like the way you're sitting' so the person next to them will do the same because then they might get the chance of the praise if that makes sense.

(Sally, Year 6 teacher, FSM 2)

One key purpose of praise mentioned by about two-thirds of the teachers at pri-mary and secondary level was to promote confidence in the students:

If you praise them when they achieve something they start to feel more confident about taking the next step.

(Gemma, Year 9 English teacher, FSM 3)

This strongly suggests that praise needed to focus on the positives before look-ing at places for improvement. For primary teachers in particular, this was related to how they framed and modelled behaviour, as well as praising academic work:

I have what I call a Good News box where the things I want the children to do I compliment and comment upon, so they then know, at three o'clock, we stop and read the Good News box, 'so and so was sitting beautifully on the carpet' so they know what I'm looking for. 'So and so was very kind and held the door open without being asked' so they know that's good practice, 'so and so was very polite today', 'so and so helped their friend when they were stuck', 'so and so went and played with somebody' . . . anything that we've seen and we stand up and we clap for the children that have done something well so the children, without actually being told, they are pick-ing up that information because we are praising the good behaviour that we expect or it may just be that 'so and so who doesn't normally come into the classroom quietly sat down beautifully' and you know, everybody gets a chance at coming up, somebody will have done something good in the day. You can ignore the bad things and just comment on one good thing and tomorrow they might do two good things, so that's the theory of it anyway.

(Wendy, Year 2 teacher, FSM 4)

Knowing students well was an essential dimension of feedback. Many teach-ers talked about the need to get the level of praise a child receives appropriate to the needs of the child – some are more 'needy of praise' than others, some are shy and prefer to receive praise more privately, and it is an important feature that the teacher can tell the difference and act accordingly. This relates back to the idea of knowing the children well as individuals and being aware of their needs, which 70 per cent of primary teachers and 60 per cent of secondary teachers said was fun-damental to their effectiveness. This was also true for the use of rewards in praise. Almost half of the primary teachers mentioned using rewards as a way of prais-ing children. Stickers were the most common means of rewards as praise, a third talked about giving these. However, only 8 per cent of the secondary teachers said that they used rewards as a means of praise and feedback, which also reflects what is appropriate for different children:

> I'm a stickler for giving out stickers for somebody who's done something really good. And I think they need to have that as a sort of concrete, as they go on through the day they think, oh yeah, I got that for doing my maths.
>
> (Chloe, Year 2 teacher, FSM 4)

For many teachers, feedback was arranged around learning objectives. With students being made more aware of their own learning objectives, many teachers built praise and feedback around the achievement of targets which the children understand and can see as measurable steps of success. Eighty per cent of the primary teachers mentioned the importance of showing the students their target or learning objective as a means of giving feedback:

> I do mark the work but perhaps in no great detail and we do have a system in the school where basically if the child has achieved the objective of the lesson we do a tick and an LO for learning objective achieved and all the children know that if they see that on their work, than basically the teacher's pleased because they've got what they were supposed to for that lesson.
>
> (Steven, Year 2 teacher, FSM 4)

Just under half of the secondary teachers also discussed the importance of using learning objectives and targets to structure the feedback they gave:

> There's a learning outcomes tracking sheet in the back of the book, they will write down an outcome on the table and [in] the corresponding row they indicate personally how they felt about reaching that target, so they don't have to tell anybody else in the class.
>
> (Keith, Year 9 English teacher, FSM 3)

Assessment for learning was an area that was reported in the literature as a key characteristic of effective practice (Mujis and Reynolds 2000; Rowe 2006). This also emerged from our data, with two-thirds of the primary teachers talking positively about assessment for learning as a method of feedback and to help them see how much students had understood. Nearly half of secondary teachers also specifically talked about assessment for, and of, learning, and three-quarters discussed formative assessment strategies that were used during and at the end of lessons. Teachers felt these helped students to take control of their own learning:

> I think assessment for learning helps the students to understand exactly what they should be aiming for and to take some control for their own learning.
>
> (Kevin, Year 9 maths teacher, FSM 3)

Both learning objectives and assessment for learning helped teachers to differentiate praise and feedback according to the needs of the students. The importance of teachers finding ways to develop each child in the way that is best for them was fundamental. Differentiating praise and feedback and setting the right targets and expectations to meet the needs of each child was important to effective practitioners:

> I think the differentiation is really crucial. Giving children work at the right level so that they can feel that they're achieving.
>
> (Elizabeth, Year 2 teacher, FSM 3)

Both oral and written feedback was discussed. A third of the primary teachers mentioned the idea of creating dialogue with the students through the exercise books, where the teacher writes a comment to which the child responds:

> I write notes in their reading diaries and they do the same back to me, so it's a continual, you know, loop of information.
>
> (Margaret, Year 2 teacher, FSM 3)

Only eight per cent of secondary teachers discussed creating a dialogue with students in this way.

Praise and feedback were given in both oral and written forms, in groups and individually. Teachers decided what was most appropriate in each case. However they were delivered, praise and feedback were important aspects of communication with students, they helped teachers frame their expectations; and having high expectations was fundamental to effective practice.

Having high expectations

All primary and secondary teachers in the study reported that high expectations which were clear, consistent and understood by students, were closely related to their effectiveness. They also emphasized the value of establishing rules and boundaries at the outset. Expectations referred to learning outcomes as well as behaviour, and also impacted on the relationships that teachers constructed with their students. Having clear expectations allowed teachers to establish good relationships with the students and still maintain control of the class. It also helped them to get the best out of all their students. This was a vital dimension of effectiveness discussed by over two-thirds of the teachers:

> My expectations are pretty high so when they do hand me something they know I'll read it and appreciate what they've done. But then I will expect it to be, you know, corrected and made into a good piece because they should be proud of what they're doing. Sloppy work is not something to be proud about. So I think I do have high expectations for that sort of thing ... And I don't molly-coddle children.
>
> (Sally, Year 6 teacher, FSM 2)

Over half the teachers discussed the importance of differentiating expectations to ensure they got the best out of students. Many teachers commented that they had high expectations and pushed each child to reach the best of their ability. This tied into the idea of setting students targets based on learning outcomes, and using these to explain their expectations to their students. More than three-quarters of primary teachers and two-thirds of secondary teachers discussed this.

Another key feature that emerged was having expectations about behaviour, and a number of methods for doing this were brought up by the teachers. Setting out clear rules and boundaries and ensuring the students knew what was expected of them was a key feature. Establishing rules and setting boundaries seemed to be most important, with two-thirds of the primary teachers commenting on this as a key part of the way they built relationships with the class. Of these, 16 per cent mentioned the importance of involving the children in the rule-making process. This enables effective teaching because class control needs only minimal effort once they know how far they can go before they cross the line:

> I'm very much, this is what I expect when you're in my classroom and we sort of work from there, really, so we've got the ground rules from the start and the boundaries and you know, you can finally relax with them a bit more.
> (Natasha, Year 2 teacher, FSM 1)

A similar proportion, three-quarters, of secondary teachers commented on the need to set rules and boundaries with students. This was seen as being closely linked to student behaviour during lessons:

> I establish some very clear ground rules at the beginning which are: they are here to do maths, they can enjoy it, we will succeed, you have to listen to me, if there's going to be any comedy, I'll be the comedian, you know. I'll warn you when you step out of line and every now and again you do have to warn them, but they're children and you do have to remind them.
> (Michael, Year 9 maths teacher, FSM 1)

All of these dimensions of effective practice set the scene for effective lessons to take place. Teachers build strong relationships through communicating high expectations and giving appropriate praise and feedback on behaviour and effort with academic work, and this allows them to plan creative, stimulating lessons.

Teaching creative, flexible and student-led lessons

The lesson and the learning environment were important dimensions of effective practice. These were created through careful and well-directed planning, but it was also important that there was room for creativity and flexibility in planning and in the classroom. Indeed, the reperatory grid data also found that flexibility was a significant dimension of effectiveness. All teachers commented on their confidence in deviating from a strict plan in order to respond appropriately to broader learning needs as they arose:

> It's nice to be able to know you can go off on a tangent if it's necessary. For example, if the class, or a group of students is having problems, you should be able to adapt the lesson to suit them.
> (Sheila, Year 9 maths teacher, FSM 1)

A key feature was the importance of flexibility in the class and the ability to know when to deviate from a plan in order to aid learning. Being able to be creative and innovative with their lessons had a significant impact on feelings of efficacy and also fed into teachers' enjoyment, as well as how they perceived the students' enjoyment. It was important that teachers felt they were in control of their own planning, and did not have things imposed upon them:

> We're very lucky here to have an element of creativity to develop our curriculum ourselves, we're given that sense of trust and that's quite nice. Whereas having something imposed to me, right you will teach it and you will teach it this way, I'm not quite so comfortable with so that's very nice to be in a school that allows that creativity.
>
> (Chloe, Year 2 teacher, FSM 4)

Successful school leaders set an environment in which teachers feel free to try new things, look for new opportunities or experiment with new ideas (Day *et al.* 2011). These effective teachers commented on the importance of this and noted that it was a highly motivating factor at both primary and secondary level:

> I think one thing probably is sort of being given freedom to experiment, try out new things and not being afraid to learn and not always just doing as it has been done or just textbook, but being encouraged to try and be creative, try out new things.
>
> (Amy, Year 2 teacher, FSM 2)

Ensuring that lessons were enjoyable for the students was another key factor. Primary teachers talked extensively about the importance of the children enjoying learning. Almost 90 per cent of the primary teachers commented on the need for lessons to be fun and varied:

> When it's at its best, it's buzzy. The kids are motivated, they're interested, they're engaged and they're stimulated, yeah.
>
> (Richard, Year 2 teacher, FSM 1)

Engaging students with activities and assignments was discussed in the previous chapter as an observation of effective practice. Teachers also talked about this, with over half of the secondary teachers commenting on making the lessons interesting, stimulating or exciting:

> You have to do your best to make the lessons as exciting as possible. There are so many other things in their lives that provide fun and excitement and they expect that here as well.
>
> (Shaun, Year 9 maths teacher, FSM 1)

Providing a variety of activities was a key aspect of how effective practitioners aimed to ensure that learning was enjoyable for the students. It allowed students opportunities to learn in different ways and for them to explore and consolidate their learning and extend it:

> You try and make it as interesting and vibrant as you can and you try and make it as varied for them as you can.
>
> (Gavin, Year 9 English teacher, FSM 3).

Alongside this was the recognition of the importance of planning for a variety of different learning styles. Almost half of the primary teachers and two-thirds of the secondary teachers discussed planning for different learning styles and commented on this as a key feature of their effectiveness. Many specifically referred to VAK (visual, auditory and kinaesthetic) learning styles:

> Well not all the children can do it physically, but what would happen is, it's more visual, so that's stuck on the board and they're seeing me move it, so what would happen then, the weaker group would have a go practically and the others, or those who haven't understood it, but yeah we do VAK. I don't know if it's been mentioned, but I do sort of remind myself of that range of ways of learning . . . it is effective and I do sort of use it when I can.
>
> (Eleanor, Year 6 teacher, FSM 2)

With the recognition that students have diverse learning needs, effective teachers liked to allow students to guide the learning process. A student-led or interactive environment for learning was reported to be essential by over a third of all teachers and the need for students to be able to be creative and to lead their own learning emerged as key themes in setting an effective learning environment:

> Through all different ways, children are encouraged to ask their own questions, they're encouraged to collaborate with one another, they're encouraged to use me as a resource and know that I'm there to be used and I think they're encouraged to drive their own learning as well so if they want to find something out, if time permits, they're allowed to do so.
>
> (Natasha, Year 2 teacher, FSM 1)

Another dimension of this was peer learning. Students are encouraged to ask questions, both to the teachers and other students, and they are encouraged to guide their own enquiry. This was a fundamental element of an effective lesson:

> I think it's quite good. They have a tendency to interact with one another anyway. They like to learn from each other and they like it when one of them brings up something and we follow it through.
>
> (Anna, Year 9 English teacher, FSM 3)

In order to encourage students to lead their own learning it was important to set up a stimulating environment in which students were confident to work together and think things through for themselves. Around a third of primary teachers commented on the use of 'starters' or 'warmers' to get the children motivated and on task, while almost three-quarters of the secondary teachers commented on the use of starter activities as a way to get students ready for problem-solving and to engage them in the learning experience:

> The starter deliberately is chosen to sort of, prod them a bit. It's a thing about multiplying numbers and I'll be multiplying 43×47 like that and coming up with an answer and challenging them to work out how I'm doing it. And they like that, because they're a top set, they're good at number.

They like the sort of puzzle problem-solving things. So I picked a starter that will deliberately challenge them and make them think.

(Geoff, Year 9 maths teacher, FSM 1)

With student-led learning plans, it was also important to ensure that students had made progress throughout the lesson. Therefore, plenaries were another key feature of most effective teachers' lessons. Almost all the teachers discussed the importance of a plenary. For more than a third of the teachers they noted that this might come in the form of mini-plenaries throughout the lesson, although for 80 per cent of the observed lessons the plenary came at the end of the lesson. These were opportunities to consolidate learning and identify areas to follow up. They were an excellent way to close an effective lesson and establish the progress towards learning objectives, and formed a point of departure for planning subsequent lessons.

Summary

In this chapter we have outlined some of the key factors that make an effective practitioner in terms of who they are and what they do. We found that there are a series of factors that relate to effectiveness, most of which are dependent on non-cognitive skills and the personality of the teacher. The importance of building strong relationships with students was fundamental to effective practice and this meant being firm and fair, positive and open, creative and supportive, demanding and flexible. These characteristics enabled them to have a strong sense of self-efficacy, high job satisfaction, motivation and a commitment to continuing professional development. They know the students well and are able to differentiate learning styles, expectations and objectives, and facilitate students to lead their own learning and engage with education. These dimensions are portrayed in the model in Figure 5.1, which demonstrates teachers' perceptions of their practice and the interrelated factors we have discussed in this chapter.

The data evidenced here clearly relates to the observation data in Chapter 4. Moreover, there is a strong resonance between these findings and the findings of previous studies presented in Chapter 2. As a summary of the accounts and perspectives of these teachers, we found ten aspects of what it means to be an effective practitioner. Effective teachers:

1   Are highly motivated and committed to their students.
2   Value professional development and look for opportunities to improve their subject knowledge and teaching practice.
3   Build strong relationships with their students and ensure they know them well, so they can understand their needs.
4   Are firm but fair, positive, open and supportive.
5   Communicate clearly with students, particularly in terms of expectations and feedback.
6   Have high expectations of their students.
7   Give positive praise and feedback to students, carefully adapted to the individual's needs.
8   Are flexible with lesson plans and are able to adapt and enrich lessons in ways appropriate for their students.

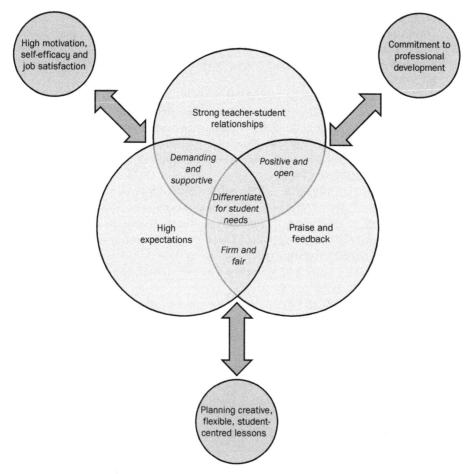

Figure 5.1   Model of an effective practitioner

9   Plan creative, enjoyable and stimulating lessons to engage students in learning, by considering a range of different learning styles.
10   Encourage students to take control of their own learning and ask questions to guide their own intellectual enquiry.

In considering student outcomes and recognizing the important role the learners themselves play in their own education, it is clear that while observing practice and talking to practitioners about how they teach are important ways to understand effective classroom practice, perhaps some of the richest data comes from the learners themselves. Therefore, in the next chapter we explore some of the above themes in more detail, but focus on students' views of effective teaching.

References

Abbott-Chapman, J., Hughes, P., Holloway, G. and Wyld, C. (1990) *Identifying the Qualities and Characteristics of the 'Effective' Teacher*. Hobart: University of Tasmania.

Barber, M. and Mourshed, M. (2007) *How the World's Best-performing School Systems Come Out on Top*. New York: McKinsey & Company.

Brouwers, A. and Tomic, W. (2000) A longitudinal study of teacher burnout and perceived self-efficacy in classroom management, *Teaching and Teacher Education*, 16(2): 239–53.

Campbell, J., Kyriakides, L., Muijs, D. and Robinson, W. (2004) *Assessing Teacher Effectiveness: Developing a Differentiated Model*. Abingdon: RoutledgeFalmer.

Day, C., Elliot, B. and Kington, A. (2005) Reform, standards and teacher identity: challenges of sustaining commitment, *Teaching and Teacher Education*, 21: 563–77.

Day C., Sammons, P., Stobart, G., Kington, A. and Gu, Q. (2007) *Teachers Matter*. Maidenhead: Open University Press.

Day, C., Sammons, P., Kington, A. and Regan, E. (2008) *Effective Classroom Practice (ECP): A Mixed Method Study of Influences and Outcomes*. Swindon: ESRC.

Day, C., Sammons, P., Leithwood, K., Hopkins, D., Gu, Q., Brown, E. and Ahtaridou, E. (2011) *Successful School Leadership: Linking with Learning and Achievement*. Maidenhead: Open University Press.

Hattie, J. (2009) *Visible Learning: A Synthesis of Over 800 Meta-analyses Relating to Achievement*. Abingdon: Routledge.

Kelly, P. and Colquhoun, D. (2003) Governing the stressed self: teacher health and well-being and effective schools, *Discourse*, 24 (2): 191–204.

Kington, A. (2009) Defining teachers' classroom relationships, in D. Stefanc and B. Harasimowicz (eds) *Social Context of Education*, Ljubljana: University of Ljubljana.

Klassen, R.M. and Tze, V.M.C. (2014) Teachers' psychological characteristics and teaching effectiveness: a meta-analysis, *Educational Research Review*, 12: 59–76.

Klassen, R.M., Perry, N.E. and Fenzal, A.C. (2012) Teachers' relatedness with students: an underemphasized component of teachers' basic psychological needs, *Journal of Educational Psychology*, 104(1): 150–65

Lortie, D. (1975) *School Teacher*. Chicago IL: University of Chicago Press.

Muijs, D. and Reynolds, D. (2000) *Effective Teaching: Evidence and Practice*. London: Sage.

Ofsted (2002) *Organising the Daily Mathematics Lesson in Mixed Reception/Year 1 Classes*. London: Ofsted.

Placek, J.H. and Dodds, P. (1988) A critical incident study of pre-service teacher beliefs about teaching success and non-success, *Research Quarterly for Exercise and Sport*, 59: 351–8.

Rowe, K. (2006) Effective teaching practices for students with and without learning difficulties: issues and implications, *Australian Journal of Learning Disabilities*, 11(3): 99–115.

Sammons, P. (2007) *School Effectiveness and Equity: Making Connections. A review of school effectiveness and improvement research and its implications for practitioners and policy makers*. Reading: CfBT.

Teddlie, C., Creemers, B., Kyriakides, L., Muijs, D. and Yu, F. (2006) The International System for Teacher Observation and Feedback: evolution of an International Study of Teacher Effectiveness Constructs, *Educational Research and Evaluation*, 12(6): 561–82.

Zembylas, M. (2003) Emotions and teacher identity: a poststructural perspective, *Teachers and Teaching: Theory and Practice*, (3): 213–38.

6 The impact of effective practice: learning from student voices

Introduction

The use of 'pupil views', sometimes referred to interchangeably as 'pupil voice', has gained popularity among educational researchers, practitioners and policy-makers in recent years. This chapter addresses the contribution of Key Stage 1, 2 and 3 (Years 2, 6 and 9) pupils' views to the Effective Classroom Practice (ECP) study, in which questionnaires and focus groups were used to access pupils' attitudes and perceptions related to their experiences of teaching and learning in their classrooms and schools.

As we discussed earlier in the research design chapter, the sample of teachers included in the ECP project was specifically designed to include those who were 'highly effective' or 'effective'.

Over the course of the project, a variety of measures incorporated adults' (i.e. teachers and researchers) perspectives, through interviews with the teachers as well as structured and unstructured lesson observations. The incorporation of pupil views, then, offered an alternative, student-centred insight into teachers' practice as well as classroom and school environments. The analyses of pupil questionnaire responses were used primarily to group teachers according to how positively they were rated by their pupils, but also to investigate relationships between pupil ratings and teacher and school characteristics (teacher gender and career phase, and school composition in terms of pupil disadvantage). Focus group data, meanwhile, allowed researchers to elicit themes and gain deeper insight into pupils' perspectives on a variety of topics relevant to their teachers, classrooms and schools.

The first section of this chapter introduces the existing literature on pupil views in education, covering the use of pupil views in policy and practice as well as some of the relevant theory and historical context for pupil views in education.

The data collection for pupil views in the ECP study is addressed in the second section, describing the samples and methods for both the attitudinal questionnaire and the focus group interviews. Following that, findings are presented and discussed, with attention to how the qualitative and quantitative results align with each other.

The chapter closes by addressing how these findings align with each other and with findings from other parts of the ECP project, ending with conclusions and implications for policy and practice.

Existing literature

History of pupil views in the UK

The increased emphasis on pupil views in education and educational research in recent years may be traced back to Article 12 of the United Nations Convention on the Rights of the Child, which states that:

> States Parties shall assure to the child who is capable of forming his or her own views the right to express those views freely in all matters affecting the child, the views of the child being given due weight in accordance with the age and maturity of the child.
>
> (UN General Assembly 1989)

In the UK in particular, the emphasis on pupil views may well have emerged as a response to direct criticism. The United Nations Committee on the Rights of the Child (CRC) – a group of 18 experts specifically charged with reporting on and making recommendations to individual states to ensure implementation of the Convention's statutes – noted in its periodic reports on the UK in 1995 and again in 2002 that children in the UK were 'not systematically consulted in matters that affect them' (CRC 2002: 3), and indicated that the government should 'take further steps to promote, facilitate and monitor systematic, meaningful and effective participation of all groups of children in society, including in school' (CRC 1995: 7). It was shortly after this that pupil views emerged as prominent features of the *Every Child Matters* agenda and later work by the national inspection agency, Ofsted, in developing a set of standards for schools (Flutter 2007).

Pupil views in practice and policy

In late 2003, UK school inspections began to include a component to gauge pupils' satisfaction with their schools. Between September 2003 and March 2005, Ofsted compiled data from 4,000 school inspections to investigate relationships between pupil satisfaction and a variety of school factors and characteristics (Ofsted 2005). Results showed that most pupils were satisfied with their schools and teachers, and that their satisfaction was associated with school type (with the highest satisfaction levels in denominational and specialist schools), socio-economic conditions based on free school meals (FSM) eligibility (with the highest ratings in schools with both the highest and lowest FSM bands), overall school effectiveness (with exceptions in a considerable number of schools that were 'a cause for concern' where students still expressed satisfaction), value-added achievement scores, consideration of and response to pupils' views, quality of teaching, opportunities for curriculum enrichment, quality of leadership, and, to a lesser extent, accommodation and resources. Pupils' satisfaction levels were often reflected in their attitudes and behaviour, and they tended to show loyalty to their schools, more so in primary than secondary schools, remaining satisfied even in many ineffective schools.

Halsey *et al.* (2006) found that the literature on pupil voice, at the time of their review, focused more on process than on impact. However, the literature that did relate to impact on policy and practice supported claims that young people's voice can impact on five key areas of policy and practice, namely: changes in organizational practices, services and facilities; strategy and policy development; budgetary decision-making; recruitment practices; and the production of materials and information resources (though it was noted that more evaluative work is required with regard to these last two items). The same review also found evidence of a variety of positive impacts of pupil voice on the pupils themselves, such as: increased confidence; social, personal and emotional competence; sense of responsibility, efficacy and autonomy; communication and collaborative skills; citizenship and community skills and values; career-relevant skills; and (based on smaller numbers of references) attendance, achievement and behaviour (Halsey *et al.* 2006). A review by Davies *et al.* (2006), however, offered the caution that most of the evidence of impact on pupils and schools was, at least at the time of the review, perceptual, and that causal claims were highly problematic.

Theoretical foundations for the use of pupil views

Contrary to what adults might assume, research has indicated that pupils' suggestions regarding teaching and learning tend to be sensible (Cooper and McIntyre 1996; Rudduck *et al.* 1996). Cullingford (2006) underscored the importance of attending to pupil views by pointing to discrepancies between the ways in which students conceptualize learning and creativity, and their actual – sometimes counterproductive – experiences of schooling.

Robinson and Taylor (2007) proposed a thorough theoretical framework for pupil voice based on four 'core values': a conception of communication as dialogue; the necessity of participation and democratic inclusivity; acknowledgement of power relations and inequality; and the potential for change and transformation. While different authors have cited a variety of theories in relation to pupil views, most seem to echo one or more of Robinson and Taylor's 'core values'.

Examples of alternative theoretical possibilities that have been used to support or guide the use of pupil views include the work of Habermas (1984) on 'communicative action' and Bandura's (1977, 1997) concept of 'self-efficacy'. Moran and Murphy (2012: 176), for example, drew on Habermas' themes to frame pupil voice as 'a basis from which to create more democratic forms of interaction between system and lifeworld', where 'lifeworld' may be interpreted as the lived experience of the learner, and 'system' connotes power and authority. From this perspective, the views of pupils are used to challenge domination by the system, engendering a more democratic and inclusive dialogue. The self-efficacy view, on the other hand, emphasizes the importance of 'outcome expectancies' (Bandura 1995). In other words, empowering pupils to participate meaningfully requires that they are able to see how their input is acted upon to produce outcomes they perceive as favourable (Gilleece and Cosgrove 2012).

Pupil views in empirical research

In the UK, the policy emphasis on pupil views has had a clear influence on the priorities of the educational research community. The Economic and Social Research

Council (ESRC) identified pupil views as an explicit focus for research in the early 2000s by creating the Phase I Network, 'Consulting Pupils about Teaching and Learning (2000–2003)' under the umbrella of the Teaching and Learning Research Programme (ESRC 2013). Some of the most prominent research on pupil views in the UK emerged out of this network (e.g. Fielding and Bragg 2003; Arnot *et al.* 2004; Rudduck and Flutter 2004; Mcintyre *et al.* 2005).

The scope of empirical research related to pupil views has included a broad range of themes. One line of enquiry has focused on how pupil perspectives may be used to inform and reflect on curriculum development and pedagogy in specific subject areas (e.g. Christidou 2011; McNaught *et al.* 2011; Wilson and Mant 2011; Lee and Johnston-Wilder 2013; Seiler 2013). Other authors have focused on best practices for the successful implementation of pupil voice in research (Christensen and James 2008) and in schools (MacBeath *et al.* 2003; Rudduck and Flutter 2004; Morgan 2011). Fielding and Bragg (2003) engaged students as researchers, and studied how this affected their learning; this line of enquiry has also been taken up by other researchers in the UK (e.g. Roberts and Nash 2009; Davies 2011) and elsewhere, such as Bland and Atweh (2007) in Australia. The potential of pupil views to contribute to teacher development has also received attention; Mcintyre *et al.* (2005) explored teachers' use of and responses to pupil views, and the extent to which these responses are productive and lasting, while Flutter (2007) used previous research findings to support teachers' use of constructive criticism from students, and to suggest ways for pupil voice to become less intimidating for teachers – for example, the introduction of pupil consultation and participation during teacher training.

Questions of how pupil characteristics influence their perceptions and experiences of school and learning have been considered in a number of studies. Blatchford (1996) studied stability of pupil views over time from ages seven to sixteen, taking into account differences by ethnicity and gender, and found little support for association between views and attainment. More recent studies have included Arnot *et al.*'s (2004) exploration of pupils' insights about how their gender, ethnicity, social class and prior achievement influenced their learning opportunities, and Gray and McLellan's (2006) survey of primary pupils' attitudes and responses to schooling, which found that girls and boys tended to be positive about different aspects (such as engagement and academic self-esteem, respectively), and identified a typology of five groups of pupils: enthusiastic and confident; moderately interested but easily bored; committed but lacking self-esteem; socially engaged but disaffected; and alienated.

Quite recently, research has emerged highlighting the views and perspectives of students in marginalized or vulnerable groups. Cefai and Cooper (2010) noted that students with social, emotional and behavioural disabilities have been largely overlooked in student voice efforts. Other researchers have also sought perspectives of students with special educational needs of varying degrees of specificity; examples include Blackman's (2011) study of Caribbean students with dyslexia, Wright's (2008) work on the views of students with multiple or complex needs and Byrnes and Rickards' (2011) more general study of the experiences of students with disabilities. This type of targeted pupil views' research has not been restricted to students with disabilities; Hopkins' (2008) emphasis on the views of disaffected and marginalized students regarding work-related learning programmes illustrates this, as does a study of exclusion and the perspectives of excluded students in a sample drawn from several prior projects by Munn and Lloyd (2005). These efforts under-score the importance of eliciting pupil views in ways that encourage a broader range of participants, not just 'typical' pupils.

According to a review by Lord and Jones (2006), qualitative methodology has been used more often than quantitative methodology to access pupil views, but many studies have combined both. The same review found that questionnaires and individual interviews were the most common approaches, but that group discussion was gaining in popularity. In fact, group interviews have been identified by young people themselves as a preferable way to express their views (Hannam 2004). This is particularly relevant to the methods and findings presented in this chapter. Less common alternatives to these methods have included visual approaches (e.g. Ryan 2009; Cremin *et al.* 2010) and card-sorting exercises (e.g. Hopkins 2010). Regard-less of the specific methods implemented, as noted by Reid *et al.* (2010), the ethical considerations involved in the collection and use of pupil perspectives are complex and crucial.

Research design and methods

Two rounds of data collection were undertaken using pupil surveys over the course of one academic year. The findings presented here are based on data collected in the second round, though analysis of data from the first round contributed to instrument development (Day *et al.* 2007a).

Access and ethics

Research involving children can be a delicate matter, involving a complex host of ethical issues; this is, perhaps, amplified as children are increasingly treated as com-petent research participants (Farrell 2005). For the research activities described in this chapter, every effort was made to consider the relevant ethical issues. The research team developed its own Code of Conduct, aligned with the ethical guide-lines of the British Educational Research Association (BERA 2011), to be followed over the course of the study. This addressed issues of participation, consent, confi-dentiality, anonymity and the right to withdraw from participation at any time.

Pupils, parents and school staff were given informational project flyers explain-ing the rationale of the research. Before participating in the study, pupils and par-ents were given information about the questionnaire and focus group interviews, including details regarding the length of time involved and the fact that interviews would be audio-recorded and subsequently transcribed.

Sample

The sample of schools was heterogeneous; schools were geographically dispersed, and made up of a mix of rural, suburban and urban schools (Kington *et al.* 2011). School composition also varied in terms of student ethnicity and socio-economic disadvantage.

Table 6.1 Pupil questionnaire returns

	Number of pupils	Number of classes	Number of schools
Year 2	302	13	12
Year 6	509	23	20
Year 9 English	226	10	5
Year 9 maths	221	10	6

Approximately 30 pupils were surveyed in each of the classes or teaching groups included in the study. In total, the questionnaire survey was administered to 1,258 students. Table 6.1 shows the total returns for pupils, classes and schools.

The focus group interviews were conducted with 414 pupils. Of these, 210 were in the primary year groups (92 in Year 2, 118 in Year 6), and 204 were in the secondary sample (84 in Year 9 maths groups, and 120 in Year 9 English groups). Forty-two primary and 34 secondary teachers participated at this stage of the research.

Questionnaire survey design

The choice of items and design of the questionnaire was based on reviews of relevant literature and survey instruments from prior studies, including VITAE[1] (Day *et al.* 2007b), PISA[2] (OECD 2005) and RAPA[3] (Levačić 2005). Items included in the survey were intended to address:

- examples of social and affective outputs of student learning;
- evidence of the relationships between effective teaching and pupil's perceptions of school and classroom climate;
- evidence of the relationship between effective teaching and pupil's perceptions of school and classroom conditions; and
- evidence of student engagement and identification with school.

The possible responses for each item ranged from one (most positive) to four (most negative). Questionnaire items were grouped under four headings: 'My school', 'My teacher', 'My classroom' and 'About you in this class', in order to glean understandings of the different aspects of pupils' experiences in, and attitudes towards, teaching and learning.

An age-appropriate version of the questionnaire was developed for each of the pupil year groups sampled (Year 2, Year 6 and Year 9). Most items remained similar or comparable across versions, but item wording was adjusted to accommodate appropriate reading levels for each age group. Some items were omitted entirely from the Year 2 questionnaire, as they were judged to be too complex for children to answer at that age (Day *et al.* 2007a).

Focus group interviews

Each focus group consisted of approximately six to eight students. The emphasis of focus group discussions was on pupils' experiences and perceptions of a lesson observed by the researchers, as well as broader conversations about their experiences and understandings of their school environments and relationships. The time spent with focus groups was dependent upon the age of the pupils involved (shorter for younger children, longer for older ones); sessions ranged from roughly 20 to 30 minutes. The research team implemented a standard set of practices to ensure that all of the focus group interview data were as consistent, accurately recorded and inclusive for participants as possible. These included:

- age-appropriate questioning techniques, reinforced through piloting prior to full implementation in the main study;
- audio-recording of focus group interviews, together with written notes; and
- topic guides outlining format, timing and content for discussions.

Approach to analysis

Questionnaire data were analysed using principal components analyses to derive sets of underlying factors from the questionnaire items for each year group. The purpose of this approach was to provide indicators of effective practice that could then be used to group the teachers in the sample, a form of 'qualitizing' these quantitative data. The next section describes the findings from these analyses in greater detail.

The pupil focus group interview data were initially coded collectively by the researchers using grounded analysis, allowing themes to emerge from the data (e.g. Glaser 1992). These qualitative data were subsequently coded and analysed in NVivo 7; this provided a tool for analysing the interviews thematically (Bazeley and Jackson 2013) and, to a certain extent, quantitatively (e.g. percentage of students who spoke positively about teacher-student relationships). Using this software also allowed for the integration of qualitative and quantitative data; summary measures from initial analysis of questionnaire data were imported into NVivo and applied as attributes for use in exploring teacher data in the larger context of the ECP study (Kington *et al.* 2011).

Findings

Questionnaire survey

The analysis of questionnaire data was undertaken with several aims in mind (Robertson *et al.* 2007):

- to find which questionnaire items clustered together to form meaningful factors;
- to identify any relationships between teachers' scores for different factors;
- to examine whether scores varied by subject (for Year 9 only);
- to find how the level of pupil social disadvantage in the school, teacher career phase and teacher gender related to pupils' views as measured by the factor scores.

Dimensions of effective practice

Pupil responses to the questionnaire items were largely positive, which indicated they had generally favourable attitudes and experiences with regard to their schools and teachers.

To address the first aim stated above, principal component analyses were conducted on each year group's responses to find underlying factors that could be used as indicators of effective practice. This was run first for all survey items in a given version of the questionnaire; for Years 2 and 6, this initial analysis was sufficient to yield clearly interpretable factors. For Year 9, subsequent analyses were deemed necessary, broken down by the four domains of the questionnaire ('My school', 'My teacher', 'My classroom' and 'About you in this class') for each subject, English and maths.

Seven factors emerged from the Year 2 data. These were compared based on the amount of variance accounted for by each of the factors. The 'strongest' factor by far was 'Overall pupil enjoyment and security', which accounted for 21.32 per cent of the total variance. 'Positive teacher support and reassurance' was a distant second, accounting for 4.94 per cent of the variance. Table 6.2 displays the factors for Year 2 along with the variance accounted for by each, and includes the items of which the strongest two factors are comprised.

In Year 6, five overall factors emerged. For this year group, 'Positive teacher support and reassurance' was the strongest factor, accounting for 29.91 per cent of the variance, followed by 'Attachment to school', accounting for 3.61 per cent of the variance (see Table 6.3 for the list of Year 6 factors, with full details for the first two).

Table 6.2   Year 2 factors

Factor 1: Overall pupil enjoyment and security	I have enjoyed being in my class My teacher is friendly My teacher makes me feel good about their teaching My teacher helps me to see why what I am learning is important This school is a friendly place My teacher is easy to get to know I feel safe in this school I like most of the lessons	21.32% variance
Factor 2: Positive teacher support and reassurance	My teacher believes that all children can do well My teacher seems to like all the children in the class My teacher makes everyone feel good about their learning My teacher listens to me I feel I learn a lot in my class	4.94% variance
Factor 3: Teacher approachability		4.37% variance
Factor 4: Clarity of teacher instruction and teacher expectations		4.25% variance
Factor 5: Attachment to school		3.94% variance
Factor 6: Pupil positive learning experience		3.50% variance
Factor 7: Working arrangements		3.24% variance

Table 6.3 Year 6 factors

Factor 1: Positive teacher support and reassurance	My teacher makes everyone feel good about their learning	29.91% variance
	My teacher makes me feel good about their teaching	
	My teacher is friendly	
	My teacher is easy to get to know	
	I feel that my teacher really knows me	
	My teacher seems to like all the children in the class	
	My teacher helps me learn new things	
	I get on well with my class teacher	
	I have enjoyed being in my class	
	I feel respected by my class teacher	
	My teacher really understands my learning needs	
	My teacher treats me fairly	
	My class teacher is very helpful	
	I feel good about myself as a learner	
	My teacher helps me to see why what I am learning is important	
	My teacher makes it clear how I can get help during the lesson	
	I have learned a lot from my teacher	
Factor 2: Attachment to school	I like being in this school	3.61% variance
	I really like this school	
	I feel that I belong in this school	
	This school is a friendly place	
	I feel safe in this school	
Factor 3: Pupil motivation and attitude to work		2.88% variance
Factor 4: Pupil understanding of work		2.54% variance
Factor 5: Teacher feedback and resources		2.36% variance

For Year 9, distinct factors emerged for each subject area within each questionnaire section. In each subject area, one factor was associated with 'My school', one with 'My teacher', six with 'My classroom' and two with 'About you in this class' (these are presented in Tables 6.4–6 for English and Tables 6.7–9 for maths).

An examination of the specific items corresponding to the factors for 'My school', 'My teacher' and 'About you in this class' shows that these are nearly identical for English and maths. The factors for 'My classroom', however, are ordered and defined differently for the two subjects (see Tables 6.5 and 6.8). For example, 'Clarity of instruction' appears to have more influence on pupils' perceptions in maths than it does in English, while factors relating to pupil behaviour exhibit the reverse. To demonstrate how factors are differently defined for the two subjects, consider the 'Teacher approachability and organization' factor for Year 9 maths, which is made up of fewer items than 'Teacher organization' for Year 9 English, while the latter includes a seemingly more diverse range of items (such as those referring to working as a class, teacher praise and mentioning life outside of school).

Table 6.4 Year 9 English factors, 'My school' and 'My teacher'

My School	My Teacher
Factor 1: Pupil enjoyment and security	**Factor 2: Teacher interest in pupils**
I like being in this school	My teacher is interested in what the students think
This school is a friendly place	My teacher believes that all students can do well
I really like this school	My teacher seems to like teaching
I feel that I belong in this school	My teacher is interested in my ideas in lessons
I feel safe in this school	My teacher believes that learning is important
I like most of the lessons	My teacher expects me to do well
	My teacher only cares about children who get good marks
57.59% variance	61.52% variance

Table 6.5 Year 9 English factors, 'My classroom'

Factor 3: Teacher organization	My teacher is friendly My teacher is easy to get to know I get on well with my class teacher I am praised or rewarded when I work hard My teacher seems to like all the children in the class My teacher praises/rewards students when they work well My teacher sometimes talks about life outside school I feel respected by my class teacher My teacher treats me fairly I feel that my contribution is valued by my teacher My class teacher is very helpful My teacher summarizes what we have learned at the end of the lesson We often work as a whole class My teacher organized the lesson well My teacher helps me learn new things My teacher makes it clear how I can get help during the lesson	42.79% variance
Factor 4: Pupil behaviour and resources	I always know what the lesson is about The work that I do in class really makes me think I usually know what to do during lessons I like learning in my class I usually know what I am supposed to learn	5.26% variance
Factor 5: Positive teacher support and reassurance		3.94% variance
Factor 6: Understanding of work and teacher feedback		3.40% variance
Factor 7: Positive teacher feedback		3.22% variance
Factor 8: Clarity of instruction		2.87% variance

Table 6.6 Year 9 English factors, 'About you in this class'

Factor 9: Pupil positive learning experience	My teacher makes me feel good about their teaching I usually enjoy my work in my class I have enjoyed being in my class I feel that my teacher really knows me My teacher makes everyone feel good about their learning I usually find the work in my class interesting I feel I learn a lot in my class I usually know my personal learning targets in this class I have managed to meet most of my learning targets I have learned a lot from my teacher	54.87% variance
Factor 10: Pupil motivation and attitude to work	I usually work hard in my class I feel confident that I can do well I usually have time to finish my work in class I have worked to the best of my ability this year I feel good about myself as a learner I feel confident to answer in my class	8.13% variance

Factor scores for pupils and for individual teachers

For each pupil, unweighted factor scores were calculated as the mean of the pupil's response values for all of the items in each factor. Teacher factor scores were then generated by calculating the means of all pupil ratings for a particular factor in a given class or teaching group. Table 6.10 gives the descriptive statistics for teacher factor scores by year group (and by subject for Year 9).

Based on the distribution of individual teacher scores for each factor, categories were defined to reflect how positively or negatively pupils from different teachers' classes rated their experiences. It should be noted that these distributions must be interpreted with some caution, as the pupils' ratings did demonstrate a

Table 6.7 Year 9 maths factors, 'My school' and 'My teacher'

My school	My teacher
Factor 1: Pupil enjoyment and security	**Factor 2: Teacher interest in pupils**
I like being in this school	My teacher is interested in what the students think
I really like this school	My teacher believes that all students can do well
I feel that I belong in this school	My teacher is interested in my ideas in lessons
I feel safe in this school	My teacher seems to like teaching
This school is a friendly place	My teacher believes that learning is important
I like most of the lessons	My teacher expects me to do well
	My teacher only cares about children who get good marks
65.81% variance	53.80% variance

Table 6.8   Year 9 maths factors, 'My classroom'

Factor 3: Teacher approachability and organization	My teacher is easy to get to know My teacher seems to like all the children in the class My teacher is friendly My teacher treats me fairly My teacher helps me learn new things My teacher makes it clear what to do when I finish my work My teacher helps me to see why what I am learning is important My teacher really understands my learning needs My teacher helps me if I make mistakes My teacher knows the way I learn best	35.81% variance
Factor 4: Positive teacher support and reassurance	Most students spend all of the lesson working All children work hard in my teacher's class The students in my class behave well most of the time My classroom has all the books and equipment I need for lessons I usually know what to do during lessons I usually know what I am supposed to learn	5.90% variance
Factor 5: Clarity of instruction		4.15% variance
Factor 6: Understanding of work		3.60% variance
Factor 7: Pupil behaviour		3.34% variance
Factor 8: Classroom rules and resources		2.95% variance

Table 6.9   Year 9 maths factors, 'About you in this class'

Factor 9: Pupil positive learning experience	I have enjoyed being in my class I feel that my teacher really knows me I usually enjoy my work in my class My teacher makes everyone feel good about their learning I feel I learn a lot in my class I usually find the work in my class interesting I have managed to meet most of my learning targets My teacher makes me feel good about their teaching I usually know my personal learning targets in this class	54.37% variance
Factor 10: Pupil motivation and attitude to work	I feel good about myself as a learner I feel confident that I can do well I usually work hard in my class I usually have time to finish my work in class I feel confident to answer in my class I have worked to the best of my ability this year	6.54% variance

Table 6.10 Teacher factor score descriptive statistics

	Mean	Standard deviation	Min.	Max.
Year 2				
Overall pupil enjoyment and security	1.27	0.14	1.07	1.53
Positive teacher support and reassurance	1.23	0.14	1.01	1.53
Teacher approachability	1.26	0.16	1.01	1.55
Clarity of instruction and teacher expectations	1.24	0.13	1.05	1.47
Attachment to school	1.38	0.21	1.08	1.70
Pupil positive learning experience	1.25	0.12	1.06	1.46
Working arrangements	1.54	0.35	1.15	2.24
Year 6				
Positive teacher support and reassurance	1.57	0.20	1.20	2.00
Attachment to school	1.62	0.23	1.20	2.02
Pupil motivation and attitude to work	1.65	0.17	1.39	2.03
Pupil understanding of work	1.84	0.19	1.58	2.27
Teacher feedback and resources	1.55	0.23	1.18	2.19
Year 9 English				
My school – Pupil enjoyment and security	2.10	0.52	1.00	4.00
My teacher – Teacher interest in pupils	1.82	0.40	1.00	3.57
My classroom – Teacher organization	1.87	0.58	1.00	3.75
My classroom – Pupil behaviour and resources	1.86	0.55	1.00	4.00
My classroom – Positive teacher support and reassurance	1.78	0.54	1.00	4.00
My classroom – Understanding of work and teacher feedback	1.89	0.55	1.00	3.80
My classroom – Positive teacher feedback	2.27	0.65	1.00	4.00
My classroom – Clarity of instruction	1.94	0.57	1.00	4.00
About you in this class – Pupil positive learning experience	1.92	0.60	1.00	3.82
About you in this class – Pupil motivation and attitude to work	1.87	0.54	1.00	4.00
Year 9 maths				
My school – Pupil enjoyment and security	2.17	0.60	1.00	4.00
My teacher – Teacher interest in pupils	1.87	0.39	1.00	3.43
My classroom – Teacher approachability and organization	1.89	0.47	1.00	3.63
My classroom – Positive teacher support and reassurance	1.86	0.53	1.00	3.64
My classroom – Clarity of instruction	1.95	0.46	1.00	4.00
My classroom – Understanding of work	1.89	0.53	1.00	4.00
My classroom – Pupil behaviour	1.90	0.45	1.00	4.00
My classroom – Classroom rules and resources	2.05	0.58	1.00	3.75
About you in this class – Pupil positive learning experience	1.97	0.55	1.00	4.00
About you in this class – Pupil motivation and attitude to work	1.89	0.54	1.00	4.00

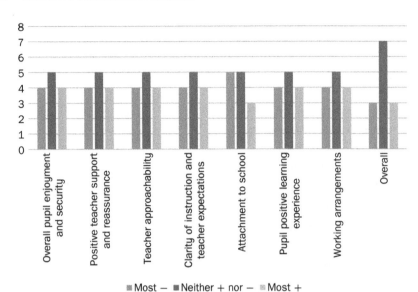

Figure 6.1 Year 2 teacher groups by factor.

considerable positive skew (Robertson *et al.* 2007). Each teacher's score for each factor was assigned to a relative grouping based on the overall distribution of scores for that factor; '+' represented the most positive group, '0' denoted a group that was neither positive nor negative, and '–' was assigned' to the most negative group. These groupings helped to clarify which factors were consistently rated more positively or negatively than others by pupils, helping to address the second and third aims (i.e. those dealing with relationships between teachers' scores for different factors, and variations between factor scores by subject for Year 9). Frequencies for the teacher groups by factor for each year group are displayed in Figures 6.1–4. In all cases, the largest group was that labelled neither positive nor negative;

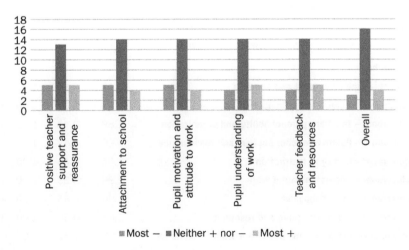

Figure 6.2 Year 6 teacher groups by factor.

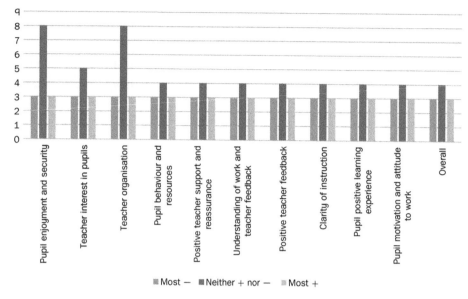

Figure 6.3   Year 9 English teacher groups by factor.

this was more pronounced for the Year 6 teacher groups, which may have been related to a relatively large sample size (there were 23 Year 6 teachers, compared to 13 from Year 2 and 10 from each subject in Year 9).

In addition, the groupings for all of the factors for a particular teacher were used to determine an overall categorization (also +, 0, or −) for that teacher. The overall or by-factor groupings were then available for reference in the context of discussions of other data about the same teachers for other strands of the ECP project, in order to inform or enrich additional comparisons.

Relationship to socio-economic status

In order to explore whether and how pupil social disadvantage related to factor scores, school FSM band was used as a proxy measure for the socio-economic

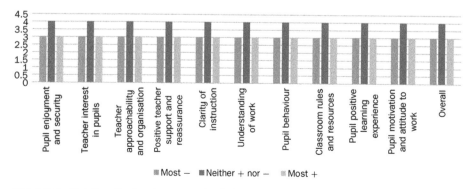

Figure 6.4   Year 9 maths teacher groups by factor.

Table 6.11   Year 2 mean factor scores by FSM band

School FSM band	N	F1	F2	F3	F4	F5	F6	F7
1	64	1.25	1.25	1.27	1.37	1.34	1.24	1.91
2	140	1.24	1.17	1.20	1.20	1.34	1.25	1.49
3	43	1.18	1.29	1.30	1.13	1.43	1.14	1.27
4	55	1.37	1.32	1.27	1.25	1.43	1.24	1.31

F1 = Overall pupil enjoyment and security
F2 = Positive teacher support and reassurance
F3 = Teacher approachability
F4 = Clarity of instruction and teacher expectations
F5 = Attachment to school
F6 = Pupil positive learning experience
F7 = Working arrangements

composition of the school in terms of the level of pupil social disadvantage of each school. Individual pupil factor scores were used to calculate mean scores for each band for each year group; the results are displayed in Tables 6.11–14 for Year 2, Year 6, Year 9 English and Year 9 maths, respectively.

The only strong relationship emerging from this analysis occurred in Year 9 maths, for which lower school FSM seemed to be associated with more positive factor scores. A 3 (FSM band) by 10 (factor) mixed measures analysis of variance confirmed that the effect of FSM band on factor scores was significant ($F(2,217) = 7.03$, MSE = 1.56, $p < 0.01$). In particular, Band 1 had significantly more positive results than the other FSM bands, based on Tukey's post-hoc analysis comparing the means for all bands ($p < 0.05$). Additionally, factor ($F(9,210) = 17.87$, MSE = 0.11, $p < 0.001$) and the interaction between factor and FSM band ($F(18,1953) = 3.37$, MSE = 0.11, $p < 0.001$) were both significant. This indicates that if FSM bands were ignored, the individual factors were scored significantly differently, and that the ratings of the various factors significantly differed in FSM bands.

In short, for the Year 9 maths sample, the pupil attitudes in Band 1 schools were more positive for every factor than those of pupils in Band 2 and Band 4 schools,

Table 6.12   Year 6 mean factor scores by FSM band

School FSM band	N	F1	F2	F3	F4	F5
1	177	1.65	1.68	1.73	1.87	1.67
2	198	1.45	1.43	1.51	1.71	1.41
3	77	1.57	1.76	1.78	1.93	1.56
4	57	1.57	1.70	1.57	1.92	1.52

F1 = Positive teacher support and reassurance
F2 = Attachment to school
F3 = Pupil motivation and attitude to work
F4 = Pupil understanding of work
F5 = Teacher feedback and resources

Table 6.13   Year 9 English mean factor scores by FSM band

School FSM band	N	F1	F2	F3	F4	F5	F6	F7	F8	F9	F10
1	75	2.03	1.78	1.74	1.81	1.77	1.86	2.48	2.02	1.80	1.85
2	113	2.02	1.85	1.96	1.88	1.80	1.93	2.26	1.87	1.99	1.88
4	38	2.51	1.80	1.83	1.89	1.76	1.82	1.91	2.00	1.95	1.87

F1 = Pupil enjoyment and security (My school)
F2 = Teacher interest in pupils (My teacher) (My classroom)
F3 = Teacher organization
F4 = Pupil behaviour and resources
F5 = Positive teacher support and reassurance
F6 = Understanding of work and teacher feedback
F7 = Positive teacher feedback
F8 = Clarity of instruction (About you in this class)
F9 = Pupil positive learning experience
F10 = Pupil motivation and attitude to work

but to differing extents depending on the particular factor. In interpreting these findings it must be remembered that the sample was drawn from more effective teachers. Band 1 were schools with the lowest proportions of disadvantaged students, and Band 4 the schools with the highest proportions.

Relationship to teacher career phase

The questionnaire results were also analysed with respect to teacher career phase. For the purposes of this analysis, five distinct career phases were defined based on number of years of teaching experience (0–3, 4–7, 8–15, 16–23 and 24+). Just as was done for the FSM band analysis, individual pupil factor scores were used to

Table 6.14   Year 9 maths mean factor scores by FSM band

School FSM band	N	F1	F2	F3	F4	F5	F6	F7	F8	F9	F10
1	70	1.89	1.81	1.70	1.83	1.74	1.79	1.92	1.87	1.75	1.80
2	78	2.24	1.85	1.87	2.04	1.90	2.00	1.99	1.96	1.89	1.89
4	73	2.36	1.95	2.02	1.97	2.01	1.90	2.25	2.08	2.03	1.98

F1 = Pupil enjoyment and security (My school)
F2 = Teacher interest in pupils (My teacher) (My classroom)
F3 = Teacher approachability and organization
F4 = Positive teacher support and reassurance
F5 = Clarity of instruction
F6 = Understanding of work
F7 = Pupil behaviour (About you in this class)
F8 = Classroom rules and resources
F9 = Pupil positive learning experience
F10 = Pupil motivation and attitude to work

Table 6.15 Year 2 mean factor scores by teacher career phase

Career phase	N	F1	F2	F3	F4	F5	F6	F7
0–3 years	28	1.29	1.26	1.32	1.21	1.41	1.17	1.24
4–7 years	160	1.27	1.27	1.26	1.25	1.39	1.24	1.59
8–15 years	53	1.24	1.21	1.23	1.29	1.48	1.31	1.58
16–23 years	20	1.08	1.01	1.01	1.05	1.11	1.06	1.15
24+ years	41	1.26	1.18	1.24	1.22	1.23	1.22	1.54

F1 = Overall pupil enjoyment and security
F2 = Positive teacher support and reassurance
F3 = Teacher approachability
F4 = Clarity of instruction and teacher expectations
F5 = Attachment to school
F6 = Pupil positive learning experience
F7 = Working arrangements

find mean factor scores for each career phase for Year 2, Year 6 and Year 9 teachers (see Tables 6.15–18).

Here again, there was not an immediately apparent relationship between career phase and factor score for Year 2 and Year 6.

Year 9 English pupils rated teachers in early and late career phases more highly than those in the middle of their careers. As described in the previous section, a mixed measures analysis of variance five (this time career phase) by ten (factor), confirmed that teachers' career phase had a significant effect on factor ratings ($F(4,220) = 9.55$, MSE $= 1.69$, $p < 0.001$). Tukey's post-hoc analysis compared career phase group means in further detail, and found that those who had taught for under three years were rated significantly more positively than teachers with eight to fifteen, or 16–23 years of experience ($p < 0.05$), and teachers with four to seven or 24 or more years of experience were also rated more positively than their counterparts with eight to fifteen years of experience ($p < 0.05$). A factor effect ($F(9,212) = 23.22$, MSE $= 0.12$, $p < 0.001$) and

Table 6.16 Year 6 mean factor scores by teacher career phase

Career phase	N	F1	F2	F3	F4	F5
0–3 years	24	1.57	1.45	1.54	1.95	1.55
4–7 years	149	1.72	1.71	1.72	1.88	1.68
8–15 years	164	1.40	1.47	1.54	1.73	1.41
16–23 years	124	1.54	1.69	1.67	1.86	1.60
24+ years	48	1.57	1.57	1.61	1.78	1.36

F1 = Positive teacher support and reassurance
F2 = Attachment to school
F3 = Pupil motivation and attitude to work
F4 = Pupil understanding of work
F5 = Teacher feedback and resources

Table 6.17 Year 9 English mean factor scores by teacher career phase

Career phase	N	F1	F2	F3	F4	F5	F6	F7	F8	F9	F10
0–3 years	69	2.08	1.68	1.62	1.67	1.60	1.73	1.98	1.87	1.76	1.83
4–7 years	67	2.08	1.76	1.69	1.81	1.70	1.81	2.19	1.92	1.77	1.76
8–15 years	27	2.21	2.16	2.50	2.35	2.24	2.29	2.68	2.20	2.43	2.08
16–23 years	40	2.15	1.93	2.13	1.91	1.86	1.98	2.43	1.78	2.14	2.03
24+ years	23	2.03	1.77	1.89	1.88	1.89	1.93	2.66	2.17	1.84	1.77

F1 = Pupil enjoyment and security (My school)
F2 = Teacher interest in pupils (My teacher) (My classroom)
F3 = Teacher organization
F4 = Pupil behaviour and resources
F5 = Positive teacher support and reassurance
F6 = Understanding of work and teacher feedback
F7 = Positive teacher feedback
F8 = Clarity of instruction (About you in this class)
F9 = Pupil positive learning experience
F10 = Pupil motivation and attitude to work

interaction between career phase and factor ($F(36,1980) = 5.21$, MSE = 0.12, $p < 0.001$) were also found to be significant. In simpler terms, the extent of the effect of teacher career phase, much like that of school FSM, varied between factors.

The results of this analysis for Year 9 maths were slightly different. Among the pupils in this sample, the pupils taught in classes by teachers who were in the later stages of their careers tended to give more positive ratings than those in the earlier career phases. Another (again five by ten) mixed-measures analysis of variance

Table 6.18 Year 9 maths mean factor scores by teacher career phase

Career phase	N	F1	F2	F3	F4	F5	F6	F7	F8	F9	F10
0–3 years	16	2.36	1.95	1.86	2.07	1.82	1.78	2.02	2.02	1.94	1.94
4–7 years	53	2.32	1.96	2.18	2.18	2.18	2.08	2.41	2.19	2.16	2.06
8–15 years	20	2.33	1.94	1.94	1.82	1.89	1.90	2.29	2.03	1.93	1.89
16–23 years	52	2.24	1.80	1.78	1.95	1.85	1.94	1.83	1.87	1.84	1.87
24+ years	80	1.93	1.81	1.69	1.81	1.73	1.78	1.90	1.87	1.73	1.78

F1 = Pupil enjoyment and security (My school)
F2 = Teacher interest in pupils (My teacher) (My Classroom)
F3 = Teacher approachability and organization
F4 = Positive teacher support and reassurance
F5 = Clarity of instruction
F6 = Understanding of work
F7 = Pupil behaviour
F8 = Classroom rules and resources (About you in this class)
F9 = Pupil positive learning experience
F10 = Pupil motivation and attitude to work

Table 6.19 Year 2 mean factor scores by teacher gender

Teacher gender	N	F1	F2	F3	F4	F5	F6	F7
Female	270	1.26	1.24	1.26	1.23	1.37	1.23	1.51
Male	32	1.17	1.11	1.11	1.26	1.39	1.21	1.61

revealed that the effect of career phase was significant for Year 9 maths ($F_{(4,220)}$ = 7.78, MSE = 1.46, p < 0.001), and post-hoc analysis clarified further that pupils in classes taught by the most experienced teachers (those in the 16–23 and 24+ career phases) gave significantly more positive ratings than pupils in classes taught by teachers with four to seven years of experience (p < 0.05). There was, yet again, a significant factor effect ($F_{(9,207)}$ = 12.76, MSE = 0.11, p < 0.001) and a significant interaction between career phase and factor ($F_{(36,1935)}$ = 2.68, MSE = 0.11, p < 0.001), which is unsurprising based on the English results. So if career phases were ignored, factors would still be rated significantly differently, and the extent to which career phase had an effect on ratings varied by factor.

Relationship to teacher gender

A similar analysis to those described above was undertaken to explore whether any significant relationships existed between teachers' gender and factor ratings (see Tables 6.19–21). Because some of the subsamples contained gender imbalances, this analysis was somewhat more problematic. In Year 2, for instance, there was only one male teacher. In Year 9, a more equal balance of genders was achieved by combining subjects (maths and English). This meant that, for the purposes of this analysis, only the factors that both subjects had in common (Factor 1, 'Pupil enjoyment and security' and Factor 2, 'Teacher interest in pupils') could be considered.

In Year 6, no major differences were apparent between the factor ratings for female and male teachers. For Year 9, pupils seemed to have more positive scores for female teachers than male teachers. A two (gender) by two (factor) mixed-measures analysis of variance showed significant main effects for gender ($F_{(1,445)}$ = 4.90, MSE = 0.33, p < 0.05) and factor ($F_{(1,445)}$ = 138.97, MSE = 0.14, p < 0.001), but not for the interaction between the two. Ultimately, because different genders were overrepresented in each subject area, any conclusions from these results are tentative at best; what appears to be an effect of teacher gender, in this context, may instead have more to do with whether teachers taught English or maths.

Table 6.20 Year 6 mean factor scores by teacher gender

Teacher gender	N	F1	F2	F3	F4	F5
Female	285	1.56	1.60	1.66	1.85	1.54
Male	224	1.54	1.60	1.60	1.78	1.53

Table 6.21   Year 9 mean factor scores by teacher gender for common factors across subjects

Teacher gender	N	F1	F2
Female	215	2.08	1.81
Male	232	2.19	1.87

Focus group interviews: experiences in observed lessons

Focus group discussions covered a wide variety of topics. The conversations were focused on the pupils' experiences in the specific lesson observed by researchers.

(i) Teachers

The vast majority of pupils (92 per cent in Year 2, 94 per cent in Year 6, 86 per cent in Year 9 maths and 95 per cent in Year 9 English) described their teachers using positive terms. For primary pupils, this included the use of words with very general positive meanings like 'brilliant', 'great' and 'lovely', as well as words with more specific implications about teachers' practice (e.g. 'hard-working') and emotional relationships with students (e.g. 'caring' and 'considerate'). Secondary pupils used arguably more specific positive terms to describe their teachers, such as 'understanding', 'sensitive', 'clever' and 'energetic'.

Many students (78 per cent in Year 2, 97 per cent in Year 6 and 77 per cent in Year 9 for both maths and English) also indicated that they felt their teachers knew them well. The majority of primary pupils who felt well-known by teachers also claimed that their teachers had mentioned something about their lives outside of school.

The factors from the questionnaire data for Year 2 that most closely reflect these comments are 'Teacher approachability', including items such as 'I get on well with my class teacher' and 'I feel liked by my class teacher', and 'Positive teacher support and reassurance', including 'My teacher seems to like all the children in the class' and 'My teacher makes everyone feel good about their learning'. For Year 6, the factor from the questionnaire data that most closely relates to the interview responses on this theme is 'Positive teacher support and reassurance', as this includes items such as 'My teacher is friendly', 'I feel that my teacher really knows me' and 'My class teacher is very helpful'. For Year 9 English, the factors 'Teacher organization' for the English groups and 'Teacher approachability and organization' for the maths groups (including items such as 'My teacher is friendly') and 'Pupil positive learning experience' for both groups (including 'I feel that my teacher really knows me') seem to correspond to the focus group interview responses.

(ii) Involvement

Over 90 per cent of students in each age and subject group reported feeling involved in the lesson. What was meant by this was different for pupils in the various subgroups of the study. Year 2 pupils mentioned questioning ('being asked questions'), feedback ('the teacher talking to me about the work') and praise ('saying well done').

Year 6 pupils mentioned different kinds of interactivity and active involvement, including 'going up to the whiteboard', 'giving the working out to a question' and 'being allowed to come up with my own questions'. Among Year 9 maths and English students, both included 'going up to the whiteboard' or 'getting us to do the work on the whiteboard'; maths pupils also gave examples of praise and fostering competition among pupils, while English pupils mentioned collective experiences such as 'reading to the group'. Both primary (88 per cent in Year 2, 86 per cent in Year 9) and secondary (94 per cent in maths, 93 per cent in English) pupils alike said that teachers made sure that pupils worked well with one another.

The focus group interview responses about involvement seem to relate closely to the factor 'Pupil motivation and attitude to work' for Years 6 and 9 (including items such as 'I work hard in my class'). For Year 2, the most relevant factor appears to be 'Pupil positive learning experience', including items such as 'The work that I do in class really makes me think'. A number of other factors also relate to some of the students' comments about involvement; for example, 'Teacher organization' in Year 9 contains the item 'We often work as a whole class'.

(iii) Classroom environment

Most pupils in Years 2 and 6 said that their teachers worked hard to make the classroom an interesting place (90 and 92 per cent, respectively). Many (85 per cent in Year 2, 75 per cent in Year 6) mentioned specific aspects such as student work, engaging displays, or dedicated physical spaces (e.g. reading areas or information technology (IT) corners). Most of the pupils who referred to specific details about the environment also claimed that this helped them to learn more.

Year 9 English pupils responded similarly: 91 per cent agreed that their teachers made an effort with the classroom environment. This was noticeably less the case in maths, for which only 79 per cent of students felt that teachers made an effort with the environment.

The factors from the questionnaire data for most groups are not so clearly linked to the interview comments about classroom environment. The Year 6 factor 'Teacher feedback and resources' and the Year 9 maths factor 'Positive teacher support and reassurance', both of which contain the item 'My classroom has all the books and equipment I need for lessons', do relate somewhat to this theme. For Year 9 English, the factor 'Clarity of instruction', including the items 'My classroom has all the books and equipment I need for lessons' and 'I find the displays very helpful in my learning', more closely reflects the pupils' responses in focus groups about the environment. It is interesting to note that while many primary pupils mentioned specific displays in their focus group interviews, this did not correspond to any of the items included in the primary groups' factors from the quantitative data.

(iv) Interest in the lesson

Over 80 per cent of students in every category found the observed lesson interesting. This was attributed to a variety of features. Many primary pupils, for example, mentioned the pace of the lesson, while secondary pupils mentioned the lesson structure. 'I liked it because it was fast and we went from one thing to another but it all made sense' (Year 2 pupil).

The activities that pupils considered interesting were different for each year group. Year 2 pupils cited working on the whiteboard as a class and illustrating their work. Year 6 pupils mentioned specific subject activities, including whole-class maths tasks, creative writing, and history and geography research. Year 9 maths responses related back to comments on involvement; these pupils were interested in working on the whiteboard as a class and participating in class competitions. English pupils, on the other hand, gave examples that included sharing out their work by reading it to the class and finding ways to make the set texts relevant to today.

The questionnaire item 'I usually find the work in my class interesting', which is most directly connected to the theme of interest in the lesson, was included in the factor 'Pupil positive learning experience' in Years 2 and 9. This item is not reflected in the factor breakdown for Year 6. Some of the other questionnaire items are also relevant to this theme (e.g. 'We often work as a whole class' in the Year 9 English factor 'Teacher organization'), but are scattered across a variety of factors for each year group.

(v) Pupil behaviour

A very large number of pupils (98 per cent in Year 2, 89 per cent in Year 6) mentioned that they did not like the behaviour of some of their peers. Many of those who shared this complaint also felt that it got in the way of learning.

Secondary pupils (82 per cent in maths and 94 per cent in English) also tended to dislike the behaviour of one or two of their peers in the class or teaching group, but the older pupils claimed that they tried to ignore this rather than allow it to interfere with their own learning.

All pupils were able to describe the consequences if a pupil behaved badly. Among the primary pupils, 74 per cent of those in Year 2 and 60 per cent of those in Year 6 said that poor behaviour was quickly dealt with by teachers. Approximately two-thirds of secondary pupils (67 per cent in maths and 63 per cent in English) indicated that their teachers had specific strategies for managing poor behaviour that usually worked.

The factors emerging from the primary pupils' questionnaire responses do not contain items that are directly related to the teachers' management of behaviour, at least in terms of the ways in which behaviour was addressed in the focus groups. The Year 9 English factor 'Positive teacher feedback', however, does seem closely related, containing items such as 'The students in my class behave well most of the time'. For Year 9 maths, 'Positive teacher support and reassurance' also includes the item 'The students in my class behave well most of the time'. Additionally, the Year 9 English factor 'Clarity of instruction', including 'I know what happens if I misbehave in class', is reflected in the pupils' interview responses.

(vi) Relevance

Most pupils said that the majority of their work in class was relevant to them; this seemed roughly to increase between primary and secondary school (from 88 per cent in Year 2 and 83 per cent in Year 6, to 98 per cent in Year 9 maths and 90 per cent in Year 9 English). The majority of primary students also mentioned that activities they did not enjoy were those that they judged to be irrelevant. Most pupils recalled their teachers using examples from other aspects of life, while the majority of secondary students mentioned teachers using illustrations or examples from their own lives.

The Year 2 factor 'Overall pupil enjoyment and security', the Year 6 and Year 9 English factor 'Positive teacher support and reassurance' and the Year 9 maths factor 'Teacher approachability and organization' all include the item 'My teacher helps me to see why what I am learning is important'. Relevance was not heavily represented in the questionnaire itself, but the fact that this item was included in factors for each year group, along with the pupils' comments in focus group interviews, does indicate that relevance plays an important role in their learning across all age groups. Additionally, the item 'My teacher sometimes talks about life outside school', which appears within the Year 6 factor 'Pupil motivation and attitude to work' as well as the Year 9 English factor 'Teacher organization', certainly addresses a dimension of relevance, though it did not appear in the factor groupings for all pupil age categories.

(vii) Difficulty of tasks

Most primary pupils said that the work done in class was at an appropriate level of difficulty for them. About half of the secondary pupils in both maths and English, by contrast, claimed that the work could have been slightly more difficult – 38 per cent of maths pupils reported finding something about the work challenging, and being pleased with this.

Task difficulty is not so directly related to the questionnaire items (and hence the factors emerging from student survey responses) as some of the other themes addressed in this section. The factors relating most closely to the difficulty of tasks include 'Pupil positive learning experience' in Year 2 (containing the item 'The work that I do in class really makes me think'), 'Pupil understanding of work' in Year 6 (including the item 'I usually know what I am supposed to learn'), 'Pupil behaviour and resources' in Year 9 English and 'Positive teacher support and reassurance in Year 9 maths (both of which include the same item mentioned for Year 6).

(viii) Communication

All of the primary pupils claimed to understand what their teachers said to them most of the time. Secondary pupils indicated unanimously that they understood everything the teacher said to them all of the time. Primary pupils used terms like 'friendly', 'clear', 'kind' and 'straightforward' to describe the ways in which their teachers talked to the class, and the vast majority reported that teachers communicated in positive ways. Secondary pupils also reported that teachers spoke to the class in a positive manner, and they described this communication using words such as 'clear', 'sensitive' and 'comprehensive'.

Connecting factors from the questionnaire data to pupil interview responses about communication are more straightforward than in the case of many of the other themes. In Year 2, the factor 'Clarity of teacher instruction and expectations', including the item 'My teacher is good at explaining our work', clearly relates to communication as discussed in the interviews. In Year 6, 'Positive teacher support and reassurance', with items such as 'My class teacher is very helpful' and 'My teacher makes it clear how I can get help during the lesson', is highly relevant to this theme. In Year 9 English, the factor 'Teacher organization' addresses a number of aspects of teacher communication, as does a combination of the Year 9 maths factors 'Teacher approachability and organization' and 'Classroom rules and resources'.

(ix) Engagement

The majority of primary pupils (83 per cent in Year 2, 73 per cent in Year 6) reported always feeling engaged in lessons. A smaller majority of secondary pupils mentioned positive involvement in lessons in reference to their own engagement (76 per cent in maths, 69 per cent in English).

Over 90 per cent of pupils in Year 2 and Year 6 said that their teachers always tried to involve every student in lesson activities, and a similar percentage in Year 9 maths noted that the teachers' encouragement contributed to them feeling involved. Year 9 English pupils stood out as less positive about this; 78 per cent of them said that they felt involved because of the teachers' encouragement.

Most students said that the class was quiet when they needed to do their work. The proportion of students responding positively about this issue seemed to be positively related to age (60 per cent in Year 2, 69 per cent in Year 6, 77 per cent in Year 9 maths and 74 per cent in Year 9 English).

Questionnaire items addressed engagement somewhat differently. In Year 2, the factors do not relate particularly closely to this theme, though 'I have enjoyed being in my class' within the factor 'Overall pupil enjoyment and security' might be seen as indirectly related. In Year 6, 'Pupil motivation and attitude to work' (containing the item 'I usually work hard in my class') and 'Pupil understanding of work' (including 'Most children spend all of the lesson working') clearly relate to engagement. In Year 9 English, 'Positive teacher feedback' contains relevant items including 'All children work hard in my teacher's class' and 'Most students spend all of the lesson working', while in Year 9 maths, these same items appear within 'Positive teacher support and reassurance'. For both Year 9 subject groups, 'Pupil motivation and attitude to work' includes the item 'I usually work hard in this class', which also connects to engagement.

(x) Feedback

Nearly all pupils in both primary and secondary school said that they received prompt feedback on their work, and that this feedback was given in both verbal and written forms. The majority of primary pupils (91 per cent in Year 2 and 86 per cent in Year 6) also mentioned that teachers tended to find positive approaches to feedback, 'even if there was a negative comment too' (Year 6 pupil).

There are a number of factors that relate less directly to teacher feedback from the questionnaire data, such as the Year 2 factor 'Working arrangements' containing the item 'My teacher is pleased when I work hard'. More directly linked, however, are the factors containing items related to teacher praise, which include 'Teacher organization' for Year 9 English and 'Pupil behaviour' for Year 9 maths.

Discussion

Findings from both the focus group interviews and the questionnaire survey demonstrate pupils' largely positive perspectives about their teachers, classrooms and schools.

In the previous section, an attempt was made to show how results from the quantitative survey data and the qualitative interview data align. Although this was not specifically an effort to perform any type of strict triangulation, the finding that some of the strongest factors arising from the questionnaire can be easily connected to the main themes emerging from the interviews bolsters the results of both.

This can be taken a step further, to consider how the findings from pupil views relate to some of the other findings from the ECP research. The analysis of teacher interviews, for example, indicates that teachers identify what makes them effective as: relationships consisting of knowing pupils well; good rapport; listening to and communicating with pupils, and maintaining respect, fairness and consistency; praise and feedback; expectations, characterized as high, clear and consistent; professional learning and development; and organization and planning, including being responsive and flexible to the interests of the class, learning styles and needs (Day *et al.* 2008). With the exception of professional learning and development, which might not be directly observable by pupils, each of these categories is clearly reflected in the factors emerging from the pupil questionnaire data. In addition, many of the same themes (e.g. relationships, feedback and communication) are echoed in the pupil focus group interview findings.

Some similar parallels can be drawn to the quantitative teacher observation data as well. Teachers score highly on factors including 'Clear and coherent lessons in a supportive learning climate', 'Engaging students with assignments and activities', 'Positive classroom management', 'Purposive learning' and 'Quality questioning and feedback for students' from the ISTOF[4] instrument, and 'Supportive lesson climate', 'Proactive lesson management', 'Well organized lesson with clear objectives' and 'Environmental and teacher support' from the QoT[5] scales, as we discuss in the Chapter 4 (Day *et al.* 2008). Again, these mirror the emphases of the pupil questionnaire factors, despite different wording (e.g. factors are framed in terms of 'supportive' climate or environment in the teacher observation data and 'teacher support' in the pupil questionnaire data, but these clearly refer to similar if not identical constructs).

This implies that pupils and teachers share some similar understandings of what constitutes key features of effective teaching and learning.

Summary

On the surface, the findings presented in this chapter offer a starting point for understanding effective classroom practice from pupils' perspectives. They also demonstrate, as discussed above, that pupils' ideas about teaching and learning are not so far removed from those of their teachers.

The qualitative data in particular also demonstrates pupils' ability to conceive of and articulate considerably complex concepts (e.g. engagement and involvement) and to reflect on how these relate to, and play out in, their own learning.

In relation to policy and practice, both the findings and the methods outlined in this chapter have the potential to inform and influence what teachers and schools do, and how effective practice is understood. First of all, teachers, principals and policy-makers might reasonably use the themes and factors presented here to

THE IMPACT OF EFFECTIVE PRACTICE: LEARNING FROM STUDENT VOICES **127**

guide teacher professional development or to reflect on current practice. This was, in fact, a feature of the study itself, as pupil feedback was aggregated at the class level and shared with participating teachers (Day *et al.* 2008).

Alternatively, the methods of data collection implemented for the purposes of this study might also be used, albeit on a smaller scale, by teachers or schools wishing to gain insight into the views of their own pupils. The caveat, in this case, is that pupils might respond differently to discussing the same topics or responding to the same items if they know the results will be viewed by authority figures from the school community rather than researchers. It is here that purposes and confidentiality are important features that may encourage pupils to be honest in their reporting and comments.

Ultimately, if pupil views are seen to align with, as well as add insight to, teacher data, this suggests that perhaps children's input deserves to be more systematically included in any discussion of teacher effectiveness, whether it is rooted in research or practice, and supports the arguments for incorporating their perspectives and voice into research on schools and teaching.

Notes

1. The Variations in Teachers' Work, Lives and Effectiveness project (2001–5).
2. The OECD's Programme for International Student Assessment.
3. The Resourcing and Pupil Attainment Study.
4. ISTOF is the abbreviation for International System for Teacher Observation and Feedback.
5. QoT is the abbreviation for Quality of Teaching.

References

Arnot, M., McIntyre, D., Pedder, D. and Reay, D. (2004) *Consultation in the Classroom: Developing Dialogue About Teaching and Learning.* Cambridge: Pearson Publishing.
Bandura, A. (1977) Self-efficacy: toward a unifying theory of behavioral change, *Psychological Review*, 84(2): 191–215.
Bandura, A. (1995) *Self-efficacy in Changing Societies.* Cambridge: Cambridge University Press.
Bandura, A. (1997) *Self-efficacy: The Exercise of Control.* New York: W.H. Freeman.
Bazeley, P. and Jackson, K. (2013) *Qualitative Data Analysis with NVivo.* London: Sage.
BERA (British Educational Research Association) (2011) *Revised Ethical Guidelines for Educational research,* London: BERA, www.bera.ac.uk/publications/Ethical%20 Guidelines.
Blackman, S. (2011) Using pupil perspective research to inform teacher pedagogy: what Caribbean pupils with dyslexia say about teaching and learning, *Journal of Research in Special Educational Needs*, 11(3): 178–85.
Bland, D. and Atweh, B. (2007) Students as researchers: engaging students' voices in PAR, *Educational Action Research*, 15(3): 337–49.

Byrnes, L.J. and Rickards, F.W. (2011) Listening to the voices of students with disabilities: can such voices inform practice? *Australasian Journal of Special Education*, 35(01): 25–34.

Cefai, C and Cooper, P. (2010) Students without voices: the unheard accounts of secondary school students with social, emotional and behaviour difficulties, *European Journal of Special Needs Education*, 25(2): 183–98.

Christensen, P. and James, A. (2008) R*esearch with Children: Perspectives and Practices*, 2nd edn. Abingdon: Routledge.

Christidou, V. (2011) Interests, attitudes and images related to science: combining students' voices with the voices of school science, teachers, and popular science, *International Journal of Environmental and Science Education*, 6(2): 141–59.

Cooper, P. and McIntyre, D. (1996) *Effective Teaching and Learning: Teachers' and Students' Perspectives*. Maidenhead: Open University Press.

CRC (Committee on the Rights of the Child) (1995) *Concluding Observations of the Committee on the Rights of the Child: United Kingdom of Great Britain and Northern Ireland*, CRC/C/15/Add.34 (15 January). Geneva: United Nations, ny.un.org/doc/UNDOC/GEN/G95/153/97/PDF/G9515397.pdf?OpenElement.

CRC (Committee on the Rights of the Child) (2002) *Concluding Observations of the Committee on the Rights of the Child: United Kingdom of Great Britain and Northern Ireland*, CRC/C/15/Add.188 (9 October). Geneva: United Nations, http://daccess-dds-ny.un.org/doc/UNDOC/GEN/G02/453/81/PDF/G0245381.pdf?OpenElement.

Cremin, H., Mason, C. and Busher, H. (2010) Problematising pupil voice using visual methods: findings from a study of engaged and disaffected pupils in an urban secondary school, *British Educational Research* Journal, 37(4): 585–603.

Cullingford, C. (2006) Children's own vision of schooling, *Education*, 3–13, 34(3): 211–21.

Davies, L., Williams, C. and Yamashita, H. (2006) *Inspiring Schools: Impact and Outcomes*. London: Esme Fairburn Foundation & Carnegie UK Trust.

Davies, P.M. (2011) Student participation in school ICT policy-making: a case of students as researchers, *Management in Education*, 25(2): 71–7.

Day, C., Sammons, P., Kington, A., Regan, E., Gunraj, J. and Towle, J. (2007a) *Effective Classroom Practice: A Mixed Methods Study of Influences and Outcomes: Interim Report Submitted to the ESRC*. Swindon: ESRC.

Day, C., Sammons, P., Stobart, G., Kington, A. and Gu, Q. (2007b) *Teachers Matter: Connecting work, Lives and Effectiveness*. Maidenhead: Open University Press.

Day, C., Sammons, P., Kington, A., Regan, E., Ko, J., Brown, E. and Robertson, D. (2008) *Effective Classroom Practice: A Mixed-methods Study of Influences and Outcomes: Full Research Report*, ESRC End of award report. Swindon: ESRC, doi:RES-000-23-1564.

ESRC (Economic and Social Research Council) (2013) *Consulting students about teaching and learning: process, impacts and outcomes*. Research catalogue, retrieved 15 December 2013, from www.esrc.ac.uk/my-esrc/grants/L139251006/read/outputs/Date/25/1.

Farrell, A. (2005) *Ethical Research with Children*. Maidenhead: Open University Press.

Fielding, M. and Bragg, S. (2003) *Students as Researchers: Making a Difference*. Cambridge: Pearson Publishing.

Flutter, J. (2007) Teacher development and pupil voice, *The Curriculum Journal*, 18(3): 343–54.

Gilleece, L. and Cosgrove, J. (2012) Student civic participation in school: what makes a difference in Ireland? *Education, Citizenship and Social Justice,* 7(3): 225–39.

Glaser, B.G. (1992) *Basics of Grounded Theory Analysis: Emergence vs. Forcing.* Mill Valley, CA: Sociology Press.

Gray, J. and McLellan, R. (2006) A matter of attitude? Developing a profile of boys' and girls' responses to primary schooling, *Gender and Education,* 18(6): 651–72.

Habermas, J. (1984) *The Theory of Communicative Action.* Boston, MA: Beacon Press.

Halsey, K., Murfield, J., Harland, J.L., Lord, P. and National Foundation for Education Research (2006) *The Voice of Young People: An Engine for Improvement? Scoping the Evidence.* Reading: CFBT Education Trust, www.nfer.ac.uk/nfer/publications/VIM01/VIM01.pdf.

Hannam, D. (2004) *Listening Up: Hearing What Students Have to Say About Learning.* London: QCA.

Hopkins, E. (2008) Work-related learning: hearing students' voices, *Educational Action Research,* 16(2): 209–19.

Hopkins, E. (2010) Classroom conditions for effective learning: hearing the voice of Key Stage 3 pupil, *Improving Schools,* 13(1): 39–53.

Kington, A., Sammons, P., Day, C. and Regan, E. (2011) Stories and statistics: describing a mixed methods study of effective classroom practice, *Journal of Mixed Methods Research,* 5(2): 103–5.

Lee, C. and Johnston-Wilder, S. (2013) Learning mathematics – letting the pupils have their say, *Educational Studies in Mathematics,* 83(2): 163–80.

Levačić, R. (2005) *Estimating the Relationship Between School Resources and Pupil Attainment at Key Stage 3.* Nottingham: DfES Publications.

Lord, P. and Jones, M. (2006) *Pupils' Experiences and Perspectives of the National Curriculum and Assessment.* Slough: NFER.

MacBeath, J., Demetriou, H., Ruddock, J. and Myers, K. (2003) *Consulting Pupils: A Toolkit for Teachers.* Cambridge: Pearson Publishing.

Mcintyre, D., Pedder, D. and Ruddock, J. (2005) Pupil voice: comfortable and uncomfortable learnings for teachers, *Research Papers in Education,* 20(2): 149–68.

McNaught, C., Ng, S.S.W. and Chow, H. (2011) Literacies in the humanities: the student voice, *Higher Education Research & Development,* 31(2): 139–54.

Moran, P. and Murphy, M. (2012) Habermas, pupil voice, rationalism, and their meeting with Lacan's Objet Petit A, *Studies in Philosophy and Education,* 31(2): 171–81.

Morgan, B. (2011) Consulting pupils about classroom teaching and learning: policy, practice and response in one school, *Research Papers in Education,* 26(4): 445–67.

Munn, P. and Lloyd, G. (2005) Exclusion and excluded pupils, *British Educational Research Journal,* 31(2): 205–21.

OECD (Organization for Economic Cooperation and Development) (2005) *PISA 2003 Data Analysis Manual.* Paris: OECD Publishing, doi:10.1787/9789264010666-en.

Ofsted (Office for Standards in Education) (2005) *Pupils' satisfaction with their school.* London. Retrieved from www.ofsted.gov.uk/assets/3944.pdf.

Reid, K., Challoner, C., Lancett, A., Jones, G., Rhysiart, G.A. and Challoner, S. (2010) The views of primary pupils on school attendance at Key Stage 2 in Wales, *Educational Studies,* 36(5): 465–79.

Roberts, A. and Nash, J. (2009) Enabling students to participate in school improvement through a students as researchers programme, *Improving Schools,* 12(2): 174–87.

Robertson, D., Sammons, P., Kington, A., Day, C., Regan, E. and Gunraj, J. (2007) *Analysing Pupil Attitudes to Teaching and Learning: An ECP Working Paper*. Nottingham: ESRC, University of Nottingham, doi:ECP/01.

Robinson, C. and Taylor, C. (2007) Theorizing student voice: values and perspectives, *Improving Schools*, 10(1): 5–17.

Rudduck, J., Chaplain, R. and Wallace, G. (1996) *School Improvement: What Can Pupils Tell Us?* London: David Fulton.

Rudduck, J. and Flutter, J. (2004) *How to Improve Your School: Giving Pupils a Voice*. London: Continuum.

Ryan, D. (2009) Pupils' views on inclusion: 'inclusion is more than a place': exploring pupil views and voice in Belfast schools through visual narrative, *British Journal of Special Education*, 36(2): 77–84.

Seiler, G. (2013) Reconstructing science curricula through student voice and choice, *Education and Urban Society*, 45(3): 362–84.

UN General Assembly (1989) *Resolution Adopted by the General Assembly: Convention on the Rights of the Child*. Geneva: United Nations, retrieved 15 December 2013 from www.ohchr.org/EN/ProfessionalInterest/Pages/CRC.aspxhttp://www.ohchr.org/EN/ProfessionalInterest/Pages/CRC.aspx.

Wilson, H. and Mant, J. (2011) What makes an exemplary teacher of science? The pupils' perspective, *School Science Review*, 93(342): 121–5.

Wright, K. (2008) Researching the views of pupils with multiple and complex needs. Is it worth doing and whose interests are served by it? *Support for Learning*, 23(1): 32–40.

PART 3

7 Career phase and teacher effectiveness

Introduction

In Part 1 of this volume we presented three key components of the discussion of effective teaching practice: the changing demands facing classroom practitioners; a review of the research on teacher effectiveness; and finally the methods employed to describe, analyse and explain the variation in classroom behaviours and practices of effective teachers while considering different school contexts, professional life phases and personal contexts in the life and work of teachers.

In Part 2 we focused strongly on the evidence relating to teachers and students, and how their experience of classroom life and effective practice can be influenced by a range of factors. The data gathered via a number of qualitative and quantitative measures were combined in each chapter and used to illustrate key characteristics of effective teachers and their teaching and how, as a result, students view their schooling. But what does this mean for effective practitioners? We know that these teachers are creative educators and represent innovation by their deviation from didactics and by the academic performance of their students. The analytical approaches resulted in the identification of a number of classroom practices that, used innovatively, made a substantial contribution to the effectiveness of teachers in the sample. However, data indicates that there was also a connection between these various pedagogical and relationship factors which defined effective practice.

In Part 3, the focus shifts towards an examination of an integrated analysis centred around two specific lenses: career phase and professional identity. In this chapter we focus upon the ways in which the practices of effective teachers vary across a career and how their career phases impact on the professional and emotional contexts of effective teaching. We suggest that teacher career phase is an important determinant, and plays a crucial part in influencing teachers' effective classroom practice. In addition, we also return to the concept identified in Chapter 4, of effective and highly effective teachers, to establish the importance of professional and personal influences. The chapter is structured into three key sections.

First, the conceptualization of career phase and the ways in which effective/highly effective teachers' practice varies within this framework are described. Second, we explore the variation in core aspects of effective teaching using this lens, illustrating the characteristics of early-, mid- and late-career phase. Last, the personal and emotional contexts of effective/highly effective teachers are presented, complete with brief profiles of effective/highly effective teachers in each career phase.

Conceptualizing career phase

Studies on teacher experience focusing on changes during the entire teaching career are scarce. Most studies on teacher development focus on short time spans such as pre-service teacher education (Bennett and Carré 1993; Price 2001; Conway and Clark 2003) or the beginning of the teaching career (Zeichner and Tabachnick 1985; So and Watkins 2005; Woolfolk Hoy and Burke Spero 2005). Other studies explore differences between novice and expert teachers (Meyer 2004; Kington 2012) or veteran teachers (Day and Gu 2009).

Although these studies were not designed to describe changes over time, they implicitly start from the assumption that becoming an expert teacher follows some kind of developmental process (Carter et al. 1988; Castejou and Martinez 2001; Jay 2002). There have been studies, notably Sikes et al. (1985), that have viewed teachers' career patterns from the perspective of age ranges. Sikes et al. argue that 'teachers are first and foremost people, and like everyone else they are subject to changes which are associated with ageing, and how the process is viewed in the society' (p. 56). However, what is overlooked to an extent are factors independent of age and, therefore, studies with a singular focus can be limited in their ability to explain the complexity of teacher professional life development.

Another approach used in the study of teacher development suggests phases which a teacher experiences over the course of a career. The model suggested by Super (1957) essentially posits four identifiable stages: exploration, establishment, maintenance and disengagement. Although related to sequential life cycle theories (e.g. Erikson 1964), Super and others have emphasized strongly that individuals do not proceed through the phases in a linear manner. Not only is there considerable variation in the timing of the stages, individuals can miss stages, revert to 'earlier' stages or remain in a single stage during a career (Huberman 1989; Super 1990; Smart and Peterson 1997). It follows that the term 'stage' may not be consistent with recent theoretical conceptualizations.

Integrating Super's (1957) model with his own, Huberman (1989) argued for a career stage model specifically for teachers' professional work, and his study on the lives of Swiss secondary school teachers has been widely cited for its development of a non-linear, empirically based schematic model of a five-phase teaching career cycle (career entry, stabilization, experimentation, conservatism, disengagement). One major contribution of Huberman's research was his identification that 'a large part of development is neither externally programmed nor personally engineered but rather discontinuous' (Huberman 1993: 195). Huberman asserts that teachers' professional career journeys are 'not adequately linear, predictable or identical' (1993: 264).

Career phase as an analytical lens

Since Huberman's seminal work in this area, a number of empirical studies focusing on teaching during the professional careers of teachers have been conducted (Henke *et al.* 2000; Pigge and Marso 2000; Wilhelm *et al.* 2000; Brown 2001; Craig 2001; Stinebrickner 2001; Manuel, 2003; Agee 2004; Mulholland and Wallace 2005; Verjovsky and Waldegg, 2005). However, there are two limitations to these studies; first, that they are largely based on self-reports of teachers; and second, none of these studies included a focus on change in practice based on the perceptions of students.

In a study by Day *et al.* (2007), the impact of the interaction between professional and personal contexts on teachers' career development, as well as the possibility of distinctive key influences relevant to teachers in different phases of their careers were considered. In this study, teachers' careers were divided into six phases[1] based upon an extensive review of previous studies on teachers' careers and professional development. This analysis interpreted teachers' experiences, identities and professional trajectories in light of a wide range of influences relating to both their professional lives and personal worlds. The evidence from this investigation into teachers' work and lives revealed that, for the majority of teachers, their original call to teaching was articulated as linked to the opportunity to work with children, and that those students remained the main source of their motivation and commitment. The research also found that teachers derive commitment and resilience to sustain such commitment from differing sources in different contexts and in different phases of their professional and personal lives. Their functional positions/role-related career advancement only comprises part of these. 'Professional life phase' refers to the number of years that a teacher has been teaching. The notion of teachers' professional lives, rather than careers, therefore, enabled an understanding of the complex factors which influence teachers in different phases of their work and how these affected their commitment.

As we discussed in Chapter 3, these professional life phases were also utilized within the Effective Classroom Practice (ECP) study. The original six professional life phases (detailed in Day *et al.* 2007) are:

1   Professional life phase 0–3 – commitment: support and challenge.
2   Professional life phase 4–7 – identity and efficacy in classroom.
3   Professional life phase 8–15 – managing changes in role and identity: growing tensions and transitions.
4   Professional life phase 16–23 – work-life tensions: challenges to motivation and commitment.
5   Professional life phase 24–30 – challenges to sustaining motivation.
6   Professional life phase 31+ – sustaining/declining motivation, ability to cope with change, looking to retire.

However, when undertaking the integrated analyses, it became evident that the key differences between, and influences upon, effective practitioners were more clearly identifiable when examined in relation to the early, mid and late stages of a career. Therefore, the six phases were conflated into three broad career phases (3–7 years, 8–23 years, 24+ years)[2] to better represent the sample of teachers involved in the study while retaining the characteristics of the original phases. The preliminary conceptual framework for understanding teacher-pupil relationships on the basis of career phase was elaborated and grounded in empirical data. These findings provide a baseline to analyse changes of individual teachers during their career and can help diagnose special situations of individual teachers at a given point in their career or regarding their development in a certain period.

The analysis of early-, mid- and late-career phases revealed important influences on teachers' work, lives and effectiveness. Understanding the variations in the practices of effective teachers across a career has important implications for understanding the mediating factors on both perceived and relational effectiveness.

Although there were perceptions of relationships that were common across all three phases, there also appears to be a significant developmental transition occurring for teachers in the early- and mid-career phases and those in the late-career phase. For example, early-career teachers felt that the relationships with their pupils were central to their motivation and commitment, sense of self-efficacy and job satisfaction, while the mid-career teachers were generally more positive about pupil behaviour than other phases. Both the mid- and late-career phases had over half the teachers stating that interactions and expectations influenced their relationships in a positive way, whereas the early-career teachers were more likely to have a problem with pupil behaviour. On the basis of these data, there are three generalizations that can be made regarding variations in teacher-pupil relationships across a career.

Early-career phase: motivated, committed and self-efficacious

Just under one-fifth (23 per cent, N = 19) of teachers were in this phase (see Figure 7.1), with over half coming from primary schools and the majority coming from schools defined as FSM 1 and 2. The dominant characteristics of this group of teachers included being highly motivated, committed and self-efficacious.

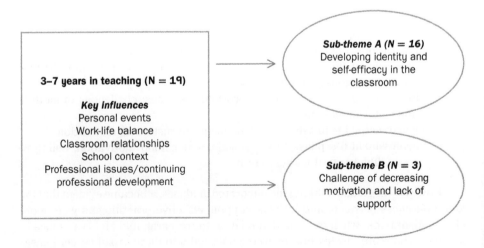

Figure 7.1 Early-career phase.

The majority of teachers in this phase of their career were identified as being in sub-theme A. However, the three primary teachers who were experiencing feelings of demotivation and lack of support from colleagues were still performing effectively according to their head teachers and saw themselves as confident professionals.

In this early phase, teachers were concerned about the quality of the personal relationships they established with pupils, being accepted by pupils, and with understanding their needs. As part of this, they focused on qualities which facilitated empathy with pupils, as they reported the value of knowing and being familiar with pupils and understanding their backgrounds. In this sense, the findings confirm the view that teachers in the beginning phase (Huberman 1993) benefited from a combination of influences that were mostly positive. That said, teachers in this group reported the negative impact of poor pupil behaviour on their work as a teacher.

Peter, a Year 9 English teacher, has just started his career and is teaching in a challenging school. His pupils have very positive views of him. A high level of teacher interaction with the pupils was observed as was a high level of pupil response. Peter used scaffolding techniques, pupil ideas and opinions, and praise with the whole class and individual students. The students were highly engaged by the tasks set for them and Peter monitored progress throughout the lesson. He focused on interactions with students, relationships in the classroom, use of humour and discipline during the lesson. Student behaviour was good and the teacher-pupil relationships were positive. The learning objectives were displayed and discussed at the start of the lesson.

Teachers in the latter part of this career phase demonstrated a primary concern over their confidence and feelings of having effective relationships with pupils, which is only partly in accord with Huberman's findings that teachers with four to six years of career experience were found to be going through a phase of 'stabilization, consolidation of a pedagogical repertoire' (1993: 13). In contrast with the teachers with zero to three years of experience, there were more frequent references made by teachers to heavy workload which was seen as reducing the time they had to spend with pupils. In line with Day *et al.*'s (2007) study, many of these teachers reported that they had benefited from leadership support which helped to reduce the impact of workload, although there were a small number who had experienced a lack of support from the school leadership. This indicates that, even at this early stage, school leaders are a key mediating influence on the relationships between teachers and pupils. If we revisit Julia, an effective primary practitioner showcased in Chapter 5, the observational field note data illustrates the highly effective nature of her classroom practice. Like other teachers in her career phase, she demonstrates the centrality of positive teacher-pupil relationships to her motivation, commitment and self-efficacy as a teacher.

A Year 6 lesson on Victorian coal mining

In her lesson on Victorian coal mining, exploring the life of child coal-miner Lottie, Julia is able to have some fun while maintaining firm voice and demeanour. The class seating is arranged in rows, just for today's lesson, to show how the Victorian classroom was arranged.

Julia is firm in her voice and expectations. She also is very aware of pupils' needs and interacts one-to-one with many throughout the lesson . . . 'You've got one minute to write the LO down. Please take care with your hand-writing. I don't want to see any silly work like yesterday' . . . Julia circulates the tables giving individual learning and instruction (ILI). 'Year 6, you were all working quietly, now I can hear some chat.' Julia corrects students and asks them to work quietly to get at least five sentences written . . . Julia and the teaching assistant bring out the model of a tunnel which is 26 inches in diameter. The teacher asks if anyone wants to see if they are small enough to do Lottie's job . . . Julia asks Samuel to see if he can crawl through the tunnel. She then asks a taller a boy called Matthew if he can fit through . . . The teacher continues reading dramatically. She gets 'Lottie' to stand up and act out the role. She chooses another student to play the housekeeper and she then plays the role enthusiastically.

(Field notes, R1)

Mid-career phase: effective, committed, challenges to motivation

This second phase was the largest group (N = 35) and was predominantly female (82 per cent). The size of the schools in which this group of teachers worked was varied but they were more likely to be in FSM 3 schools, which is reflected in the key influences on this phase (see Figure 7.2).

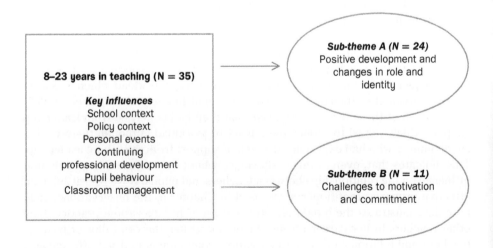

Figure 7.2 Mid-career phase.

We found that most teachers in this phase were highly committed and saw themselves as effective. They welcomed the developments and changes in their roles and the impact that these had on their professional identity. A third of these teachers (31 per cent, $N = 11$) were identified as experiencing challenges to their motivation and commitment, but this seemed to be largely due to events in their personal lives such as bereavement, becoming a carer or divorce.

For mid-career teachers, the intensity and strength of the relationship depended on the teacher's willingness to exhibit genuine feelings to the pupils rather than play a role. The teachers who felt more successful in the development of their relationships were those who acknowledged and accepted the fact that, although the relationship could be reciprocal, it was unequal and this inequity should not be abused within the classroom environment. This encouraged a continuous negotiation of the relationship which was achieved by constant discussion with pupils which, in turn, allowed the discovery of boundaries while maintaining authority and influence.

George

George is in his mid-career stage, and has a high level of motivation and commitment. He teaches in a challenging school and his identity is in balance. During his lessons, there was a high level of teacher interaction and a focus on his use of humour. George displayed the learning objectives at the beginning of the lesson, used scaffolding techniques, and used pupil ideas and opinions. There was a high level of pupil engagement and George experienced good teacher-pupil relationships.

Positive pupil-teacher relationships for this group of teachers were also characterized by low levels of behavioural problems and high levels of closeness, supporting children's motivation to explore, as well as their growing ability to regulate social, emotional and cognitive skills (Kutnick and Kington 2005). This behaviour was grounded in the care and consistency demonstrated over a period of time, in which a teacher's concern was reflected in response to an individual pupil and the actions they were prepared to take in order to support and develop the child and their relationship.

Huberman (1993: 7) discusses a phase of experimentation and diversification after the 'stabilization'/'pedagogical consolidation' phase. He posits that teachers, with between seven and 25 years' experience, 'having made an initial tour of duty in the classroom' set off in search of new challenges and new stimulations (1993: 8). For the mid-career teachers in this study, these challenges were in the form of promotion and additional responsibilities (Day et al. 2007) which had started to play a significant role in the relationships developed with individual pupils. Promotion at this career phase supports research by Hilsum and Start (1974) who noted that the first promotion was usually achieved for primary teachers after seven years, and Maclean (1992) who found that the average number of years for promotion was 11 years. However, in this study (and in common with the early-career teachers), the challenge of new roles was combined with excessive paperwork and heavy workload which were seen as key hindrances to their relationships in the classroom. In contrast to the earlier phase, school leadership was not considered a supportive factor.

Revisiting Richard from Chapter 5, we see how a mid-career phase teacher manages his classroom climate and pupil behaviour in his lessons. Like other mid-career teachers he was positive about pupil behaviour and classroom management.

A Year 2 lesson on instructional writing

This lesson is a very creative lesson as Richard combines humour to teach the students instructional writing. The students must use their imagination to create a humorous set of instructions for making a Halloween sandwich. Richard needed only to remind pupils of the behaviour that was expected of them. 'Very calm, warm teacher with high expectations about behaviour, which he constantly reminds the students about in a non-confrontational manner.' . . . The teacher counts down from five to one; 'shush', and when he gets quietness he says 'noses' and the students quieten down and look towards him . . . The teacher uses a tambourine to gain attention and then counts down from five . . . *Whole-group Instruction:* The teacher claps his hands and tells the class that there is too much noise and that he can't do the thinking that he wants to do. He then asks the students to do their work without voices. The students continue with their work up a whisper . . . *Small-group instruction:* The teacher takes another group to the mat for instructions by reviewing previous work. One student is very slow to come to the carpet and the teacher corrects her behaviour in a quiet way by saying, 'Just put that on the table and come here now please, nothing will happen to you while you are here.' The teacher reads some instructions from the students' work and guides this group to add some adjectives to spell out their instructions. For example, slimy worms, smidgy brains etc. . . . Whole-group instruction: The teacher instructs the class to colour in the telling words in their instructions when they have completed them. He then gives differentiated instructions: 'If you are in these three tables, colour the word which is adding more detail' . . . He then tells the students that he is going to show them the instructions that he has written. The instructions that he has written are for making a sandwich for Halloween . . . For example; one of the instructions says, 'Spread a little gunpowder on one slice of bread'. He uses humour. The students laugh at the last instruction which reads, 'Eat your sandwich carefully and get ready to take off' . . . Richard uses humour to give further instructions and uses a funny voice to get the students to think about what they could put into their own Halloween sandwich . . . Richard speaks with one student and says: 'I hope I'm not going to be sick reading your sandwich.' Teacher-pupil interaction is humorous and the student just shakes her head and smiles.

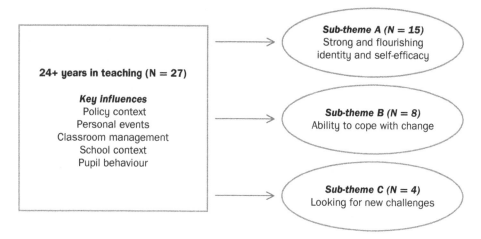

Figure 7.3 Late-career phase.

Late-career phase: strong identity, efficacy and ability to cope with change

In the third phase (N = 27), over half (56 per cent, N = 15) of the teachers worked in secondary schools. While their motivation levels generally remained high, they were also very positive about change, especially with regard to policy and leadership (see Figure 7.3).

Of the 27 teachers in this phase, nearly three-quarters (72 per cent) taught in socially disadvantaged schools (FSM 3 and 4). These teachers were still highly motivated, committed and self-efficacious, and had a strong sense of identity.

Marion

Marion is in the later stages of her career and works in a challenging school. She has managed to maintain a high level of commitment, and her identity is in balance. Her pupils have very positive views of her. In the lessons observed, there was a high level of teacher interaction with the pupils and a high level of pupil response. Marion used scaffolding techniques, used pupil ideas and opinions, and praised students, both as individuals and as a whole class, when they achieved academically. She displayed the learning objectives at the beginning of the lesson and conducted a plenary at the end of the lesson. Marion was very focused on the interactions in the classroom and relationships with pupils. Pupil behaviour was good, relationships were positive and the pupils were highly engaged in the tasks.

Teaching was seen by late-career teachers as an interrelated whole. By this phase, teachers appeared to have replaced the early-career phase view of pupils 'as people' with a view of pupils 'as learners', and were more likely to empathize with their pupils' needs and efforts in terms of their academic performance and desired academic outcomes. For these teachers, development of relationships was perceived to be based on interconnections between patterns of interaction and other elements. Moreover, positive interactions, behaviours, influences and expectations developed through familiarization, shared construction and knowledge of the relationship. However, this did not guarantee that a 'good' relationship would develop; it seemed that teachers needed to see, hear and interact with pupils sufficiently often in order to recognize the aspects of them that would contribute to a sustained relationship. This supports findings by Kington (2005, 2009) that suggest that if the teacher is unable to communicate with pupils frequently, and considers there to be differences between the self and the other (themselves and the pupil), the means for establishing a common activity may be hindered. Diane's teaching cameo shows how, as a late-career phase teacher, she is positive regarding her classroom relationships and pupil behaviour. Diane is a Year 6 teacher who teaches in a medium-sized school that has a high proportion of FMS (4). She is in the late stages of her teaching career, having been teaching for over 25 years.

Diane's Year 6 lesson on connectives

Diane asks questions throughout the lesson to elicit examples of connectives but also to ascertain the students' views on the story and their understanding of terminology. She is a very calm teacher in an extremely busy classroom of students of varying levels of engagement. She distributes lots of praise for behaviour and work, and values the contributions of the children in her lessons. She maintains a disciplined classroom by employing lots of changes in activity in the lesson and her use of humour. She deals with one 'problem' student in a very interesting way in the first lesson observed.

[The student] reads her a story and Diane stands beside her and looks at her work as she reads. Diane tells [the student] that that was the best work that she has ever done. She gives [the student] lots of praise and tells her that she will never get away with doing just a little bit of work ever again . . . Diane corrects [the student] for talking out of turn again and says: 'Only one voice please' . . . A lot of the students are whispering, they then quieten down when the teacher begins to speak . . . Diane asks Alicia to move to a chair closer to the screen so that she stops talking with another group of students. She is given a chair to sit on away from the other students.

Classroom management in Diane's case is displayed when the students show respect for her authority by ceasing their chatter when she begins to speak, the students call on her by first name, and the teacher can use humour in the classroom and sustain pupil engagement. The pupils in her classes respond well to her humour.

The opportunity and time children had to interact with the teacher was an important factor in relation to late-career phase teachers' development of relationships. Limited positive interactions and controlled impositions by the teacher (proximity or interruptions of interactions) sometimes diminished the shared opportunities with the teacher and opportunities to experience reciprocity in their relationship. Conversely, teachers perceived that pupils whose development led to an increased number of social encounters enjoyed more opportunities to learn about others and about relationships. This group also acknowledged a lesser use of proximity which may suggest a greater confidence in relationship development based on experience as a practitioner.

In common with the mid-career teachers, external policies and initiatives continued to demonstrate a strong negative impact on teachers' relationships with pupils. Although they were able to manage it, deteriorating pupil behaviour was a key influence on teachers in this cohort. As a consequence, they were more likely to be facing challenges to sustaining positive relationships with individual pupils. However, teachers reported that pupils' progress and positive teacher-pupil relationships were the main source of job satisfaction in this phase. Huberman (1993) maintains that there is a phase of 'disengagement' towards the end of teachers' careers. However, this was not confirmed by the teachers in this study who reported a continued commitment to maintain positive relationships and engage fully with pupils.

The preliminary conceptual framework for understanding teacher-pupil relationships on the basis of career phase was elaborated and grounded in empirical data. These findings provide a baseline to analyse changes of individual teachers during their career and can help diagnose special situations of individual teachers at a given point in their career or regarding their development in a certain period.

Career phase and effective classroom practices

Having outlined each of the career phases, we wanted to interrogate the integrated data set against the core characteristics (Chapters 4, 5 and 6) such as relationships, praise, creativity and expectations, as well as the personal factors associated with effective practice (see Chapter 5), such as motivation, commitment and well-being. Here we look at each of these characteristics and factors and consider the nuanced differences of each within the different career phases.

Core aspects of effective classroom practice

Teacher-student relationships

The ability to build and sustain good relationships with students was an issue that emerged from the vast majority (96 per cent, N = 78) of teachers across all three phases as contributing to their effectiveness. A number of factors influenced this – for example, getting to know the students well, establishing good rapport and interaction, using humour, listening to what the students had to say and communicating effectively with them.

In their early career, teachers reported a concern about the quality of the relationships established with students. They were concerned with being accepted by students and with understanding them:

> It's all about building a relationship with them and getting to know them and them getting to know you . . . They like to know about you as well, you know what I mean, that you've got a life and things like that.
>
> (Early-career teacher)

While developing these relationships, early-career teachers highlighted the need for them to be based on fairness and consistency, and offered in a supportive and caring way: 'It's important to me that the children know they can come to me for support or if they need to talk. I don't want them to think of me as just the teacher' (early-career teacher). A great many mid-career teachers were also concerned about discipline, yet at the same time understood that too much discipline could undermine the quality of the relationships.

> It is so important to start off with discipline and boundaries so that they know what is expected from them in terms of behaviour. You have to be careful not to go over the top though or else they think it's a joke and don't listen. There is a very fine line between good and bad discipline.
>
> (Mid-career teacher)

However, by the mid-career phase, teachers were starting to make numerous observations about the personal needs and circumstances of students, and express a desire to help them.

> I differentiate my approaches to students a lot more now than I did. I know all about each child and tailor the way I teach them all. It takes longer to plan that way, but by now I can take some of what I was having to plan for granted and focus on the individual needs a bit more.
>
> (Mid-career teacher)

This study found that in almost 80 per cent of the mid-career teachers, there were signs of a conflict between maintaining this 'individual' approach and meeting instructional and management concerns: 'It can get very difficult trying to juggle the individual needs of pupils and the overall management of the class, but you're expected to do it after a while' (mid-career teacher). As with early-career teachers, this included the need for teacher-pupil relationships to be based on fairness, consistency and support: 'I think if you are there for them and they know they can go to you for support, and that you will be consistent, that is the thing' (mid-career teacher). The data showed that the mid- and late-career teachers gave more time to developing individual relationships with students, and focused upon building self-esteem, engendering trust and maintaining respect.

> What you have to make sure is that every child in that class believes that you've been talking to them, and that you are with them and not anyone else. It's to do with moving around the room, it's to do with eye contact, it's to do with calling out names, trying to get as many people as you can answering questions.
>
> (Late-career teacher)

By the late-career phase, many teachers appeared to have similarly replaced the early-career view of students as 'people' with a view of students as learners. Late-career teachers were also more likely to empathize with their students' needs and efforts in terms of their academic performance and desired academic outcomes:

'I think I see a greater need for the children to achieve academically now. I am very focused on getting them through school as successfully as possible in terms of outcomes' (late-career teacher).

Praise and feedback to students

Many of the effective teachers (91 per cent, N = 74) identified praise and feedback as a means of building relationships with students. Early-career teachers also defined this factor as one that supported learning targets or objectives, assessment for learning and other forms of informal assessment.

> There has to be clear feedback to students otherwise they won't be able to improve and it's another way of building a rapport with them. If you make sure good work is acknowledged then it does make them feel special and as if they can trust you.
>
> (Early-career teacher)

Mid-career teachers talked about the importance of responding to and acknowledging that some children needed more public praise while others preferred feedback to be more private:

> I have some students that need praise a lot and others who just don't like any feedback in front of the rest of the class. So, in terms of comments, it's all done when marking their books, or during more private discussions about their work.
>
> (Mid-career teacher)

Examination of the data showed that the late-career teachers, like their early- and mid-career colleagues, used praise extensively to promote positive relationships, develop rapport and establish boundaries. In addition, praise offered opportunities to reflect, self-evaluate and engage in dialogue about learning:

> My skill is to walk around the room, listen to their questions and then make a decision that they haven't actually understood this fully and I might stop the group and talk to the group again or it might be just one or two of them need a little bit of a hint.
>
> (Late-career teacher)

This group of teachers were clearly trying to use this technique to help students recognize their own improvements, giving them additional confidence, and influencing their own learning.

Teacher expectations of students

All primary and secondary teachers in the study, regardless of level of career phase, reported that high expectations which were clear, consistent and understood by students was an important issue that was closely related to their effectiveness. They also emphasized the value of establishing rules and boundaries at the outset.

Early-career teachers reported that they made behavioural expectations clear from the start of the year by formalizing them in a document or as part of a display: 'We had a talk at the beginning of the school year and went through all the rules for the class and what I was not willing to put up with, like shouting, and then they all signed it' (early-career teacher). They explained that they based their academic expectations around targets or learning objectives which provided a consistent way to demonstrate their aspirations for the class. This was also the approach taken by the majority of late-career teachers who said they differentiated expectations according students' abilities:

> You have to be so careful when developing expectations of students because it can either motivate or demotivate them. I try to keep everything connected to what they are capable of and not project a standardized set of outcomes on all of them.
>
> (Late-career teacher)

Further to this, late-career and mid-career teachers were also more relaxed about stating the behaviour expectations to the students. Maybe due to experience, they explained that there was an assumption that students knew how to behave and dealt with any problems if they occurred. However, they were clear that poor behaviour was not acceptable: 'It's a self-fulfilling prophecy, I think. If you act as if behaviour has to be good, then it usually is' (late-career teacher).

Mid-career teachers also focused on expectations that were individualized, consistent, sequential and differentiated, but tried to give students more control over their learning: 'It's having high expectations of children and making sure that you know the level of each child and can make sure that they know what the expectations are for the next level so they can aspire to them' (mid-career teacher).

Teacher creativity and flexibility

Unsurprisingly, early-career teachers were less confident about this issue than the other phases. However, they defined this factor in terms of the impact of creativity in lessons on pupil engagement:

> Students don't want you to stick to a set of lesson plans they want to know how things are relevant to them . . . and talking about real-life issues. It can be really scary, but when I have had a lesson like that, I always come out of it amazed by how engaged they all were.
>
> (Early-career teacher)

Mid-career teachers said that flexibility was vital and that often plans could change throughout a lesson depending on the needs or interests of the class. They also spoke about learning from mistakes and being reflective about their practice:

> Obviously there's a need to be flexible and depend on how things are going. But even if it's not, you know, doesn't quite go according to plan, at least then I'll learn from it and can change it to make it better for next time.
>
> (Mid-career teacher)

We found that the late-career teachers had a more consistent approach to balancing creativity, task-centred progress and fun with the maintenance of discipline:

> You've got to be flexible. You mustn't do, sort of the trainee teacher lesson which is 'I'm going to teach you this, and you're not going to put me off', if you're going to be a good teacher you have to be confident about taking off on a tangent, and if you are taking off on a tangent, know how far you take it and whether it's going to be useful or not.
>
> (Late-career teacher)

In terms of these core characteristics the practice of these effective teachers had similarities across all phases, and they were all clearly important regardless of the career phase. However, as we have seen, there were some interesting differences between teachers in each career phase in terms of how they interpret and enact these dimensions of their practice, and indeed how they build on and develop their practice throughout their career. The classroom practice of these teachers not only illustrated unique pedagogical practices, but also demonstrated innovation through modification and adaptation and was influenced by mediating factors. These factors included school leadership, school culture and support from colleagues, which were seen to be vital in the development and maintenance of effectiveness, especially with regard to pupil relationships and overall climate for learning.

While a small minority of teachers (11 per cent, N = 9) did not feel that they worked in a particularly supportive environment, most made positive comments. These included the supportive or caring nature of line managers and the senior leadership team, the encouragement given to engage in professional development, and the chance to improve their practice through feedback from observations. Primary teachers were more likely to discuss the provision of resources by the leadership as having an impact on effectiveness, with almost three quarters (71 per cent, N = 32) saying how classroom or teaching assistants had a very significant and positive impact on their effectiveness. This group of core factors confirmed findings from previous research, for example by McBer (2000) and Hattie and Timperley (2007). The findings also concur with those of Mortimore *et al.* (1988) who found that the key classroom factors of effective teachers included communication involving high levels of interaction, the facilitation of pupil responsibility and independence, providing challenging work, a positive classroom environment and high levels of praise and encouragement.

Personal factors

Motivation, commitment and job satisfaction

This theme emerged from the series of factors that revolved around a central idea that personal satisfaction may, or may not, be gained from undertaking the work of teaching. Maintaining high levels of motivation, job satisfaction and commitment to teaching was key to teachers across all phases. The majority of teachers (89 per cent, N = 72) talked about having a high level of motivation and commitment and enjoying the challenges and high standards expected from the job.

Early-career teachers defined this factor by discussing the pleasure attained from teaching a good lesson, pupil engagement and support from colleagues:

> I get very motivated by knowing that the class have enjoyed the lesson, have learned something, that's what I trained to do after all.
>
> (Early-career teacher)

> My colleagues keep me going – they keep me motivated, committed to my job and add to the satisfaction gained from the classroom.
>
> (Early-career teacher)

Teachers in the mid-career phase reported that they maintained a high level of motivation and commitment by seeking new challenges, and continuing professional development: 'I want to find out about new ways of doing things, so ICT courses have been great and I would like to do a masters degree soon' (mid-career teacher).

Whereas late-career teachers stated that seizing opportunities to be involved in a variety of activities in the school, and developing and sustaining positive relationships with colleagues, were the main influences on motivation and job satisfaction: 'I'm always looking out for something to be involved in – could be a course or a group. It keeps you known throughout the school as someone who'll get involved and you get to spend time with other teachers' (late-career teacher). This suggests that for teachers in all phases, satisfaction relating to work is an important aspect of their construct systems which helped to mitigate against negative influences on their work such as tiredness, pressure from external demands and managing different roles within the school.

Well-being

This factor centred on the idea that the participants were experiencing (or had felt in the past) feelings that constituted some form of threat to their physical or emotional well-being. Overall, the majority (90 per cent, N = 73) of teachers felt that their work and life were fairly balanced in spite of competing demands, although this fluctuated throughout the year. Feelings of well-being were enhanced for early-career teachers by freedom to make decisions in the classroom (which they had not experienced during training), opportunities for development and feeling a commitment to the community surrounding the school: 'I feel great and well-balanced, and hopeful for the future. It's a great feeling to have everything in front of you at last' (early-career teacher).

Although a higher proportion of the teachers in the early-career phase felt a positive sense of well-being, compared with the other two phases, the mid- and late-career teachers defined well-being in terms of being able to adopt strategies in order to help them manage workload and keep life in balance. As one teacher stated, 'I do what I need to do to get through each day and achieve everything I need to achieve' (mid-career teacher).

Feelings of self-efficacy

Bandura (1995) described self-efficacy as the individual's confidence in her/his ability to complete a specific task or behaviour successfully. Early-career teachers tended to define this as having enough confidence in their job to be able to cope with unexpected situations.

> When I started training, I didn't ever think I would feel confident enough to stand up in front of a class and now I do and have the added confidence to deal with things that happen that are not planned.
>
> (Early-career teacher)

Mid-career teachers thought that it was connected to a level of knowledge and understanding built up over time that allows them to deal with the complex work involved with teaching: 'I'm now at the point of my career when I have developed a system that works for me and that has come with time because you can't learn everything before you start teaching' (mid-career teacher). This strong belief in ability and skills was echoed by late-career teachers, who also felt that time had allowed them to build up a bank of strategies to facilitate effective practice in the face of changing demands:

> I wouldn't say I could do it in my sleep, but it's nearly at that point – it's experience. And that has also helped in dealing with the things that happen outside the classroom – the policies, the senior management, the changes that take place, etc.
>
> (Late-career teacher)

Mid- and late-career teachers both also referred to the ability to cope with the organizational requirements of the workplace and being able to deal with this effectively. The majority of teachers (89 per cent, N = 72) talked about having a high level of motivation and commitment and enjoying the challenges and high standards expected from the job (Kington *et al.* 2008). Continuing professional development was reported to be one of the main influences on job satisfaction, and teachers commented upon a rise in motivation and well-being as a result of time for planning, preparation and assessment, and having more support in the classroom. On further analysis, this factor increased in dominance for the participant teachers and, in addition to having a bearing on all career phases (see Figures 7.1–3), was seen as influential in terms of professional identity, discussed in Chapter 8.

As we can see from the evidence, there were some perceptions regarding effective practice displayed by teachers across all career phases. For example, a high level of support from the school leadership and colleagues was seen as a vital construct for a large proportion of teachers and the ways this support was defined showed no variations in the expectations of staff.

For early-career teachers there was a consensus of opinion regarding the high levels of enthusiasm, commitment and motivation coupled with feelings about their relationships with children and understanding of pupil needs which were developing. Likewise, mid-career teachers were said to be enthusiastic and motivated, as well as having positive relationships with children and a greater understanding of their needs. The majority of teachers in the early- and mid-career phases thought that enthusiasm and motivation started to diminish with experience. However, this was not evident from the observational and interview data collected from those in the later phase.

Table 7.1 Characteristics of career phases

	Effective/highly effective	Key influences
Early (N = 19)	12 x effective	**Personal:** motivated by teaching, efficacy based on confidence in ability to cope
	7 x highly effective	**Situational:** quality of relationships (understanding of students, acceptance, fairness and consistency), clear upfront behavioural expectations, anxious about flexibility, highly supported
		Professional: leadership support, workload
Mid-career (N = 35)	22 x effective	**Personal:** motivated by new challenges and continuing professional development, efficacy based on experience and bank of strategies
	13 x highly effective	**Situational:** quality of relationships (disciplinary balance, personalized teaching versus management concerns, fairness and consistency, developing self-esteem), consistent behavioural expectations, flexible and creative, highly supported
		Professional: new roles and excessive paperwork
Late-career (N = 27)	18 x effective	**Personal:** motivated by opportunities and relationships, efficacy based on experience and bank of strategies
	9 x highly effective	**Situational:** quality of relationships (students as learners, empathy with students' needs, developing self-esteem), relaxed about behavioural expectations, balancing creativity and discipline, highly supported
		Professional: sustained engagement, positive relationships

When examining the data relating to pedagogic and emotional aspects of effective practice, there are also similarities. However, the names given to particular items or factors derived from statistical techniques are only labels and it is the qualitative analyses of the meaning behind those labels that reveal the considerable variation in the ways in which these evolve over time and change depending on career phase. In addition, grounded analysis provided support for a developmental approach to teacher effectiveness. By this we mean that teachers focus on different aspects of their teaching practices at different stages of their career (see Table 7.1).

Effective/highly effective teachers: the professional versus the emotional

Using this combination of qualitative and quantitative methods of data collection and analysis, we found key differences in the effectiveness of teachers in the sample, which led to the identification of a group of highly effective teachers. The identification of these teachers as highly effective was based on a combination of factors:

1 Value-added data collected over three years or more which showed pupil progress as above expectation.
2 Social, affective and behavioural data collected via a pupil questionnaire survey that indicated a positive attitude to school, lesson and the teacher.
3 Judgement ratings based on the International Instrument for Teacher Observation and Feedback (ISTOF) and Quality of Teaching (QoT) observation schedules that were predominantly strong.

Nearly one-quarter of primary (N = 11) and half of secondary teachers (N = 18) in the study were classified as highly effective. Effective and highly effective teachers displayed key characteristics which were identified via the observations of classroom practice (Chapter 4), the in-depth interviews with teachers (Chapter 5) and the student responses (Chapter 6). However, the ways in which these manifested themselves and were combined with other practices defined the two groups. To some extent, the findings from this analysis supports the literature which indicates that teachers make changes to their professional and personal approaches to teaching as they transfer from one career phase to another (Day *et al.* 2007). However, what we also found was that the journey taken by teachers over the course of a career is a complex one, involving not only effective professional practice, but also 'emotional effectiveness'.

Professional practices

Both the effective and highly effective teachers in the sample were effective in all 'core' aspects of teaching practices, and observational findings provide support for the view that there is an overall (or generic) concept of teacher effectiveness (as discussed in Chapter 4). However, the qualitative analyses reveal that there is considerable variation in the ways in which these are enacted. In addition, qualitative data provides support for a differentiated concept of teacher effectiveness which suggests that effective and highly effective teachers can show both strengths and weaknesses in different aspects of their teaching practices and might vary in their effectiveness over time, in different lessons and for different pupil groups.

While many elements of effective classroom practice were utilized by both the effective and the highly effective teachers, the highly effective teachers possessed and combined a greater range of teaching and learning strategies and, in defining these factors, drew attention to consistency, reflexivity and context. They were also more likely to define their practice in terms of engaging in co-learning with the students, and were interested in the intellectual stimulation of the students (Slavin 1983). Those teachers identified as highly effective gave individual and personalized support to pupils in order to address their needs, leading them to be motivated to engage in learning and ensure inclusion. Furthermore, the highly effective teachers constructed their practice in terms of clearly sequenced, segmented and purposively paced lessons, with well-managed transitions between tasks, and a plenary was conducted in their lessons, supporting the findings of Hattie (2003), Sammons and Ko (2008), Muijs and Reynolds (2005) and Reynolds and Muijs (1999) who presented similar evidence.

Highly effective teachers had an increased focus upon giving individual and personalized support to students in order to address their needs, leading them to be motivated to engage in learning and ensure inclusion. Some aspects of their pedagogy, such as the facilitation of independent learning, opportunities for students to reflect, self-evaluate and engage in dialogue about learning, and the opportunity to recognize their own improvements in giving students additional confidence in influencing their own learning, reflected previous work (see Schoenfeld 1987).

Emotional effectiveness

Effective and highly effective teachers referred to a strong sense of motivation, commitment, self-efficacy and well-being with regard to their effectiveness. These factors confirmed findings from previous research, for example, Day *et al.* (2007) who reported that teacher identity, resilience and belief in themselves to do the job were vital to being a successful and effective practitioner, and supports further work in the areas of teacher self-efficacy (Brouwers and Tomic 2003), commitment (Zembylas 2003; Day *et al.* 2005) and well-being (Kelly and Colquhoun 2003).

As with professional practices, the effective and highly effective teachers defined these emotional factors differently. Effective teachers were more likely to still be developing a teacher identity and finding their place within the team. They felt able to do the job, but knew that there were still aspects of teaching they needed to focus on and were highly motivated and committed to doing this. Although the pressure of a teaching career was high, the effective teachers did not think that it affected their well-being and felt a high level of job satisfaction. The highly effective teachers reported that they maintained a high level of motivation and commitment by seeking new challenges, seizing opportunities to be involved in a variety of activities in the school, and developing and sustaining positive relationships with colleagues.

Effective and highly effective teachers reported high levels of self-efficacy and that their well-being was less likely to suffer due to external demands on their time such as partners, children and other family commitments. Both of these aspects contributed, in turn, to a more stable sense of professional identity. However, the highly effective teachers were also seen to be more able to adopt strategies in order to help them manage workload and keep life in balance. Unlike previous research (Day *et al.* 2007), neither the effective or highly effective teachers in the late-career phase reported a decline in motivation, commitment or job satisfaction as they felt respected by other members of the staff, and fulfilled an advisory role for those new to the profession. The classroom practice of these teachers not only illustrated unique pedagogical practices, but also demonstrated innovation through modification and adaptation strategies in order to keep them professionally and emotionally effective.

Summary

It may appear, on first reading, that there is nothing particularly innovative about the effective teaching described in this chapter; that these classroom factors are considered and addressed by all teachers. However, what is notable is that the effective and highly effective teachers in this study use these practices consistently, with success, resulting in positive student achievement. Many additional demands were placed on these teachers, not only in relation to the organization of their classroom activities but also in managing relationships and interactions with family, colleagues and school leadership, but in spite of these demands, all of the participant teachers demonstrated and articulated a commitment to their profession. We have indicated that as effective teachers develop through their careers, there are areas of tension which may have an impact on future practice. These areas include decisions regarding classroom management techniques, enhancing learning outcomes and how to respond to individual pupil needs. Underpinning these areas of tension is the apparent conflict effective teachers have between effective professional practice and their emotional effectiveness.

In summary, the analyses of classroom practices have supported the claim that, for effective and highly effective teachers across the early-, mid- and late-career phases, these practices can change over time and as a result of different experiences and school contexts and, in addition, can be accompanied by changes in school/classroom factors. These factors include teachers' personal experience, the leadership of the school and wider socio-cultural influences which can impact positively or negatively on the context of the school. Examination of the interplay between these different elements is essential in illustrating how an individual teacher draws on a variety of professional, contextual and personal elements for support in their classroom practice in order to sustain effectiveness.

The key messages from this chapter, in particular from the evidence from classroom observations, reinforce the differences between effective and highly effective teachers outlined in previous chapters. These include:

Teacher-student relationships

- Effective teachers promote positive teacher-pupil relationships and sustain these through the use of praise and feedback strategies, developing close, positive rapport and establishing boundaries with pupils.
- In addition, more effective teachers give more time to developing individual relationships with pupils, and focus upon building self-esteem, engendering trust and maintaining respect.
- Effective teachers develop a positive learning climate by focusing on positive classroom relationships, a dynamic and organized classroom environment, and persistently high and clearly communicated expectations of pupils.
- In addition, more effective teachers create a positive climate for learning by challenging pupils' ideas, inspiring them, being more innovative in their practices and differentiating among pupils according to abilities and interests where appropriate. Pupils have more control over their learning and more opportunities to achieve success.

Praise and feedback to students

- Effective teachers are aware of the learning objectives and use feedback and review strategies to evaluate the extent to which these were being achieved throughout the lesson. Monitoring and evaluation strategies are used to record the achievement of all pupils and to foster motivation among pupils.

- In addition, more effective teachers offer regular opportunities for pupils to reflect, self-evaluate, engage in dialogue about learning and recognize, appreciate and share with other pupils their own improvements (giving pupils additional confidence in influencing their own learning).

Teacher expectations of students

- Effective teachers have high expectations, use three- or four-part lessons and include a starter activity and plenary. The lessons are well-structured and have good transition between tasks.
- In addition, more effective teachers focus on expectations that are individualized, consistent, sequential and differentiated, giving pupils active engagement with and a higher degree of decision-making over their learning. They do not limit themselves to the use of three- or four-part lessons.

Teacher creativity and flexibility

- Effective teachers cater for a variety of pupil learning styles (visual, verbal, aural and kinaesthetic) and are aware of the learning and personal needs of groups and individuals. They pay attention to inclusivity and differentiation.
- In addition, more effective teachers give individual and personalized support to pupils in order to assess and address their needs, leading them to engage in learning with their peers, and to ensure inclusion.
- Effective teachers focus on structured and well-paced lessons, used questioning and scaffolding techniques and make pupils aware of the learning objectives. They also work on maintaining a high level of pupil engagement.
- In addition, more effective teachers instigate new challenges for pupils aimed at facilitating independent learning. They engage in co-construction of knowledge and cognitive structure with the pupils, and pupils, in turn, participate more and demonstrate more sustained engagement in the lessons and in their own learning.

Notes

1. The six phases were 0–3, 4–7, 8–15, 16–23, 24–30 and 31+ years.
2. There were no teachers involved in the study who had been teaching for two years or less.

References

Agee, J. (2004) Negotiating a teaching identity: an African American teacher's struggle to teach in test-driven contexts, *Teachers College Record*, 106: 747–74.

Bandura, A. (ed.) (1995) *Self-efficacy in Changing Societies*. New York: Cambridge University Press.

Bennett, N. and Carré, C. (1993) *Learning to Teach*. London: Routledge.

Brouwers, A. and Tomic, W. (2000) A longitudinal study of teacher burnout and perceived self-efficacy in classroom management, *Teaching and Teacher Education*, 16(2): 239–53.

Brown, K. (2001) Mentoring and the retention of newly qualified language teachers, *Cambridge Journal of Education*, 31: 53–68.

Carter, K., Cushing, K., Sabers, D., Stein, P. and Berliner, D. (1988) Expert-novice differences in perceiving and processing visual classroom information, *Journal of Teacher Education*, 38: 25–31.

Castejou, J.L. and Martinez, M.A. (2001) The personal constructs of expert and novice teachers concerning the teacher function in the Spanish educational reform, *Learning and Instruction*, 11: 113–31.

Conway, P.F. and Clark, C.M. (2003) The journey inward and outward: a re-examination of fuller's concerns based model of teacher development, *Teaching and Teacher Education*, 19: 465–82.

Craig, C.J. (2001) The relationship between and among teachers' narrative knowledge, communities of knowing, and school reform: a case of 'the monkey's paw', *Curriculum Inquiry*, 31: 303–32.

Day, C. and Gu, Q. (2009) Veteran teachers: commitment, resilience and quality retention, *Teachers and Teaching: Theory and Practice*, 15(4): 441–57.

Day, C., Elliot, B. and Kington, A. (2005) Reform, standards and teacher identity: challenges of sustaining commitment, *Teaching and Teacher Education*, 21: 563–77.

Day, C., Sammons, P., Stobart, G., Kington, A. and Gu, Q. (2007) *Teachers Matter*. Maidenhead: Open University Press.

Erikson, E.H. (1964) *Childhood and Society*, 2nd edn. New York: Norton.

Hattie, J. (2003) Teachers make a difference: what is the research evidence? Paper presented at the Annual Conference of the Australian Council for Educational Research, Australia, October.

Hattie, J. and Timperley, H. (2007) The power of feedback, *Review of Educational Research*, 77(1): 81–112.

Henke, R., Chen, X., Geis, S. and Knepper, P. (2000) Progress through the teacher pipeline: 1992–93 college graduates and elementary/secondary school teaching as of 1997, *Education Statistics Quarterly*, 2: 91–8.

Hilsum, S. and Start, K.B. (1974) *Promotion and Careers in Teaching*. Atlantic Highlands, NJ: NFER Publishing Company.

Huberman, M. (1989) The professional life cycle of teachers, *Teachers College Record*, 91(1): 31–57.

Huberman, M. (1993) *The Lives of Teachers*. London: Cassell.

Jay, J.K. (2002) Points on a continuum: an expert/novice study of pedagogical reasoning, *Professional Educator*, 24: 63–74.

Kelly, P. and Colquhoun, D. (2003) Governing the stressed self: teacher health and well-being and effective schools, *Discourse*, 24(2): 191–204.

Kington, A. (2005) Qualities, formation and development of teacher-pupil relationships in the primary school, in B. Kozuh, T. Beran, A. Kozlowska and P. Bayliss, (eds), *Measurement and Assessment in Educational and Social Research*. Exeter-Calgary-Cracow.

Kington, A. (2009) Defining teachers' classroom relationships, in D. Stefanc and B. Harasimowicz (eds) *The Social Context of Education*. Ljubljana: Valentin Bucik.

Kington, A. (2012) Narratives of variation in teacher-pupil relationships across a career, *European Journal of Educational Studies*, 4(2): 189–201.

Kington, A., Reed, N., Regan, E., Sammons, P., Day, C. and Gunraj, J. (2008) *Initial Findings from the Repertory Grid Data. Working paper ECP/03*. Nottingham: University of Nottingham.

Kutnick, P. and Kington, A. (2005) Children's friendships and learning in school: cognitive enhancement through social interaction?, *British Journal of Educational Psychology*, 75(4): 521–38.

Maclean, R. (1992) *Teachers' Careers and Promotional Patterns: A Sociological Analysis*. London: Falmer Press.

Manuel, J. (2003) Such are the ambitions of youth: exploring issues of retention and attrition of early career teachers in New South Wales, *Asia-Pacific Journal of Teacher Education*, 31: 139–51.

McBer, H. (2000) *Research into Teacher Effectiveness: A Model of Teacher Effectiveness*, Report to the Department for Education and Employment. London: DFEE.

Meyer, H. (2004) Novice and expert teachers' conceptions of learners' prior knowledge, *Science Education*, 88: 970–83.

Mortimore, P., Sammons, P., Stoll, L., Lewis, D. and Ecob, R. (1988) *School Matters: The Junior Years*. Wells: Open Books.

Muijs, D. and Reynolds, D. (2005) *Effective Teaching: Evidence and Practice*. London: Sage.

Mulholland, J. and Wallace, J. (2005) Growing the tree of teacher knowledge: ten years of learning to teach elementary science, *Journal of Research in Science Teaching*, 42: 767–90.

Pigge, F. and Marso, R.N. (2000) Development of attitude toward teaching career, *Mid-Western Educational Researcher*, 13(2): 2–9.

Price, J.N. (2001) Action research, pedagogy and change: the transformative potential of action research in pre-service teacher education, *Journal of Curriculum Studies*, 33: 43–74.

Reynolds, D. and Muijs, R.D. (1999) The effective teaching of mathematics: a review of research, *School Leadership and Management*, 19(3): 273–88

Sammons, P. and Ko, J. (2008) Using systematic classroom observation schedules to investigate effective teaching: overview of quantitative findings, in *Effective Classroom Practice (ECP) ESRC Project Report* (RES-000-23-1564). Swindon: ESRC.

Schoenfeld, A. (1987) *Cognitive Science and Mathematics Education*. Hillsdale, NJ: Lawrence Erlbaum Associates.

Sikes, P.J., Measor, L. and Woods, P. (1985) *Teacher Careers: Crises and Continuities*. London: Falmer Press.

Slavin, R.E. (1983) *Cooperative Learning*. New York: Longman.

Smart, R. and Peterson, C. (1997) Super's career stages and the decision to change careers, *Journal of Vocational Behaviour*, 51: 358–74.

So, W.W.M. and Watkins, D.A. (2005) From beginning teacher education to professional teaching: a study of the thinking of Hong Kong primary science teachers, *Teaching and Teacher Education*, 21: 525–41.

Stinebrickner, T.R. (2001) A dynamic model of teacher labor supply, *Journal of Labor Economics*, x: 196–230.

Super, D.E. (1957) *The Psychology of Careers*. New York: Harper.

Super, D.E. (1990) A life-span, life-space approach to career development, in D. Brown and L. Brooks (eds) *Career Choice and Development: Applying Contemporary Theories to Practice*, 2nd edn. San Francisco, CA: Jossey-Bass.

Verjovsky, J. and Waldegg, G. (2005) Analyzing beliefs and practices of a Mexican high school biology teacher, *Journal of Research in Science Teaching*, 42: 465–91.

Wilhelm, K., Dewhurst-Savellis, J. and Parker, G. (2000) Teacher stress? An analysis of why teachers leave and why they stay, *Teachers and Teaching: Theory and Practice*, 6: 291–304.

Woolfolk Hoy, A. and Burke Spero, R. (2005) Changes in teacher efficacy during the early years of teaching: a comparison of four measures, *Teaching and Teacher Education*, 21: 343–56.

Zeichner, K. and Tabachnick, B.R. (1985) The development of teacher perspectives: social strategies and instructional control in the socialization of beginning teachers, *Journal of Education for Teachers*, 11: 1–25.

Zembylas, M. (2003) Emotions and teacher identity: a poststructural perspective, *Teachers and Teaching: Theory and Practice*, 9(3): 213–38.

8 Professional identity and effective classroom practice

Introduction

Chapter 7 highlighted that for each of the career phases (early-, mid-or late-career), identity played a key positive role. However, while many elements of effective professional and emotional classroom practice were utilized by all of the teachers in the study (see previous chapters) there were two factors that were seen to have a significant influence on teachers' professional identity across career phases: teacher-student relationships and self-efficacy.

In Chapter 5 we looked at the elements of effective practice across all career phases, and indeed, self-efficacy was a feature that was seen to play an important role in teachers' motivation and commitment. In terms of how the practitioners understood the more effective elements of their practice, we found that teacher-student relationships were central and they also fed into how they set expectations, both academic and behavioural, and how they approached praise and feedback. Given the importance of these aspects of teacher identity and practice, it is useful to delve a little deeper into how different scenarios of teacher identity impact on the ways teachers negotiate relationships with their students. This chapter is divided into three main sections. First, we explore research on teacher identity. In the second section the conceptualization of teacher identity applied within the project is explained. Last, teacher identity is examined in the context of teacher-student relationships and teacher self-efficacy. Three stories from illustrative teachers showcase the key outcome of the mixed method strategy of combining quantitative and qualitative measures and preserving the individual amid the summarizing of data. Building on the exploration of relationships across career phases in the previous chapter, we also discuss the connection between self-efficacy and career phase.

Previous research on teacher identity

There has been an increased focus within many of the social sciences towards questions of identity (Calhoun 1994; Connelly and Clandinin 1999). These include psychological perspectives such as Bruner (1987) and Erikson (1959) who consider identity to be a reflection of an individual's narrative, and Schriffin (1996) who examines the construction of identity from a sociolinguistic perspective. Education is not excluded from this development, which has generated changes in educational policy and reforms in many countries during the last 15 years (Hammersley 2002; Woods and Jeffrey 2002; Day *et al.* 2005). These changes are believed to 'challenge teachers' individual and collective professional and personal identities' (Day 2002: 678). Consequently, many researchers with a concern for teachers and teacher education have promoted the investigation of teachers' work and teacher identity within this developing policy context. For some studies the question of construction and development of teacher identity is connected to the teaching of subject matter (Drake *et al.* 2001), while others investigate student teachers' development and conception of teacher identity (Walkington 2005). Studies of teacher identity are also often closely connected to those that also focus on teacher knowledge (Connelly and Clandinin 1999; Beijaard *et al.* 2004), teacher professionalism and professional development (Roberts 2000).

Identity, as people's source of meaning and experience, is different from *roles*, which organize people's functions within institutions and organizations (Castells 2004). Teachers play a variety of roles within and outside the classroom and their roles are an indispensable part of their professional identities (Day and Kington, 2008; Beijaard *et al.* 2004). People continually negotiate their identity in order to balance the actions they consider normal and reasonable, what they do and what they wish to do (Calhoun 1994). Identity is thereby not something ready-made that we can find or develop, but something we create and recreate through our relations to the world and other people.

Despite the number of studies involving primary teacher identity, the concept of 'identity' is often treated as unproblematic and singular and is therefore in many cases not explicitly defined (Weber and Mitchell 1995; Beijaard *et al.* 2004; Sfard and Prusak 2005). Those studies that do attempt to define or describe teacher identity draw on several traditions and understandings, making it difficult to identify specific conceptions. In spite of these differences, most current studies seem to consider teacher identity as a relational phenomenon. Teacher identity is thus considered to be shaped and changed by, and within, a multitude of contextual and personal elements (Flores and Day 2006). Some studies approach identity as a stable feature rooted in core sets of values and practices, while others approach identity as unstable, flexible and dependent on contextual or personal changes (Day *et al.* 2006). Other researchers (Hargreaves 1994; Nias 1996; Sumsion 2002) have noted that teacher identities are not only constructed from technical and emotional aspects of teaching and their personal lives, but, also, '. . . as the result of an interaction between the personal experiences of teachers and the social, cultural, and institutional environment in which they function on a daily basis' (Sleegers and Kelchtermans 1999: 579).

MacLure (1993) argued that the teachers in her study appeared to be more varied in their senses of themselves, much less secure in their identities as teachers and less committed to teaching as a career. She proposed the concept of an 'active' agential teacher self, which is formed and informed through the 'discursive practices' and interactions in which individuals engage. Here identity is not viewed as a stable quality that people possess, but rather is constructed within social relations and used by individuals as an interactional resource where instabilities, whether of a personal, professional or situated nature, or a combination of these, create stresses or 'a continuing site of struggle' (p. 312) in the fabric of identity and need to be managed.

Day *et al.* (2007) outline four limitations with previous research into teachers' professional identities: disagreement over whether identities are substantive or contingent stable/unstable; lack of longitudinal real-time data; do not explore the link between identity and teacher effectiveness; and more or less cognizance taken of macro-, miso-, micro-structures, personal biographies or emotional factors. The current study uses a constructivist approach, as it is founded on the understanding that people construct their identities through relations, choices, practices and language (Elliott 2005). Within a constructivist approach to identity the challenge for the teacher is not to find a single teacher identity, but rather to integrate the different roles and fragments of his or her professional and personal life in a meaningful way. In their job, teachers are confronted with different roles through which they will construct and reconstruct their teacher identity through a constant negotiation. To what extent this negotiation of identity is experienced as conflicting or difficult will however vary individually (Calhoun 1994). Within this constructivist framework, the study builds on the concepts of primary teachers' professional identity and career phase developed by Day *et al.* (2007), Day (2011) and Kington *et al.* (2012) and makes major conceptual and empirical contributions to understandings about the nature of teacher commitment and resilience, and the challenges of sustaining positive professional identities at different times in their lives and careers and in different school contexts. The findings have profound implications for knowledge of teachers' quality retention and the governments' raising standards agendas.

Conceptualization of teacher identity

The Variations in Teachers' Work, Lives and their Effects on Pupils (VITAE) research found that teachers' capacity to sustain their commitment and effectiveness were moderated by their identities (and professional life phases), and that these were mediated by the 'scenarios' or contexts in which they lived and worked. The VITAE findings suggested that identity itself is a composite concept comprising interaction between professional, situational and personal factors (Day *et al.* 2007). These were further developed such that identity itself is a composite of three clusters of influences: socio-cultural/policy, workplace and personal. Each of these influences is itself made up of interactions between a range of sometimes competing factors which have to be managed in the staffroom and classroom. How a teacher manages these will determine his or her professional identity:

1   **Socio-cultural/policy.** This cluster of influences reflects cultural, social and policy expectations of teachers and teaching, and the educational ideals, ethical and moral purposes of the teachers. It is open to the influence of changing policy and social trends as to what constitutes a good teacher, classroom practitioner, etc., and may contain a number of competing and conflicting elements such as local or national policy, continuing professional development, workload, roles and responsibilities, etc.

2   **Workplace or socially located influences.** These are located in the micro-politics and social relationships of specific school, department or classroom contexts and are affected by local conditions, i.e. pupil behaviour, the quality of leadership, support and feedback in teachers' immediate work context.
3   **Personal influences.** These are located in life outside school and are associated with personal histories, present lives, family, social relationships and personal sense of efficacy and vulnerability.

Teachers may experience tensions within and between these three clusters of influence at any given time and each cluster is itself subject to a number of positive and negative influences. The strength of teachers' job satisfaction, well-being, self-efficacy and vulnerability, commitment and resilience, and their ability to exercise agency, will be affected but not necessarily determined by these influences, for each of these may be mediated by teachers' cultural traditions, sense of vocation/moral purpose/values and agency and the interaction between these and their working environment. Any one (or more) of these three clusters of influence may, however, at a particular time, become dominant, thus challenging the relative stability of the other two and influencing teachers' existing sense of professional identity. Managing such new (or persisting) negative instabilities and tensions will require additional time and emotional energy from the teacher, and this may affect their capacity to sustain their positive sense of professional identity. These dimensions are not static, and change in one dimension affected teachers' abilities to manage the others.

Identity scenarios

Within this framework, it is the degree of dominance which these influences have on each dimension of identity and the way teachers manage them which determine the relative stability or instability of teachers' composite identity and whether this is positive or negative. In addition, VITAE identified four identity scenarios (Day and Kington 2008):

Scenario 1: dimensions in relative balance
Scenario 2: one dominant dimension
Scenario 3: two dominant dimensions
Scenario 4: three conflicting dimensions

The extent to which the scenarios were managed by the teachers depended in part on the level of disturbance or fluctuation, and in part on the combination of internal and external influences. Analysis of the key features of teachers' professional lives and work facilitated the grouping of VITAE teachers into one of these four scenarios on the basis of the degree of dominance of a particular influence. In the case of the Effective Classroom Practice (ECP) project, teachers were allocated to the first three scenarios only and no teachers exhibited the last scenario where all three dimensions are in conflict.

The first scenario shows an identity that is stable with the three dimensions being held in balance, as depicted in Figure 8.1. Although there would be mild

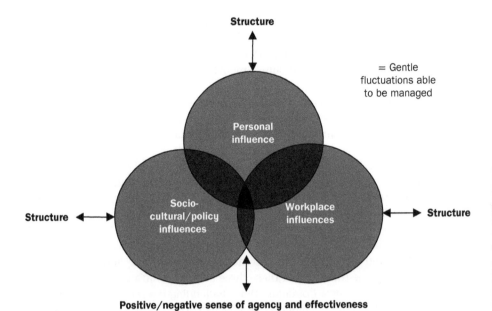

Figure 8.1 Scenario 1 – dimensions in relative balance.

fluctuations within and between these from time to time, no action would need to be taken unless stability is negative. In this model, identity becomes unstable when one or more dimension is disturbed by internal or external events. Over half (53 per cent, N = 43) of the teachers in the current study were in this group.

In Scenario 2 (see Day and Kington 2008), one of the three dimensions of identity dominates, which distorts one or both of the other dimensions, for instance, the dominance of workplace influences over both personal and socio-cultural influences. In most cases of Scenario 2, fluctuations are managed in the short term, depending on the individual teacher's motivation, commitment, self-efficacy, support from colleagues and leadership. Analysis of the interview data revealed that there were 31 teachers (38 per cent) in the second scenario where one dimension was dominant. Key positive features of this scenario include promotion or additional roles, departmental support, motivated colleagues/pupils, teamwork, pupil behaviour and life events. Negative features include increased workload, external policies, poor pupil behaviour, lack of parental support, poor in-school communication and life events such as illness or relationship problems.

Within Scenario 3, two of the three dimensions of identity dominate which puts pressure on the other dimension, for instance, fluctuations in personal and workplace. Fluctuations may be managed in the short term, depending on internal and external factors (e.g. self-efficacy, support from home/colleagues). Key positive features of this scenario include ambition, career advancement, staff morale, pupil relationships, buying a house or becoming a parent. Negative influences include unsuccessful promotion, new leadership and family illness. In our

Table 8.1   Characteristics of professional identity scenarios

	Career phase (effective + highly effective)	Effective/highly effective	Key influences
Scenario 1 (N = 43)	10 × early (7 + 3) 18 × mid (13 + 5) 15 × late (11 + 4)	31 × effective 12 × highly effective	**Personal:** self-efficacy, marriage, pregnancy, bereavement, divorce
Scenario 2 (N = 31)	8 × early (4 + 4) 15 × mid (7 + 8) 8 × late (3 + 5)	14 × effective 17 × highly effective	**Workplace:** teacher-pupil relationships, new role, school leadership
Scenario 3 (N = 7)	1 × early 2 × mid 4 × late	7 × effective	**Sociocultural/political:** retirement plans

analysis of the interview data 9 per cent (N = 7) of teachers were in Scenario 3 where two dimensions dominated and impacted on the third. The characteristics of the professional identity scenarios present in our sample, complete with a breakdown of the sample according to career phases and effectiveness, are illustrated in Table 8.1.

The proportion of teachers in Scenario 1 might seem fairly low given the effective nature of our sample. However, there were two main reasons for this: first, that in Scenarios 2 and 3 the dominant dimensions were (for the most part) positive, for example, marriage, new role or promotion; and, second that, as discussed in the last chapter, the highly effective teachers thrived on challenge and found ways to manage the influencing factors as required. That said, Scenario 3 was made up exclusively of effective (rather than highly effective) teachers.

Key concepts that impact on professional identity

Teacher-student relationships

Teachers are acknowledged as adults whose relationships with children contribute to the social, emotional and cognitive development of those children (Birch and Ladd 1998; Hamre and Pianta 2001; Kington 2005). The relationship that a child has with his or her teacher in the primary phase of schooling is associated with a range of child outcomes, including children's competent behaviour in relationships with peers, as well as their relationships with future teachers (Howes and Hamilton 1993; Howes et al. 1994; Birch and Ladd 1998). Aspects of the teacher-child relationship are also linked to school adjustment and academic achievement (Howes et al. 1994; Pianta et al. 1995; Birch and Ladd 1997). In addition, positive teacher-child relationships can serve as a buffer against risk (Lynch and Cicchetti 1992; Pianta et al. 1995; Mitchell-Copeland et al. 1997).

Past research has also focused on associations between teachers' perceptions of their relationships with children and their judgements about children's feelings of satisfaction with school (Baker 1999), as well as pupils' social status in the classroom (Skinner and Belmont 1993). There have also been a number of studies regarding elements of classroom activity which doubtless have an impact upon teacher-pupil relationships, such as the creation of productive classroom environments (Hook and Vass 2000), the role of authority in the classroom (Robertson 1996) and how pupils interact with one another in the classroom, both academically (e.g. Kutnick and Kington 2005) and socially (Hartup 1998). Findings such as these indicate that positive early teacher-child relationships may help place children on a trajectory towards higher levels of school adjustment and competence, whereas negative early relationships with teachers forecast a less promising trajectory for children (Kington 2005, 2009; Kington et al. 2013).

A further strand of research is concerned with the importance of relationships between students and teachers in shaping the quality of students' motivation and classroom learning experiences. Several reviews of the literature have examined the importance of teachers' instructional practices (Wigfield et al. 1998) as well as the affective and intellectual contexts of classroom learning (Perry and Weinstein 1998; Osterman 2000; Turner and Meyer 2000). Additionally, reviews have examined the role students may play in shaping the social context of learning through their beliefs, judgements, goals and attempts to regulate social behaviour (Urdan and Maehr 1995; Patrick 1997; Pianta 1999; Wentzel 1999).

The growing body of literature examining the nature of teacher-child interaction suggests that teacher relationships make a unique contribution to children's social and cognitive development through adolescence (Resnick et al. 1997). Operating as socializing agents, teachers can influence the quality of students' social and intellectual experiences via their abilities to instil values in children such as the motivation to learn (Brophy and Kherr 1985; Brophy 1998; Oldfather and Dahl 1994); by providing classroom contexts that stimulate children's motivation and learning (Ames 1992; Perry 1998; Ryan et al. 1998; Turner et al. 1998); by addressing children's need to belong (Connell and Wellborn 1991; Wentzel 1997, 1998); by developing a social identity (Alderman 1999; Wentzel 1993); and by serving a regulatory function for the development of emotional, behavioural and academic skills (Birch and Ladd 1997; Pianta 1997, 1999; Yowell and Smylie 1999).

Similarities and differences in approaches with pupils

Analysis of data revealed a number of underlying factors associated with teacher-pupil relationships and professional identity. Teachers in all three scenarios identified the following characteristics:

1 The ability to build and sustain good relationships with pupils was said to be crucial for the majority (93 per cent, N = 75) of teachers across all three scenarios. A number of factors influenced this – for example, getting to know the pupils well, establishing good rapport and interaction, using humour, listening to what the pupils had to say and communicating effectively with them.

2   All teachers were concerned about the quality of the relationships established with pupils, being accepted by pupils and understanding them. They also highlighted the need for relationships to be based on fairness and consistency, and offered in a supportive and caring way.

3   The majority of teachers (86 per cent, N = 70) were concerned about discipline, yet at the same time understood that too much discipline could undermine the quality of the relationships.

4   Finally, these teachers (84 per cent, N = 68) empathized with their pupils' needs and efforts in terms of their academic performance and desired academic outcomes.

Further analysis revealed a number of important themes that highlighted similarities and differences between the three scenarios – interaction, expectations, behaviour and proximity.

Scenario 1

All teachers in Scenario 1 stated that they try to combine a number of approaches when interacting with pupils and often used humour and a relaxed, informal approach to teaching in order to utilize their relationships with pupils during the learning process. They felt that the more relaxed children were during lessons, '. . . the more they enjoy it and the more they learn' (late-career teacher). The highly effective teachers also reported that they played a role in shaping relationships through the emotional quality of their interactions with children, as well as their responsiveness in terms of frequency and consistency to children's needs. This was seen by teachers as particularly important to pupils in the later stages of primary school who are often undergoing profound shifts in their sense of self and are struggling to negotiate changing relationships with their parents and peers.

Many of the teachers in Scenario 1 identified proximity as a means of maintaining positive interactions with pupils, indicating that this factor not only supported learning targets or objectives, and forms of informal assessment, but the highly effective teachers also noted an impact upon pupil behaviour. Perceptions of pupil behaviour occupied the thoughts of all teachers in this scenario more than those in Scenarios 2 or 3. It was this group of teachers who believed more strongly that aspects of their relationships with pupils were related to pupil behaviour so that ' . . . if I work hard on the relationship aspect, the good behaviour will follow – there is definitely a connection between the two things' (early-career teacher). Teachers in this scenario focused on expectations that were individualized, consistent, sequential and differentiated, but tried to give pupils more control over their learning. In addition, the highly effective teachers spoke about how the 'history' of the relationship was a component that affected expectations between teacher and pupil. The history was significant because ' . . . when you know something about a pupil, either because you have taught them before or from a colleague, you can be more realistic about communications and expectations' (mid-career teacher), thereby connecting the familiarity and shared knowledge which had developed between participants.

Scenario 2

Teachers in Scenario 2 tended to focus their attention on academic-related interactions, but also reported that they maintained their personal interest in pupils outside of lesson time. One early-career teacher stated '. . . even though I like to keep classroom talk about work, I like to keep in touch with what they're doing in their own time as well, so try to talk to them in the playground and on breaks'. Although a higher proportion of the teachers in this scenario felt more positive about pupil behaviour compared with the other two scenarios, the highly effective teachers in this group defined good behaviour in terms of strategies adopted in order to help them manage any disruptive behaviour and maintain pupil discipline, saying that it was not just about promoting good behaviour because that should be '. . . the default setting' (mid-career teacher).

Effective and highly effective teachers reported that they made behavioural expectations clear from the start of the year by formalizing them in a document or as part of a display. They explained that they based their academic expectations around targets or learning objectives which provided a consistent way to demonstrate their aspirations for the class. Examination of the data showed that the highly effective teachers in this scenario, like those in Scenario 1, used classroom seating and proximity with pupils to promote positive relationships, 'develop rapport, and establish boundaries' (late-career teacher). In addition, this organization offered opportunities for the teachers to engage with pupils in dialogue about learning. One of the strategies used by teachers in this group was to stand close to children who were known to get distracted – 'It means I can reinforce the rules if necessary without having to stop the lesson and draw attention to it' (mid-career teacher).

Scenario 3

Teachers in Scenario 3 were more likely to define their interactions with pupils as positive if there was a certain level of humour and rapport, with the aim of getting to know the pupil and establish a level of familiarity. This kind of interaction was thought to make it '. . . easier to develop relationships with some children, especially when it flows over into the classroom' (mid-career teacher). However, this group of teachers was more likely to become dissatisfied with pupil behaviour which they reported was brought on by the high demands placed on pupils. Although seen as a manageable situation which was usually handled easily by these effective teachers, there was an acknowledgement that it could become a threat to a positive classroom atmosphere. Late-career teachers felt more strongly about this, with one stating, 'Behaviour becomes more and more difficult the longer I teach. The things that used to work when I was younger don't work now so I have to be stronger and impose more discipline as soon as I think behaviour is changing for the worse' (late-career teacher). As a consequence, these teachers stated that they strived to find additional strategies to deal with the situation which, in turn, took more of their time away from other aspects of their practice. One of these strategies was to differentiate expectations according to pupils' abilities even though they were aware that to do this could 'either motivate or demotivate them' (early-career teacher). Further to this, teachers in Scenario 3 were also more relaxed regarding their perceptions of proximity compared with the first two scenarios. Interestingly, late-career teachers were less likely to make strategic use of proximity to maintain relationships.

Teacher self-efficacy

Self-efficacy refers to individuals' beliefs about their capabilities to carry out a particular course of action successfully (Bandura 1997). Bandura proposed that self-efficacy beliefs are context-specific rather than a generalized expectancy. Consequently, teachers' sense of efficacy has been examined in relation to a number of school-level variables, such as the climate and structure of the school, the leadership of the principal and the collective efficacy of the organization. Self-efficacy theory, applied in the educational arena, has generated a body of research focused on the connection between teachers' feelings of self-efficacy, their actions and the eventual outcomes (Tschannen-Moran et al. 1998). These researchers report that, in assessing beliefs about their teaching ability in a particular context, teachers make two related judgements. The first is related to the requirements needed for a specific teaching task which will include student factors such as their perceived ability, motivation and socio-economic status; and contextual factors such as school leadership, collegial support and the availability of resources. The second is an assessment of their personal teaching competence in light of those requirements.

A potentially important element of teachers' environments related to self-efficacy is the climate of the school. Stronger self-efficacy beliefs have been found among teachers who perceived a positive school atmosphere (Moore and Esselman 1992) and a strong press for academic achievement among the staff in their school (Hoy and Woolfolk 1993). Receiving positive feedback on teacher performance and collaboration with other teachers were significantly associated with teachers' sense of efficacy, as were parent involvement in the school and school-wide coordination of student behaviour (Rosenholtz 1989). Researchers have also found that teachers' self-efficacy influences their teaching behaviours and their students' motivation and achievement (Tschannen-Moran and Woolfolk Hoy 2001; Skaalvik and Skaalvik 2007). Teachers with low self-efficacy experience greater difficulties in teaching, higher levels of job-related stress (Betoret 2006) and lower levels of job satisfaction (Klassen et al. 2009).

Variations in teachers' sense of self-efficacy

The stories related here have been chosen to illustrate the key influences on teachers' perceptions of their effective practice across the three professional identity scenarios. The three teachers described were all identified as being highly effective in relation to their value-added data collected over three years (above expectation), social, affective and behavioural data collected via a student questionnaire survey (positive attitude to school, lesson and the teacher) and judgement ratings based on the International Instrument for Teacher Observation and Feedback (ISTOF) and Quality of Teaching (QoT) observation schedules (predominantly strong).

Barry's story: seizing opportunities to sustain a strong sense of self-efficacy (Scenario 1)

Barry was a Year 6 teacher in a large, primary school of 490 pupils located in an inner-city area with a high level of ethnic diversity, pupils with English as a second language, and social and economic disadvantage (FSM 4). Barry was 29 years old and had been teaching for six years, four of which were in this school. He was also a key stage manager and a member of the senior management team. In his personal life, Barry was married with three sons and was primarily attracted to teaching because he wanted to 'be part of children's education and to inspire them'.

Initially Barry saw relationships with students as the factor that had the biggest negative impact on his work as a teacher. However, after the first year of teaching this had changed. He spoke of how, in his early career, he had worked hard on developing creative strategies for dealing with poor communication and interaction in class and this had resulted in increased respect from the students. He also talked about his effectiveness in terms of managing pupil expectations and behaviour management and, alongside excellent student results, his work was being noticed within the senior management team. This recognition had had an impact on his levels of motivation and commitment to his work and he was eager to find further opportunity to 'get involved' in school life. For example, he applied and was successful in becoming a key stage manager and thrived on the additional responsibilities, saying that his effectiveness was 'increasing all the time'. Barry also took on the role of mentor to other colleagues who were struggling with particular aspects of their practice. This was combined, once more, with the feeling that his work and dedication were being acknowledged within the school and he reported that his feeling of professional identity was as strong as it had ever been.

One year before the ECP study, there had been a change in the school leadership and Barry was initially a little anxious about this, but after a short time he had felt reassured that the structures that had been in place before were to remain. The new head teacher continued to call upon Barry's professional judgement regarding issues of effective practice within Key Stage 2 and his enthusiasm and job satisfaction continued to increase. He also stated that the positive feeling he had about work was reflected in his personal life and he started socializing more frequently. Barry said that he now enjoyed the day-to-day interactions with pupils and the intensity of his roles within school. His colleagues were supportive and this had been an influential factor in him considering a move to deputy headship in the near future.

Andrea's story: positive changes in professional and personal roles (Scenario 2)

Andrea was 46 years old and had been teaching for 25 years at her first school, a medium-sized community primary school with 252 pupils on roll, situated in an area of low socio-economic disadvantage (FSM 1). It was located in a suburban area where the majority of pupils were from white British backgrounds. Andrea was originally attracted to teaching because of the security it offered, which still applied. She was a Year 2 teacher as well as history and music coordinator.

Andrea described the pupils in the school as 'challenging, lively and interesting' and said that the staff probably put up with a 'percentage of behaviour not tolerated elsewhere'. She had experienced pupil behaviour problems in the past, but had gradually found that her classroom management strategies had worked with the pupils. She had always regarded herself as approachable and affable but had continued to work on her relationships with the class, increasing positive interactions with pupils and engaging with them on an individual level. Andrea gained great satisfaction from the progress of her 'most stressful class' and this seemed to have raised her profile in the school, leading to a perceived increase in her motivation and commitment. Other effective strategies adopted in the classroom by Andrea included a more flexible approach to planning, greater use of a variety of teaching styles and attention to individual pupil needs.

Her growing professional experience had increased her perceived effectiveness as a teacher. Further, her self-efficacy and confidence in managing the classroom had improved since she began teaching. At the beginning of the project year she was highly committed to teaching and was very pleased to see that she could make a difference to pupils both academically and personally. She saw teaching as 'a life as well as a job'. Not surprisingly, she enjoyed an extremely high level of job satisfaction. Andrea suggested that three critical incidents had improved her effectiveness as a teacher in her early years in teaching: gaining a permanent contract, recovering from a broken relationship and taking on new responsibilities after a recent inspection by Ofsted.

Andrea had been considering a possible move to Italy. However, she had started having doubts and saw this as a 'turning point' in her career path. Gaining a greater sense of success in teaching, she welcomed the support of colleagues and had made substantial improvements over the previous two years in terms of her time management skills and her knowledge of 'the mindset' of primary school-age children. This had been recognized by the head teacher which had resulted in a positive impact on Andrea's relationship with him. The head teacher stated that he was always available and willing to help and his feedback seemed to focus on positive aspects of Andrea's practice, thus increasing her morale and self-efficacy. As a result, Andrea was looking to take on more responsibility, possibly in another school, and maintained a high level of motivation and commitment to her teaching and future plans.

Charlotte's story: increasing belief in ability to be an effective practitioner (Scenario 3)

Charlotte was a teacher in a large comprehensive school of 935 pupils in a relatively disadvantaged urban area (FSM 3). She was married with two children (aged five and eight). Apart from being a Year 9 English teacher, Charlotte was also assistant head teacher and a key stage manager, which sometimes put pressure on her personal life. She was 42 years old and had taught for 17 years. In general, Charlotte stated that she had been progressing well in terms of career development and had received positive feedback on her teaching. However, she had clear expectations of the kind of teacher she wanted to be and felt that she was not achieving this in spite of excellent exam results for her students across all ability groups.

Charlotte claimed that teaching had always been her 'ideal profession' and she received considerable encouragement from her family to enter the profession. At the beginning of her career, Charlotte was confident that she possessed what she thought were the qualities of a good teacher: patience, the ability to listen and the appropriate personality. Charlotte did have some positive things to say about her work. She found some colleague-led inputs into her career, such as those on behaviour management, to be valuable, and she acknowledged the support of some colleagues, one of whom was always available when she needed him. However, although Charlotte viewed the senior management team as positive, she felt less positive about the leadership in her department. Nevertheless, members of staff were 'incredibly supportive and friendly' and she enjoyed the pleasant environment in the school. Charlotte had also established a good relationship with her pupils, but found that, overall, pupil behaviour had become more challenging.

Responsibilities relating to work and to home life were proving difficult to manage but Charlotte was committed to continue in teaching. This involved asking her husband to reduce the amount of time he worked away from home, making it easier to combine school work and domestic responsibilities. She stated that she had 'never worked so hard trying to balance everything out' but that it had all paid off and now she 'even had time for a social life'. By the end of the year, Charlotte was more comfortable talking about her effectiveness and she was aware that, according to various measures of effectiveness (including SAT scores), she was highly effective in her practice. However, Charlotte's experience illustrates how a lack of support, heavy workload and personal factors can impact on feelings of self-efficacy.

Connections between self-efficacy and career phase

The three case studies presented provide some insights regarding the obstacles, both personal and professional, that can impede a teachers' self-belief in their effectiveness. Although Bandura (1997) hypothesized that self-efficacy beliefs remain relatively stable once established, it has been noted that 'little evidence exists about how [teachers'] efficacy beliefs change or solidify across stages of a career' (Tschannen-Moran *et al.* 1998: 238). Ross *et al.* (1996) found mixed support for the influence of experience on teachers' self-efficacy, and Ghaith and Yaghi (1997) found negative correlations between years of experience and teacher self-efficacy. Woolfolk Hoy and Burke Spero (2005) conducted a longitudinal study in which results showed a significant rise in teachers' self-efficacy during teacher training, followed by a decline at the end of their first teaching year. A study by Wolters and Daugherty (2007) examined the influence of teaching experience on teachers' self-efficacy and goal structures. Results showed modest effects of experience on self-efficacy for instructional strategies and self-efficacy for classroom management, but no effect of experience on self-efficacy for student engagement.

The developmental course of occupational self-efficacy is not uniform from early to late adulthood, and teachers' self-efficacy may ebb and flow over the course of a career as it is influenced by life, career events and challenges (Klassen *et al.* 2009). Bandura (1997) suggested that some workers at mid-to-late career stages may restructure or scale down overambitious goals due to waning self-efficacy. Other factors thought to influence self-efficacy are support of school leaders for developing colleagues such as through distributed or transformational leadership (Bandura 1997; Bass 2000; Penlington *et al.* 2008) borne out by our data, as well as physical and psychological factors (Kooij *et al.* 2008), especially in the early career stages (Tschannen-Moran and Woolfolk Hoy 2007).

Andrea, Barry and Charlotte had much in common. The three teachers had certain prior expectations of teaching which were initially met, but which changed, positively and negatively, at different stages of their career. All of them relied on the support of colleagues and the school leadership to mitigate the impact of workload, the hours that had to be invested, the demands of planning and the burden of administration. They also valued the 'feedback' on their teaching in relation to effectiveness and in order to sustain a high level of commitment and motivation. Andrea and Barry felt that behaviour and the maintenance of positive relationships with students was a factor in their effectiveness and had developed strategies in the classroom. Charlotte also felt positively about her ability to deal with behaviour issues but acknowledged that this was an area that was causing increasing difficulty in the classroom. Likewise, while all three teachers shared an overall satisfaction with the support of the head teacher, all had different opinions on the reasons for this. Andrea had tried to negotiate this issue by using effective strategies to get noticed by the head teacher and colleagues in order to further her career opportunities in the school. In contrast, Barry had achieved good results due to his effective practices and additional roles, and had received support to progress his career further.

Importantly, there were clear opportunities for collegial support and for teachers to work alongside others among the broader sample of teachers. In these circumstances, where the participants were exhibiting an emergent sense of themselves as capable teachers, there were allocations of time, staffing and resources to support that work. These arrangements reflected a shared and intentional approach to supporting teachers by surrounding them with opportunities to share the emotional, professional and practical implications of their teaching. As Pietsch and Williamson (2010) highlight, these opportunities are not always available to teachers, and the circumstances of teachers' employment (in any career phase) can make a considerable difference. The lack of access to colleagues, professional learning opportunities and resources can confine teachers to the periphery of the profession and can hold them in a state of survival rather than allow them to thrive. Wenger (1998: 5) also highlights that when teachers (particularly early career teachers) participate in the 'social configurations' of their professional communities, they gain access to the shared dialogue and iteration of the group and therefore benefit from the collective meaning that is made and conveyed within the group.

The ECP study supports the argument posited by Huberman (1989) that promotion and recognition are key influential factors on teachers' sense of effectiveness and career advancement. Teachers' promotions are discussed in Hilsum and Start's (1974) and Maclean's (1992) studies on teachers' career patterns. Hilsum and Start noted that the first promotion could be achieved after 3 years in teaching for secondary teachers and after promotion for primary teachers. In contrast, Maclean found that one-quarter of primary teachers in his study obtained their first promotion after between 3 and 6 years of teaching experience, but with an average level of 11 years. Although these three cases represent the career spectrum, they still reflect this to varying degrees and, as a result, these practitioners had developed a strong sense of belief in their ability as effective practitioners (Glickman and Tamashiro 1982).

Evidence from this study strongly suggests the crucial importance of promotion and recognition to the professional development of teachers. Across the entire sample, 69 out of 81 had additional responsibilities (85 per cent) and, of these, 67 (97 per cent) indicated the significance of promotion to their increased motivation, confidence and perceived efficacy. It is apparent that teachers had greatly benefited from their consolidated experience in the classroom which was a contributing factor to their growing sense of efficacy. The roles that teachers perform subsequently carry a significant emotional component, which reflects both their personal motivations to be teaching and the level of emotional investment required to do the job well (O'Connor 2008). Teachers' capacity to navigate these responsibilities is therefore connected to the opportunities provided and the support given to do this work well (Peters and Pearce 2012).

Whereas previous researchers have noted that self-efficacy increases with teachers' experience (e.g. Wolters and Daugherty 2007), Bandura (1997) proposed that self-efficacy beliefs remain relatively stable once established, and although this stability may be true within a specific career stage, the results from our study suggest that teachers gain confidence in their teaching skills through their careers. In many ways this trajectory of self-efficacy reflects as much about the professional contexts of the participant teachers as it does about their effectiveness. Understandings of teachers and their sense of self-efficacy therefore need to be viewed in relation to the contexts in which they work, the nature of professional and personal support provided for them, and how responsibility is shared for making this influential time of development beneficial.

Summary

In this chapter we have delved into the ways in which teachers negotiate classroom relationships and their notions of self-efficacy in three different teacher identity scenarios derived from a constructivist framework of teachers' professional identity and career phase developed by Day *et al.* (2007) and Kington *et al.* (2012). Situated in what research currently has to say about teacher identity, classroom relationships and self-efficacy in teaching, we have highlighted the manifestations of teacher identity in highly effective and effective teachers in Years 2, 6 and 9.

Data presented in this chapter shows that over half of highly effective and effective teachers in our sample felt that their personal, situated and professional dimensions were in balance (Scenario 1), while 38 per cent presented with one dominant dimension (Scenario 2). While it has been acknowledged that teachers' work is complex, emotional and intensive (Sammons *et al.* 2007), our findings also show that professional life phase and sense of identity affect teachers in a variety of different ways. The findings illustrate that highly effective teachers seem to thrive on challenge and that they are usually highly successful in finding ways to manage the variation in work and professional life. In practice, this meant that highly effective and effective teachers possessed the ability to build and sustain good quality relationships with students based on positive interactions and firm, fair and consistent behaviour management, which allowed them to focus both on academic performance and pupils' individual needs, including building self-esteem. These results build on those previously reported by the VITAE project (Sammons *et al.* 2007; Day and Kington 2008; Day *et al.* 2008) through the new and important observational component included in the mixed method design outlined in Chapter 3.

The findings reveal, particularly through the stories of the three teachers, the key influences on teachers' perceptions of their own effective practice across three different identity scenarios and provide insights into both the obstacles that can impede their self-efficacy and the strategies adopted to sustain their effectiveness and work-life balance. In summary, many teachers gain confidence in their teaching skills throughout their careers; however, it is important to consider the contexts in which they work and the nature of personal and professional support. This resonates with findings from Sammons *et al.* (2007) and Gu and Day (2007) who report that pupils of teachers who were sustaining or continuing to build their commitment were more likely to attain results at or above the level expected and, as such, maintain their effectiveness. The highly effective teachers' positive professional identity is associated with quality teacher-pupil relationships and self-efficacy, which are fundamental to their capacities to become and remain effective. Consequently, support and development strategies will remain an important consideration from a management perspective within their organizations in order to build and sustain effective teachers in schools.

This chapter highlights the conceptual and empirical contributions to understandings about the nature of teacher effectiveness, and the challenges of sustaining positive professional identities at different times in their lives and careers and in different school contexts. We have shown how the interaction between teachers' sense of efficacy, identity and management of the personal, situated and professional dimensions of their lives contributed to their effectiveness across their professional career phases.

References

Alderman, M.K. (1999) *Motivation for Achievement: Possibilities for Teaching and Learning.* Mahwah, NJ: Lawrence Erlbaum Associates.

Ames, C. (1992) Classrooms: goals, structures, and student motivation, *Journal of Educational Psychology*, 84: 261–71.

Baker, J. (1999) Teacher-student interaction in urban at-risk classrooms: differential behavior, relationship quality, and student satisfaction with school, *The Elementary School Journal*, 100: 57–70.

Bandura, A. (1997) *Self Efficacy: The Exercise of Control*. New York: W.H. Freeman & Company.

Bass, B.M. (2000) The future of leadership in learning organizations, *The Journal of Leadership Studies*, 7(3): 18–40.

Beijaard, D., Meijer, P.C. and Verloop, N. (2004) Reconsider research on teachers' professional identity, *Teaching and Teacher Education*, 20: 107–28.

Betoret, F.D. (2006) Stressors, self-efficacy, coping resources, and burnout among secondary school teachers in Spain, *Educational Psychology*, 26: 519–39.

Birch, S.H. and Ladd, G.W. (1997) The teacher-child relationship and children's early school adjustment, *Journal of School Psychology*, 35: 61–79.

Birch, S.H. and Ladd, G.W. (1998) Children's interpersonal behaviors and the teacher-child relationship, *Developmental Psychology*, 34: 934–46.

Brophy, J. (1998) *Motivating Students to Learn*. Boston, MA: McGraw-Hill.

Brophy, J. and Kher, N. (1985) Teacher socialization as a mechanism for developing student motivation to learn, in R.S. Feldman (ed.) *The Social Psychology of Education: Current Research and Theory*. New York: Cambridge University Press.

Bruner, J.S. (1987) Life as narrative, *Social Research*, 54: 1–17.

Calhoun, C. (ed.) (1994) *Social Theory and the Politics of Identity*. Oxford: Blackwell.

Castells, M. (2004) *The Power of Identity*. Malden, MA: Blackwell.

Connell, J.P. and Wellborn, J.G. (1991) Competence, autonomy, and relatedness: a motivational analysis of self-system processes, *The Minnesota Symposia on Child Development: Self Processes and Development*, 2: 43–77.

Connelly, F.M. and Clandinin, D.J. (eds) (1999) *Shaping a Professional Identity. Stories of Educational Practice*. New York: TCP.

Day, C. (2002) School reform and transitions in teacher professionalism and identity, *International Journal of Educational Research*, 37: 677– 92.

Day, C. (2011) Uncertain professional identities: managing the emotional contexts of teaching, in C. Day and J. Chi-Kin Lee (eds), New understandings of teacher's work, *Professional Learning and Development in Schools and Higher Education*, 100: 45–64.

Day, C. and Kington, A. (2008) Identity, well-being and effectiveness: the emotional contexts of teaching, *Pedagogy, Culture and Society*, 16–23 (February).

Day, C., Elliot, B. and Kington, A. (2005) Reform, standards and teacher identity: challenges of sustaining commitment, *Teaching and Teacher Education*, 21: 563–77.

Day, C., Kington, A., Stobart, G. and Sammons, P. (2006) The personal and professional selves of teachers: stable and unstable identities, *British Educational Research Journal*, 32(4): 601–16.

Day, C., Sammons, P., Stobart, G., Kington, A. and Gu, Q. (2007) *Teachers Matter*. Maidenhead: Open University Press.

Day, C., Sammons, P., Kington, A., Regan, E., Ko, J., Brown, E., Gunraj, J. and Roberston, D. (2008) *Effective Classroom Practice: A Mixed Method Study of Influences and Outcomes*. End of Award Report, ESRC online. Swindon: ESRC.

Drake, C., Spillane, J.P. and Hufferd-Ackles, K. (2001) Storied identities: teacher learning and subject matter context, *Journal of Curriculum Studies*, 33(1): 1–23.

Elliott, J. (2005) *Using Narrative in Social Research*. London: Sage.

Erikson, E.H. (1959) *Identity and the Life Cycle*. New York: Norton.

Flores, M.A. and Day, C. (2006) Contexts which shape and reshape new teachers' identities: a multi perspective study, *Teaching and Teacher Education*, 22(2): 219–32.

Ghaith, G. and Yaghi, H. (1997) Relationships among experience, teacher efficacy, and attitudes toward the implementation of instructional innovation, *Teaching and Teacher Education*, 13: 451–8.

Glickman, C.D. and Tamashiro, R.T. (1982) A comparison of first-year, fifth-year, and former teachers on efficacy, ego development, and problem solving, *Psychology in the Schools*, 19: 558–62.

Gu, Q. and Day, C. (2007) Teachers resilience: a necessary condition for effectiveness, *Teaching and Teacher Education*, 23(8): 1302–16.

Hammersley, M. (2002) *Educational Research, Policymaking and Practice*. London: Paul Chapman.

Hamre, B. and Pianta, R.C. (2001) Early teacher-child relationships and trajectory of school outcomes through eighth grade, *Child Development*, 72: 625–38.

Hargreaves, A. (1994) *Changing Teachers, Changing Times – Teachers' Work and Culture in the Postmodern Age*. London: Cassell.

Hartup, W.W. (1998) Friendships and developmental significance, in A. Campbell and S. Muncer (eds) *The Social Child*. Hove: Psychology Press.

Hilsum, S. and Start, K.B. (1974) *Promotion and Careers in Teaching*. Windsor NJ: NFER Publishing Company.

Hook, P. and Vass, A. (2000) *Creating Winning Classrooms*. London: David Fulton.

Howes, C. and Hamilton, C.E. (1993) The changing experience of child care: changes in teachers and in teacher-child relationships and children's social competence with peers, *Early Childhood Research Quarterly*, 8: 15–32.

Howes, C., Hamilton, C.E. and Matheson, C.C. (1994) Children's relationships with peers: differential associations with aspects of the teacher-child relationship, *Child Development*, 65: 253–63.

Hoy, W.K. and Woolfolk, A.E. (1993) Teachers' sense of efficacy and the organizational health of schools, *The Elementary School Journal*, 93: 356–72.

Huberman, M. (1989) The professional life cycle of teachers, *Teachers College Record*, 91(1): 31–57.

Kington, A. (2005) Qualities, formation and development of teacher-pupil relationships in the primary school, in B. Kozuh, T. Beran, A. Kozlowska and P. Bayliss (eds) *Measurement and Assessment in Educational and Social Research*. Exeter: Calgary-Cracow.

Kington, A. (2009) Defining teachers' classroom relationships, in D. Stefanc and B. Harasimowicz (eds) *The Social Context of Education*. Ljubljana: Valentin Bucik.

Kington, A., Day, C., Sammons, P., Regan, E., Brown, E. and Gunraj, J. (2012) What makes teachers effective?: Profiles of innovative classroom practice, in C. Day (ed.) *Routledge International Handbook of Teacher and School Development*. London: Routledge.

Kington, A., Gates, P. and Sammons, P. (2013) Development of social relationships, interactions and behaviours in early education settings, *Journal of Early Childhood Research*, 11(3): 293–312.

Klassen, R.M., Bong, M., Usher, E.L., Chong, W.H., Huan, V.S., Wong, I.Y. and Georgiou, T. (2009) Exploring the validity of the Teachers' Self-Efficacy Scale in five countries, *Contemporary Educational Psychology*, 34: 67–76.

Kooij, D., de Lange, A., Jansen, P. and Dikkers, J. (2008) Older workers' motivation to continue to work: five meanings of age, *Journal of Managerial Psychology*, 23: 364–94.

Kutnick, P. and Kington, A. (2005) Children's friendships and learning in school: cognitive enhancement through social interaction? *British Journal of Educational Psychology*, 75(4): 521–38.

Lynch, M. and Cicchetti, D. (1992) Maltreated children's reports of relatedness to their teachers, in R.C. Pianta (ed.) *Beyond the Parent – The Role of Other Adults in Children's Lives: New Directions for Child Development*, pp. 81–108. San Francisco: Jossey-Bass.

Maclean, R. (1992) *Teachers' Careers and Promotional Patterns: A Sociological Analysis*. London: Falmer Press.

MacLure, M. (1993) Arguing for your self: identity as an organising principle in teachers' jobs and lives, *British Educational Research Journal*, 19,(4): 311–22.

Mitchell-Copeland, J., Denham, S.A. and DeMulder, E.K. (1997) Q-Sort assessment of child-teacher attachment relationships and social competence in preschool, *Early Education and Development*, 8: 27–39.

Moore, W. and Esselman, M. (1992) Teacher efficacy, power, school climate, and achievement: a desegregating district's experience, paper presented at the Annual Meeting of the American Educational Research Association, San Francisco.

Nias, J. (1996) Thinking about feeling: the emotions in teaching, *Cambridge Journal of Education*, 26(3): 293–306.

O'Connor, K. E. (2008) 'You choose to care': teachers, emotions and professional identity, *Teaching and Teacher Education*, 24: 117–26.

Oldfather, P and Dahl, K. (1994) Toward a social constructivist reconceptualization of intrinsic motivation for literacy learning, *Journal of Reading Behavior*, 26: 139–58.

Osterman, K.F. (2000) Students' need for belonging in the school community, *Review of Educational Research*, 70: 323–67.

Patrick, H. (1997) Social self-regulation: exploring the relations between children's social relationships, academic self-regulation, and school performance, *Educational Psychologist*, 32: 209–20.

Penlington, C., Kington, A. and Day, C. (2008) Leadership in improving schools: a qualitative perspective, *School Leadership & Management: Formerly School Organisation*, 28(1): 65–82.

Perry, K.E. and Weinstein, R.S. (1998) The social context of early schooling and children's school adjustment, *Educational Psychologist*, 33: 177–94.

Perry, N. (1998) Young children's self-regulated learning and contexts that support it, *Journal of Educational Psychology*, 90: 715–29.

Peters, J. and Pearce, J. (2012) Relationships and early career teacher resilience: a role for school principals,*Teachers and Teaching*, 18: 249–62.

Pianta, R.C. (1997) Adult-child relationship processes and early schooling, *Early Education and Development*, 8: 11–26.

Pianta, R.C. (1999) *Enhancing Relationships between Children and Teachers*. Washington, DC: American Psychological Association.

Pianta, R.C., Steinberg, M. and Rollins, K. (1995) The first two years of school: teacher-child relationships and deflections in children's classroom adjustment, *Development and Psychopathology*, 7: 297–312.

Pietsch, M. and Williamson, J. (2010) 'Getting the pieces together': negotiating the transition from pre-service to in-service teacher, *Asia-Pacific Journal of Teacher Education*, 38: 331–44.

Resnick, M.D., Bearman, P.S., Blum, R.W. *et al.* (1997) Protecting adolescents from harm: findings from the national longitudinal study on adolescent health, *Journal of the American Medical Association*, 278: 823–32.

Roberts, L. (2000) Shifting identities: an investigation into student and novice teachers' evolving professional identity, *Journal of Education for Teaching*, 26(2): 185–6.

Robertson, S. (1996) Teachers' work, restructuring and postfordism: constructing the new 'professionalism', in I. Goodson and A. Hargreaves (eds) *Teachers' Professional Lives*. London: Falmer Press.

Rosenholtz, S. (1989) *Teacher's Workplace: The Social Organization of Schools*. New York: Longman.

Ross, J.A., Cousins, J. B. and Gadalla, T. (1996) Within-teacher predictors of teacher efficacy, *Teaching and Teacher Education*, 12: 385–400.

Ryan, A., Gheen, M.H. and Midgley, C. (1998) Why do some students avoid asking for help? An examination of the interplay among students' academic efficacy, teachers' social-emotional role, and the classroom goal structure, *Journal of Educational Psychology*, 90: 528–35.

Sammons, P., Day, C., Kington, A., Gu, Q., Stobart, G. and Smees, R. (2007) Exploring variations in teachers' work, lives and their effects on pupils: key findings and implications from a longitudinal mixed-method study, *British Educational Research Journal*, 33(5): 681–701.

Schiffrin, D. (1996) Narrative as self-portrait: sociolinguistic construction of identity, *Language in Society*, 25: 167–203.

Sfard, A. and Prusak, A. (2005) Telling identities: in search of an analytic tool for investigating learning as a culturally shaped activity, *Educational Researcher*, 34(4): 14–22.

Skaalvik, E.M. and Skaalvik, S. (2007) Dimensions of teacher self-efficacy and relations with strain factors, perceived collective teacher efficacy, and teacher burnout, *Journal of Educational Psychology*, 99: 611–25.

Skinner, E.A. and Belmont, M. (1993) Motivation in the classroom: reciprocal effects of teacher behavior and students engagement across the school year, *Journal of Educational Psychology*, 85: 571–88.

Sleegers, P. and Kelchtermans, G. (1999) Inleiding op het themanummer: professionele identiteit van leraren (Professional identity of teachers), *Pedagogish Tijdschrift*, 24: 369–74.

Sumsion, J. (2002) Becoming, being and unbecoming an early childhood educator: a phenomenological case study of teacher attrition, *Teaching and Teacher Educatio*, 18: 869–85.

Tschannen-Moran, M. and Woolfolk Hoy, A. (2001) Teacher efficacy: capturing an elusive construct, *Teaching and Teacher Education*, 17: 783–805.

Tschannen-Moran, M. and Woolfolk Hoy, A. (2007) The differential antecedents of self-efficacy beliefs of novice and experienced teachers, *Teaching and Teacher Education*, 23: 944–56.

Tschannen-Moran, M., Woolfolk Hoy, A. and Hoy, W. K. (1998) Teacher efficacy: its meaning and measure, *Review of Educational Research*, 68: 202–48.

Turner, J.C. and Meyer, D.K. (2000) Studying and understanding the instructional contexts of classrooms: using our past to forge our future, *Educational Psychologist*, 35: 69–85.

Turner, J.C., Meyer, D.K., Cox, K.C., Logan, C., DiCintio, M. and Thomas, C.T. (1998) Creating contexts for involvement in mathematics, *Journal of Educational Psychology*, 90: 730–45.

Urdan, T.C. and Maehr, M.L. (1995) Beyond a two-goal theory of motivation and achievement: a case for social goals, *Review of Educational Research*, 65: 213–43.

Walkington, J. (2005) Becoming a teacher: encouraging development of teacher identity through reflective practice, *Asia-Pacific Journal of Teacher Education*, 33(1): 53–64.

Weber, S. and Mitchell, C. (1995) *That's Funny, You Don't Look Like a Teacher*. London: Routledge.

Wenger, E. (1998) *Communities of Practice: Learning, Meaning, and Identity*. Cambridge: Cambridge University Press.

Wentzel, K.R. (1993) Motivation and achievement in early adolescence: role of multiple classroom goals, *Journal of Early Adolescence*, 13: 4–20.

Wentzel, K.R. (1997) Student motivation in middle school: the role of perceived pedagogical caring, *Journal of Educational Psychology*, 89: 411–19.

Wentzel, K.R. (1998) Social relationships and motivation in middle school: the role of parents, teachers, and peers, *Journal of Educational Psychology*, 90: 202–9.

Wigfield, A., Eccles, J.S. and Rodriguez, D. (1998) The development of children's motivation in school contexts, in P.D. Pearson and A. Iran-Nejad (eds) *Review of Research in Education*. Washington, DC: AERA.

Wolters, C. A. and Daugherty, S. G. (2007) Goal structures and teachers' sense of efficacy: their relation and association to teaching experience and academic level, *Journal of Educational Psychology*, 99: 181–93.

Woods, P. and Jeffrey, B. (2002) The reconstruction of primary teachers' identities, *British Journal of Sociology in Education*, 23(1): 89–106.

Woolfolk Hoy, A. and Burke Spero, R. (2005) Changes in teacher efficacy during the early years of teaching: a comparison of four measures, *Teaching and Teacher Education*, 21: 343–56.

Yowell, C.M. and Smylie, M.A. (1999) Self-regulation in democratic communities, *The Elementary School Journal*, 99: 469–90.

9 Supporting, promoting and sustaining effective classroom practice

Introduction

The previous chapters have highlighted the multi-dimensional nature of effectiveness within teaching. They have revealed important connections between different perspectives (teachers' and pupils') and different sources of evidence that we have studied to produce robust findings identifying the features of more effective practice and illuminating what teachers do and who they are. We have also explored the core pedagogical and emotional characteristics of these effective teachers which have enabled them to remain highly resilient, motivated and committed to the profession.

As explicitly discussed in Chapters 2, 3 and 8, teaching can be stressful due to the nature of change, the long hours worked, threats to professional identity and the lack of self-efficacy. In addition, the themes in this book have discussed how early career mentoring, professional development and support can mitigate against the 'reality aftershock' of beginning teachers (Hobson 2009; McIntrye *et al.* 2009; Hobson and Ashby 2012). Nonetheless, this sample of practitioners is unusual in that they were identified as effective or more effective over several years. This final chapter will link together our main findings and then explore ways in which these areas can be addressed: areas which we would encourage the profession to continue discussing to ensure that teachers remain highly motivated and engaged, assuring sustained effectiveness.

Key findings

As outlined in Chapter 3, we started off by deciding to triangulate evidence, both qualitative and quantitative, to investigate the main features of observed practice of a sample of effective and more effective teachers. In addition to qualitative observations we used two international systematic observation schedules, International Instrument for Teacher Observation and Feedback (ISTOF) and the Quality of Teaching (QoT). From the ISTOF instrument we were able to study seven key topics:

- assessment and evaluation;
- differentiation and inclusion;
- clarity of instruction;

- instructional skills;
- promoting active learning and developing meta-cognitive skills;
- classroom climate;
- classroom management.

In addition, from the QoT we could focus on how far our sample showed the following features in their classroom practice:

- safe and orderly school climate;
- stimulating learning climate;
- clear objectives;
- clear instruction;
- activating pupils;
- adaptation of teaching;
- teaching learning strategies;
- effective classroom organization.

Our results reveal that this sample of effective and more effective teachers scored highly in terms of the following factors related to judgements of the quality of teaching from the QoT schedule (where ratings imply predominant strengths) – supportive lesson climate, proactive lesson management, well-organized lesson with clear objectives, and environmental and teacher support.

From the ISTOF observations it was also found that the sample scores very highly in terms of the following factors – clear and coherent lesson in a supportive learning climate, engaging students with assignments and activities, positive classroom management, purposive learning, and quality questioning and feedback for students. These various features can be seen as necessary and key characteristics of effective or high-quality teaching across different sectors, subjects and contexts.

From our qualitative observations we were able to create cameos of individual teachers to illuminate features of their effective classroom practice and these complement the quantitative results. Our interview data have provided rich insights from teachers' own accounts of their work and the influences on these. The interview data supports the findings of the observations in terms of the need for supportive lesson climates and proactive lesson management. These effective teachers talked about the importance of coherent, well-organized lesson plans with clear objectives, where students are engaged with the activities. Some of the key themes to emerge from the interviews were the importance of positive classroom management and providing feedback to students, both as a means of achieving learning objectives and as a way to support positive relationships.

Finally, from pupil surveys and pupil focus groups we accumulated rich data to add an additional perspective – that of the pupils' voice – to our research. The incorporation of pupil views, then, offered an alternative, student-centred insight into teachers' practice as well as classroom and school environments. The analyses of pupil questionnaire responses were used primarily to group teachers according to how positively they were rated by their pupils, but also to investigate relationships between pupil ratings and teacher and school characteristics (teacher gender and career phase, and school composition in terms of pupil disadvantage). Focus group data, meanwhile, allowed researchers to elicit themes and gain deeper insight into pupils' perspectives on a variety of topics relevant to their teachers, classrooms and schools. Findings from both the focus group interviews and the questionnaire survey demonstrated pupils' largely positive perspectives about their teachers, classrooms and schools.

We have studied how the pupil views' component of the study relates to some of the other findings from the ECP research. The analysis of teacher interviews, for example, indicated that teachers identified what makes them effective as: relationships consisting of knowing pupils well; good rapport; listening to and communicating with pupils and maintaining respect, fairness and consistency; praise and feedback; expectations, characterized as high, clear and consistent; professional learning and development; and organization and planning, including being responsive and flexible to the interests of the class, learning styles and needs. With the exception of professional learning and development, which might not be directly observable by pupils, each of these categories was clearly reflected in the factors emerging from the pupil questionnaire data. In addition, many of the same themes (e.g. relationships, feedback and communication) were echoed in the pupil focus group interview findings.

Some similar parallels can be drawn to the quantitative teacher observation data as well. Teachers scored highly on factors including 'Clear and coherent lessons in a supportive learning climate', 'Engaging students with assignments and activities', 'Positive classroom management', 'Purposive learning' and 'Quality questioning and feedback for students' from the ISTOF instrument, and 'Supportive lesson climate', 'Proactive lesson management', 'Well-organized lesson with clear objectives' and 'Environmental and teacher support' from the QoT scales. Again, these mirror the emphases arising from responses to the pupil questionnaire despite different wording (e.g. factors are framed in terms of 'supportive' climate or environment in the teacher observation data and 'teacher support' in the pupil questionnaire data, but these clearly refer to similar if not identical constructs).

This implies that pupils and teachers share some similar understandings of what constitutes effective teaching and learning. The findings offer a starting point for understanding effective classroom practice from pupils' perspectives. They also demonstrate, as discussed above, that pupils' ideas about teaching and learning are not so far removed from those of their teachers.

The qualitative data in particular also demonstrates pupils' ability to conceive of and articulate considerably complex concepts (e.g. engagement and involvement) and to reflect on how these relate to, and play out in, their own learning.

In relation to implications for policy and practice, both the findings and the methods used to study pupils' views have the potential to influence what teachers and schools do, and how effective practice is understood. First of all, teachers, principals and policy-makers might reasonably use the themes and factors presented here to guide teacher professional development or to reflect on current practice.

Having summarized the main features of our research we move on to consider the topic of education change and the implications for effective teaching.

The impact of educational change

Education is particularly prone to change as successive governments strive to implement their respective visions, through a complex and sometimes conflicting myriad of initiatives. In fact, if you rearrange the word 'teaching' it becomes 'change it'! Yet what are we aiming to change within the profession? Needless to say, perhaps the most important aspect is the empowerment of learners to progress, achieve and exceed their potential. Perhaps it is the various domains that contribute to learning, such as the cognitive, emotive and psychomotor domains. Perhaps it is to ensure that learners achieve their best through success in national assessments and examinations that enable them to progress and enter higher education. Alternately, such change may relate to the teacher ensuring that they continue to strive to improve their practice. Indeed, given the multitude of changes that teachers as professionals seek to enable and promote through their work, to what extent are these shared across the profession?

Although the focus of this book is not on educational change, such change can have a substantial impact on teacher effectiveness and classroom practice. Hence in this section we want to consider and raise many challenging questions about the impact of educational change on teacher effectiveness. It explores how teachers experience change and considers how more effective teachers respond (e.g. through resilience).

With recent curriculum and assessment reforms, new initiatives and strategies, and tensions from within and outside of the sector, the teaching profession that an early-career phase teacher enters upon graduation will not be the same profession as they progress in various later career phases. What is it that ensures a teacher can continue to operate within such a climate? Although attributed to Charles Darwin, the following quote is a paraphrase from Megginson (1963: 4), summarizing themes from Darwin's work:

> According to Darwin's *Origin of Species*, it is not the most intellectual of the species that survives; it is not the strongest that survives; but the species that survives is the one that is able best to adapt and adjust to the changing environment in which it finds itself.

In relation to the teaching profession, it is surprising that adaptability and adjustment are topics seldom addressed in respective teacher education programmes, given that teachers are being prepared for an uncertain future of potentially 40 years' service. A DfES (2006) report considered how teaching should develop to meet the demands of society in the year 2020. Within the report, five drivers of change were highlighted:

- **Demographic drivers:** in 2020 there are predicted to be more over-65-year-olds than under-16s. This will result in a younger, less experienced teaching profession.
- **Social drivers:** the report predicted that there would be greater diversity of social attitudes and a decline of traditional family structures (although not family values). Along with the greater social diversity, it is predicted

that there will be greater religious diversity, and furthermore, that a greater proportion of children will have parents who have been university educated.

- **Technological drivers:** the DfES report was written in 2006, before the advent of tablet computers, faster processors, increased mobile technology and so forth. The report did however predict that the pace of technological change would increase exponentially.
- **Economic drivers:** although the report did not predict the global recession, it did highlight that living standards would be expected to be around 30 per cent higher, with more luxuries becoming necessities. Furthermore, the report predicted that young people will need to become better qualified to secure employment. Working patterns would increasingly diversify with occupational structures becoming less hierarchical.
- **Environmental drivers:** the report predicted that there would be a continuing heightened awareness of environmental responsibilities, with decisive action required to counter proposed threats.

It is the interplay of these drivers which is important to note: as an example, the economic drivers may have a direct correlation with the technological drivers: 'superfast broadband' will be a requirement for individuals to contribute to the economy. Arguably the report has dated as the subsequent decade has progressed, yet can we even begin to predict how the professional landscape will look in another decade's time, let alone the predicted 40 or more years of service a new teacher may expect?

According to Castle and Buckler (2009) there are different changes that can occur within the professional context, for example:

- growth and expansion, where practice is enhanced through doing more of the same, perhaps on a wider basis;
- diversification, relating to adapting existing practices to incorporate new elements;
- contraction, where an existing practice may be limited or even stopped;
- discontinuity, where an existing practice is stopped;
- innovation, where something completely new is developed.

The relationship between these dimensions is equally as difficult to predict as the changing educational landscape unfolds. What practices will be contracted or discontinued, versus those that will develop or diversify over the coming years? Yet in returning to the general theme of change, this is one of the core reasons for the prevalence of stress levels within the profession. Therefore, how best can we prepare teachers for change?

Hritz (2008) discusses that when change is introduced, 25 per cent of people are resistant, while 15 per cent embrace the change. The remaining 60 per cent claim to be uncertain and can either be swayed to resist or embrace the change. If this is correlated to a staff meeting of 20 teachers, the five teachers who resist any proposed change are a greater number than the three who are ready to engage with the change: the remaining 14 will be listening to the various arguments before making their decision. Therefore, what is important is helping to ensure that change is introduced effectively through avoiding what MacBeath and Mortimore (2001) highlight as factors for failure. Such factors relate to the lack of consistent leadership, the lack of motivation, the lack of initiative, the lack of capacity and the lack of information. Indeed, often when a change is proposed, it is this latter aspect that is seldom shared to explain *why* the change is needed. All too often, the 'headline' of what change is on the horizon is apparent and yet the reasons for such change are not explained effectively. If the drivers for change were shared more explicitly, perhaps the 25 per cent of individuals resistant to change would engage more proactively.

According to MacBeath and Mortimore (2001: 17), such resistance to change can derive from one or more of the following:

- people projecting their own deficiencies;
- people clinging to past practices;
- defences built up against threatening messages from the outside;
- fear of failure;
- seeing change as someone else's job;
- hostile relationships among staff;
- seeking safety in numbers.

Various models of change management discuss the need to highlight the importance of why the change should occur; for example Pettigrew and Whipp (1993) explain that the interaction between the content (the what), the process (the how) and the context (the where) needs to be explained to ensure that individuals understand the requirements of the change. Often, only one or other elements are discussed, such as the content or the process, without the full perspective being shared. It is this full perspective which needs to be explained from the outset to all involved, which will help to ensure that the change initiative can be effectively facilitated. However, we need to recognize that not all change is good. School improvement research has demonstrated that clear priorities and a limited number of changes stand more chance of success than seeking to change many aspects simultaneously. There is much evidence that current policies are changing the structures and governance of schools, while at the same time reorganizing the curriculum and assessment frameworks, and the inspection framework is sapping morale among teachers due to the perceived pressures of externally mandated change.

Change is often perceived in relation to the cost of the change in relation to resources (whether time or financial cost) and the quality that the change will provide. Yet according to Krüger (2002), this is the tip of the metaphoric iceberg whereby the requirements of effective personal and professional management similarly need to be considered. In relation to this, the perceptions and beliefs of individuals alongside various factors relating to power and politics need addressing: if individuals think that the change will cause too much disruption and at too high a risk, or that the change will threaten their position in some way, the change will meet with resistance.

Effective change management is consequently an issue to be addressed within the education profession. Across the sector, the consideration should focus not just on what needs changing or how, but on explicitly ensuring that all those involved are

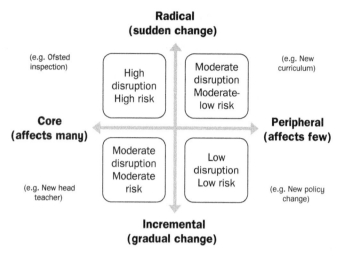

Figure 9.1   Quadrants of change (adapted from Blackwell 2003).

as informed of the drivers for change as possible. This is not to say that change is an easy process to engage with – rather, that through good information and communication, there may be opportunities to negate as many features as possible which could otherwise lead to resistance. As an example, the continuum of change can take place on a micro-, small-scale level, through to the macro-, larger-scale level. Within this another continuum relates to the change occurring either radically or incrementally, akin to either a brick thrown into a still pond resulting in large disruption, or undulating ripples from a small pebble thrown in. A further continuum is whether the change is core, or fundamental, to all involved in relation to practice, or whether it is a more peripheral change. The radical/incremental continuum and the core/peripheral continuum can be plotted to demonstrate the nature of change, as outlined by Blackwell (2003) (see Figure 9.1).

Within Blackwell's model, the change that provides the most risk with the greatest amount of disruption occurs when the change is both a radical and a core change, compared to a risk that is incremental and peripheral. Furthermore, although a change can cause high risk and high disruption to one person, they may take the responsibility for implementing the successful change initiative to ensure that there is low disruption and low risk to others. Take for example a change in a teacher's practice: they may engage with a new strategy that they have taken time to research, prepare and engage with, internalizing such practice so that they can share it with their students or colleagues, encouraging smaller steps to their practice in order to succeed.

Despite the best efforts to ensure that a change is incremental and peripheral, there will be times when a teacher is confronted with highly disruptive, high-risk changes. On a personal level, change can result in a sense of despair, as discussed in Kübler-Ross and Kessler's 'grief cycle' (2005). According to the cycle, when first facing change, the individual experiences a sense of shock that can manifest through immobilization: refusing to accept the situation, perhaps feeling paralysed through the enormity of the change. The second stage is a process of initial adjustment, whereby there is a sense of minimization in relation to the change, where perhaps the teacher only provides a scant effort in engagement. As the change becomes increasingly clear to the individual, there is a sense of an inner contradiction, that the familiar past is now confronted with the unfamiliar future, resulting in a sense of resistance and in turn, depression. This leads to an inner crisis that, while it can be can be fought against, leads the individual accepting the new reality, while relinquishing past practices. As the individual progresses with the change, there is a period of reconstruction and recovery, whereby they test the new reality of the change in an attempt to find new meaning, before the change is ingrained and internalized within their practice. Such depths of despair in relation to change are similarly discussed by Craine (2000, 2007: 45) through his change cycle (see Figure 9.2). Within the cycle, the core idea is to move individuals from the 'No zone' characterized by resistance through to the 'Go zone', where people engage with the change. The cycle does however acknowledge the 'Chasm', where the minimization, depression and inner crises evident in Kübler-Ross' grief cycle are evident.

Although both Kübler-Ross and Craine discuss the depths of the change through the inner contradictions and inner crisis, or the chasm respectively, the proposed change can be overcome through Lewin's (1947) stages of change. According to Lewin's model, the first process is to 'unfreeze' the situation through dismantling the existing mind-set that individuals and organizations can adhere to. The second stage is where the change is introduced, which as Lewin discusses can cause confusion and transition, with existing practices challenged. The final stage is a process of freezing, or crystallizing the new mind-set, to embed the change and return to a sense of equilibrium. Yet, how often does the teaching profession keep changing without this third stage being truly embedded? Just when one policy or practice appears established, another can come along with the associated threats of change.

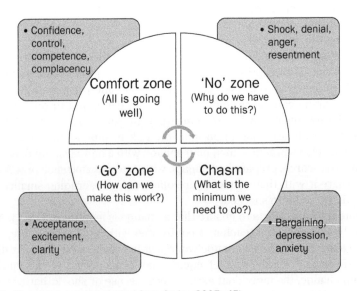

Figure 9.2   The change cycle (adapted from Craine 2007: 45).

The importance of consolidating changes has similarly been discussed by Kotter (1996) who provides an eight-step process which needs to be adhered to in order to:

- establish a sense of urgency;
- create a coalition;
- develop a clear vision;
- share the vision;
- empower people to clear obstacles;
- secure short-term wins;
- consolidate and keep moving;
- anchor the change.

In ensuring that proposed changes within teaching are successful, a shared responsibility and a sense of ownership are thus warranted. Identifying the causes of such changes is one approach to enable individuals to understand the primary or secondary causes of a change which lead to the root cause of the problem that needs changing (models such as Ishikawa's 1985 'fishbone diagram'), or through ensuring that the level of dissatisfaction with how things are (D) combined with the vision of what is possible (V) and the first steps to be taken (F) are greater than the resistance, or the cost of the change in relation to psychological resources, or resources of time, money and materials (R). This is summarized by Beckhard and Harris (1987) as the change equation: change $= (D \times V \times F) > R$.

As evident through the various models discussed, from the outset the change needs to be shared with the staff opposed to a 'top-down' directive: through providing such ownership, the change enables teachers to enhance their self-efficacy through capitalizing on the actual competence required to ensure the change works, balanced against the estimation of this competence (Bandura 1986). If such self-efficacy is not balanced, there will be a diminished motivation in facilitating the change.

One theory (of the many that exist) in relation to motivation is that of self-determination (Deci and Ryan 1985), whereby individuals can become more motivated if they feel competent in controlling their environment and are able to predict the outcomes of their actions; they feel autonomous in that they can determine their own course of action without interference from others; finally they feel a sense of relatedness equating to satisfactory engagement with others. In practice, if a new change is proposed, although resistance may occur as outlined in the previous discussion, if teachers are enabled to effect the change through deciding on how best to facilitate the change through discussion with others, in adherence to their existing skill set, the change is more likely to succeed.

The impact of stress

The scale and nature of educational change can further increase stress levels within the teaching profession. Available statistics indicate that stress is a major cause of absence from work (Kerr et al. 2009). Specifically within the teaching profession, 0.5 million working days are lost each year due to stress-related illness, with 69 per cent of teachers reporting stress (NASUWT 2010). Stress is associated

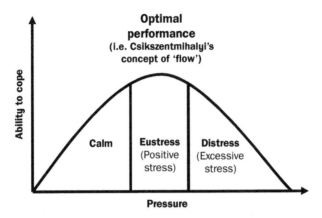

Figure 9.3 Yerkes-Dodson stress curve (adapted from Buckler and Castle 2014).

with the ability to cope with the increase in pressure as characterized by Yerkes and Dodson's (1908) association between physiological arousal and performance (see Figure 9.3).

As shown in Figure 9.3, a certain degree of stress is required to ensure optimal performance, and although individuals can exceed this level for a limited time, thus moving into the 'distress' zone, the resources required to maintain the level of performance will eventually become excessive resulting in the psychological state of 'burnout' characterized by exhaustion, demotivation, distress, ineffectiveness, and dysfunctional attitudes and behaviours (Betoret 2006; Skaalvik and Skaalvik 2007). By analogy, if when driving a car, the accelerator was pressed to the floor without changing gear, the revolution counter would quickly move to the red zone, warning of potential engine failure, or burnout of the engine, unless another gear is selected.

Castle and Buckler (2009) discuss strategies for limiting stress, specifically in relation to reducing anxiety through a five-stage process:

- Stage 1: identify the demand placed upon you;
- Stage 2: identify your perception of that demand;
- Stage 3: ascertain your psychological and physiological response to that perception;
- Stage 4: substitute inappropriate thoughts where necessary;
- Stage 5: observe/reflect/record your behaviour in response to the situation.

Although Castle and Buckler discuss stress in relation to reducing the level of anxiety, they propose a number of strategies to reduce stress levels, such as promoting relaxation through diaphragmatic breathing, using 'muscle-to-mind' and 'mind-to-muscle' relaxation strategies such as progressive muscular relaxation, the use of biofeedback, using cognitive restructuring to replace self-defeating comments with enhanced, positive comments and incorporating mental imagery within practice, alongside the importance of correct hydration, nutrition and sufficient sleep.

The interplay of constant change combined with frequently ineffective change management, and the associated risk of stress, is perhaps the greatest risk to teacher effectiveness. Yet over the course of time within the teaching profession, it is likely that you will facilitate change on a daily basis: whether this is with one learner, a group or class of learners, or indeed, colleagues and other professionals. As well as ensuring that the strategies of effective practice as highlighted are paramount, there is one further attribute to discuss: that of professional reflection.

Professional reflection

According to Brock (2006), defining the term 'professional' is a contemporary and contentious issue within many disciplines, specifically within education and management. Brock discusses the definition of the term through a review of literature before proposing seven dimensions of professionalism:

- **Knowledge:** specialist knowledge, unique expertise, experience;
- **Education and training:** higher education, qualifications, practical experience, obligation to engage in continuing professional development;
- **Skills:** competence and efficacy, task complexity, communication, judgement;
- **Autonomy:** entry requirements, self-regulation and standards, voice in public policy, discretionary judgement;
- **Values:** ideology, altruism, dedication, service to clients;
- **Ethics:** codes of conduct, moral integrity, confidentiality, trustworthiness, responsibility;
- **Reward:** influence, social status, power, vocation.

Implicitly within Brock's dimensions is the concept of reflection, an aspect that Buckler and Castle (2014) discuss as being central for teacher development alongside developing a professional philosophy. The most widely discussed model of reflection, based on the concept of experiential learning, is the Kolb cycle (Kolb and Fry 1975). The Kolb cycle is a four-stage process where any of the stages can be used as the initial stage for reflection – whether this is the concrete experience, which capitalizes on the actual process of teaching, or reflective observation, where there is a process of objectively analysing the outcome of the experience, or abstract conceptualization, where conceptual understanding is reviewed, or active experimentation, which ensures a process of aiming to find new solutions to problems – the cycle encourages reflection: without reflection, the same mistakes would simply continue to be repeated.

Another common theorist discussed in relation to reflection is Donald Schön (1983) who discusses two types of reflection: reflection *in* action (whereby the teacher adapts their teaching as the lesson progresses through a process of continual monitoring) and reflection *on* action (where the teacher considers the lesson after it has finished). According to Schön, the interplay of reflecting on or in practice enables the professional to analyse what has happened through considering the lesson from a number of perspectives. This allows the teacher to identify what worked effectively while also highlighting areas for further development. This in turn helps to develop professional knowledge and enables the teacher to consider what to do the next time they experience a similar situation.

Both Kolb and Schön's models are dependent on the individual being central to the reflection process; however, Brookfield proposed a model that capitalized on the contributions of others to engage with the reflective process though four different perspectives, or 'lenses' (Brookfield 1995). These include the individual facilitating the learning experience (the teacher), the perceptions of others (such as the learners), colleagues (other teachers or peers), as well as theoretical perspectives (from literature) to provide an informed perspective.

Although a number of reflection models have been discussed among the multitude that exist, the important point to note is that for teaching to be considered a profession, such reflection is paramount to ensure that when change is introduced, teachers are empowered to ask the question 'why?' without this being interpreted as an affront to the person leading the change. Indeed, if change is effectively facilitated and made explicit, such questions would not need to be asked of the change: instead the focus would be on how effectively the individual is able to embed the change in their practice.

Emotional resilience

Many of the effective teachers in our research showed emotional resilience, self-efficacy and a positive approach to their work. They were often individuals who seemed to be prepared to 'go that extra mile', to persist in an attempt to achieve a desired outcome, or as Loehr (1995: 11) defines it, 'the ability to stand tall in the face of adversity . . . a psychic resilience that allows you to rebound from setbacks and failures time and time again'. Through this definition, the concept of endurance and stamina is evident, yet in returning to the themes explored in this chapter, continuing to push can cause distress and burnout. It is a question of achieving a balance for the individual: resilience for one person may differ in relation to another. The interplay of effective change, stress management, reflection and investing in psychological skill training techniques can continue to enhance a teacher's performance to assure a long, productive, vibrant and successful, effective, teaching career.

Implications

Much has been learnt from Effective Classroom Practice (ECP) research that has implications for both policy and practice. It builds on other work on teacher effectiveness (Mujis and Reynolds 2010) but extends this via the focus on professional identities, self-efficacy and resilience. We have sought to analyse the concept of effectiveness and point to its complexity. We caution against simplistic assumptions that assume it is a simple matter to identify more or indeed less effective teachers and to use such information to reward 'good' performance or sanction 'poor' performance. Analysing data about pupil outcomes and progress using value-added approaches can be a helpful source of evidence for self-evaluation and reflection, but it is not reliable enough to make high-stakes judgements about teacher performance, as we have shown in the earlier Variations in Teachers' Work Lives and their Effects on Pupils (VITAE) study (Sammons *et al.* 2007). Research in the USA and elsewhere has also drawn similar conclusions about measurement and the need to be aware of how far measures are reliable and valid. The same caveats apply to using observations of teachers for high-stakes decisions and this in turn highlights the need to have a more nuanced approach, recognizing that a differentiated perspective is more appropriate (Darling-Hammond *et al.* 2010).

Our research points to the value of such information as a developmental tool for teachers, to be used in a supportive environment. This fits with recent reviews that seek to support schools and teachers in improving their practice by drawing attention to what enables effective production and transformation of evidence and what enables schools to make effective use of externally produced evidence (Nelson and O'Beirne 2014). The need to ensure research evidence on educational effectiveness is not lost in translation has been drawn to our attention recently by Harris *et al.* (2013). They argue strongly for the 'need to combine different research methodologies and make more use of multi-method analyses that tell a compelling story about exactly how to lever better performance effectively and sustainably at all levels in the system' (p. 15). The results of the ECP research are based on just such a powerful combination of methodologies. Our multi-methods combine stories and statistics and have enabled us to produce robust findings that can act as a guide to inform and support schools and teachers concerned to promote improvement and facing the pressures of externally driven change. Our findings also point to the value of listening to the pupil voice, as well as using performance data on pupil outcomes of classroom practice to study and promote effectiveness. Taken together with teachers' own voices, these different perspectives and sources of evidence can inform teacher educators and support ongoing professional development. Our findings thus provide a powerful guide to the features of high-quality and effective teaching, as well as insights into how to help teachers maintain their professional identities, their job satisfaction, motivation and commitment, and develop their resilience over the course of their careers.

Recent reviews of teacher effectiveness have drawn attention to the value of linking the knowledge base with that of professional learning and note the need to view teachers as adaptive experts in systems with high adaptive capacities (Muijs *et al.* 2014). This review suggests a cycle or ongoing process of professional learning informed by research results on what supports better outcomes for pupils, and has change at the heart of the ongoing process with monitoring and feedback loops supporting reflective practice and self-regulated learning for teachers. The ECP research methodology and findings supports such a process of fostering self-regulated and reflective practice.

We anticipate that the ECP findings will support school leaders and teachers as they seek to enhance the quality of learning and teaching in their schools and cope with ever increasing, complex demands and pace of change in educational systems across the world.

References

Bandura, A. (1986) *Social Foundations of Thought and Action: A Social Cognitive Theory*. Englewood Cliffs, NJ: Prentice Hall.

Beckhard, R. and Harris, R. (1987) *Organizational Transitions: Managing Complex Change*. Reading, MA: Addison-Wesley.

Betoret, F.D. (2006) Stressors, self-efficacy, coping resources, and burnout among secondary school teachers in Spain, *Educational Psychology*, 26: 519–39.

Blackwell, R. (2003) *Guidelines for Promoting and Facilitating Change*. York: LTSN.

Brock, A. (2006) Eliciting early years educators' thinking: how do they define and sustain their professionalism? *EECERA Conference*, Reykjavik, Iceland, 30 August–2 September.

Brookfield, S. (1995) *Becoming a Critically Reflective Teacher*. San Francisco, CA: Jossey-Bass.

Buckler, S. and Castle, P. (2014) *Psychology for Teachers*. London: Sage.

Castle, P. and Buckler, S. (2009) *How to be a Successful Teacher: Strategies for Personal and Professional Development*. London: Sage.

Craine, K. (2000) *Designing a Document Strategy: Documents, Technology, People*. Hurs: MC2 Books.

Craine, K. (2007) Managing the cycle of change, *The Information Management Journal*, September/October: 44–50.

Darling- Hammond, L., Dieckmann, J., Haertel, E., Lotan, R., Newton, X., Philipose, S., Spang, E., Thomas, E. and Williamson, P. (2010) Studying teacher effectiveness: the challenges of developing valid measures, in G. Walford, E. Tucker and M. Viswanathan (eds) *The Sage Handbook of Measurement*. London: Sage.

Deci, E.L. and Ryan, R.M. (1985) *Intrinsic Motivation and Self-determination in Human Behaviour*. New York: Plenum.

DfES (2006) *2020 Vision: Report of the Teaching and Learning in 2020 Review Group*. Nottingham: DfES Publications.

Harris, A., Chapman, C., Muijs, D., Reynolds, D., Campbell, C., Creemers, B., Earl, L., Kyriakides, L., Munoz, G., Stoll, L., Stringfield, S., van Velzen, B. and Weinstein, J. (2013) Getting lost in translation?: An analysis of the international engagement of practitioners and policy-makers with the educational effectiveness research base, *School Leadership and Management*, 33(1): 3–19, 10.1080/13632434.2012.723622.

Hobson, A.J. (2009) On being bottom of the pecking order: beginner teachers' perceptions and experiences of support, *Teacher Development: An International Journal of Teachers' Professional Development*, 13(4): 299–320.

Hobson, A.J. and Ashby, P. (2012) Reality aftershock and how to avert it: second-year teachers' experiences of support for their professional development, *Cambridge Journal of Education*, 42(2): 177–96.

Hritz, C. (2008) Change model: three stages to success, *Leadership Excellence*, May: 14.

Ishikawa, K. (1985) *What is Total Quality Control? The Japanese Way* (translated by D.J. Lu). Upper Saddle River, NJ: Prentice Hall.

Kerr, R., McHugh, M. and McCrory, M. (2009) HSE Management Standards and stress-related work outcomes, *Occupational Medicine*, 59: 574–9.

Kolb, D.A. and Fry, R. (1975) Toward an applied theory of experiential learnin, in C. Cooper (ed.) *Theories of Group Process*. London: John Wiley.

Kotter, J. (1996) *Leading Change*. Watertown, MA: Harvard Business School Press.

Krüger, W. (2002) *Excellence in Change*. Wiesbaden: Gabler.

Kübler-Ross, E. and Kessler, D. (2005) *On Grief and Grieving: Finding the Meaning of Grief Through the Fiive Stages of Loss*. London: Simon & Schuster.

Lewin, K. (1947) Frontiers in group dynamics: concept, method and reality in social science, social equilibria and social change, *Human Relations*, 1: 5–41.

Loehr, J.E. (1995) *The New Mental Toughness Training for Sports*. New York: Penguin.

MacBeath, J. and Mortimore, P. (eds.) (2001) *Improving School Effectiveness*. Maidenhead: Open University Press.

McIntyre, J., Hobson, A.J. and Mitchell, N. (2009) Continuity, support, togetherness and trust: findings from an evaluation of a university-administered early professional development programme for teachers in England, *Professional Development in Education*, 35(3): 357–79.

Megginson, L.C. (1963) Lessons from Europe for American business, *Southwestern Social Science Quarterly*, 44(1): 3–13.

Muijs, D., and Reynolds, D. (2010) *Effective Teaching: Evidence and Practice*, 3rd edn. London: Sage.

Muijs, D., Kyruakides, L., van der Werf, G., Creemers, B., Timperley, H. and Earl, L. (2014) State of the art – teacher effectiveness and professional learning, *School Effectiveness and School Improvement*, 25(2): 231–56.

NASUWT (2010) *Teachers' Mental Health: A Study Exploring the Experiences of Teachers with Work-related Stress and Mental Health Problems*. Redhill: NASUWT.

Nelson, J. and O'Beirne, C. (2014) *Using Evidence in the Classroom: What Works and Why?* Slough: NFER.

Pettigrew, A. and Whipp, R. (1993) *Managing Change for Competitive Success*. Oxford: Wiley-Blackwell.

Sammons, P., Day, C., Kington, A., Gu, Q., Stobart, G. and Smees, R. (2007) Exploring variations in teachers' work, lives and their effects on pupils: key findings and implications from a longitudinal mixed methods study, *British Educational Research Journal*, 33(5): 681–701.

Schön, D. (1983) *The Reflective Practitioner*. New York: Basic Books.

Skaalvik, E. M. and Skaalvik, S. (2007) Dimensions of teacher self-efficacy and relations with strain factors, perceived collective teacher efficacy, and teacher burnout, *Journal of Educational Psychology*, 99: 611–25.

Yerkes, R.M. and Dodson, J.D. (1908) The relation of strength of stimulus to rapidity of habit-formation, *Journal of Comparative Neurology and Psychology*, 18: 459–82.

Index

BAD EDUCATION
Debunking Myths in Education

Philip Adey and Justin Dillon (Eds)

9780335246014(Paperback)
2012

eBook also available

We all know that small classes are better than large classes; that children are best taught in groups according to their ability; that some schools are much better than others and that we should teach children according to their individual learning styles ... or do we?

This book asks awkward questions about these and many other sacred cows of education. Each chapter tackles a persistent myth in education, confronting it with research evidence and teasing out any kernel of truth which may underlie the myth.

Key features:

- The 17 chapters each deal with one topic and are written by an established authority in the field
- The arguments are defensible and underpinned by sound
- Covers topical issues such as the class size debate - *Class Size: Is Small Better?* and the question *Are there "Good" and "Bad" Schools?*

www.openup.co.uk

OPEN UNIVERSITY PRESS
McGraw - Hill Education